ISLAND PARADOX

Island Paradox
Puerto Rico in the 1990s

FRANCISCO L. RIVERA-BATIZ
CARLOS E. SANTIAGO

Russell Sage Foundation · New York

The Russell Sage Foundation

The Russell Sage Foundation, one of the oldest of America's general purpose foundations, was established in 1907 by Mrs. Margaret Olivia Sage for "the improvement of social and living conditions in the United States." The Foundation seeks to fulfill this mandate by fostering the development and dissemination of knowledge about the country's political, social, and economic problems. While the Foundation endeavors to assure the accuracy and objectivity of each book it publishes, the conclusions and interpretations in Russell Sage Foundation publications are those of the authors and not of the Foundation, its Trustees, or its staff. Publication by Russell Sage, therefore, does not imply Foundation endorsement.

Library of Congress Cataloging-in-Publication Data

Rivera-Batiz, Francisco L.
    Island paradox : Puerto Rico in the 1990s / Francisco Rivera-Batiz
and Carlos E. Santiago.
        p.   cm.
    Includes bibliographical references and index.
    ISBN 0-87154-721-X (alk. paper)
    1. Puerto Rico—Population. 2. Puerto Rico—Economic conditions—
1952– 3. Puerto Rico—Social conditions—1952– 4. Puerto Rico—Emigration
and immigration. 5. Puerto Ricans—United States. I. Santiago, Carlos Enrique.
II. Title.
HB3555.R58 1996
306'.097295—dc20   96-21094
                                                                                                    CIP

The paper used in this publication meets the minimum requirements of American National Standard for Information Sciences—Permanence of Paper for Printed Library Materials. ANSI Z39.48-1992.

Text design by Rozlyn Coleman.

RUSSELL SAGE FOUNDATION
112 East 64th Street, New York, New York 10021
10 9 8 7 6 5 4 3 2 1

For
Sandra
and
Azara

Contents

Acknowledgments

THIS BOOK forms part of the 1990 census research project funded by the Russell Sage Foundation, the Ford Foundation, the Andrew W. Mellon Foundation, the Spencer Foundation, the National Science Foundation, and the National Institutes of Aging. Assistance was also provided by the Social Science Research Council, the Bureau of the Census, and the Population Studies Center of the University of Michigan. The project was under guidance of a National Advisory Board chaired by Eric Wanner, president of the Russell Sage Foundation, and with members: William Butz, U.S. Bureau of the Census, Jorge Chapa, University of Texas at Austin, Richard Easterlin, University of Southern California, Reynolds Farley, University of Michigan, David Featherman, Social Science Research Council, James Johnson, University of North Carolina at Chapel Hill, Evelyn Kitagawa, University of Chicago, Karen Mason, East-West Center, and Charles Westoff, Princeton University.

The staff of the Russell Sage Foundation, Columbia University, and the University at Albany provided essential support, allowing the successful completion of this project. The authors are grateful to Nancy Cunniff-Casey, the project officer at the Russell Sage Foundation, for her valuable assistance throughout all stages of the project. At Columbia University, the research assistance of Roberto Agodini, Anabelle Guerrero, Lillian Martí, and Deboyioti Sarkar is gratefully acknowledged. At the University at Albany, Kisalaya Basu provided efficient research assistance while discussions with Edna Acosta-Belén, Margarita Benítez, José Cruz, Samuel Figueroa-Sifre, and Colbert Nepaulsingh concerning Puerto Rico proved invaluable.

Suggestions and comments were received from a number of scholars and researchers, including, Jorge Chapa, University of Texas at Austin, Jaime del Valle, University of Puerto Rico at Río Piedras, Reynolds

Farley, University of Michigan, Peter Guarnaccia, Rutgers University, Jeffrey Passel, the Urban Institute, Raquel Rivera Pinderhughes, San Francisco State University, Clara Rodríguez, Fordham University, and Stewart Tolnay, University at Albany. The authors thank them for their investment of time and effort, and for their many comments and suggestions for improvement.

Francisco L. Rivera-Batiz
Carlos E. Santiago

ILLUSTRATION: PUERTO RICO'S PLACE IN THE CARIBBEAN

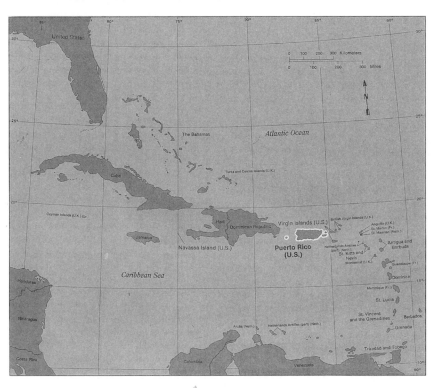

CHAPTER 1

Island Paradox:
Puerto Rico in the 1990s

PERHAPS nowhere else in the Western Hemisphere do the sharply different economies and societies of Latin America and the United States encounter one another as closely as in Puerto Rico. Halfway between North and South America, this Caribbean island of three and a half million people is literally situated between two worlds. But it is history, culture, and politics—more than geography—that account for Puerto Rico's present situation.

Puerto Rico was a Spanish colony from the early sixteenth century until the end of the nineteenth century, by which time it had a Spanish-speaking population of about one million made up of a mixture of races and ethnicities, with African, European, and Taíno/Arawak components. In 1898, after the Spanish-American War, the island became a territory of the United States. Subsequently, Puerto Rico's economic, social, and political ties with the United States became stronger than the ties between the United States and any other country in Latin America. Even Mexico's relationship with the United States in the aftermath of the North American Free Trade Agreement pales by comparison.

The island's current political status was forged in the 1940s by the Puerto Rican leader Luis Muñoz Marín and his Popular Democratic Party. In 1952, Puerto Rico became the Commonwealth of Puerto Rico, or, as officially referred to by the government, a "free state associated with the United States" (*Estado Libre Asociado*). Under the commonwealth formula, Puerto Rico is neither a state of the American union nor an independent country. It has a popularly elected governor and legislature, but its residents are exempt from federal taxes, have no voting representatives in Congress, and may not vote in national elections. Puerto Rico uses the U.S. dollar as its currency, and its foreign

1

and immigration policies are controlled by Washington. Persons born in Puerto Rico hold U.S. citizenship and may move freely between the island and the mainland. This has led to massive population flows in and out of Puerto Rico. Slightly over three and a half million persons now reside on the island, but close to three million Puerto Ricans live in the continental United States. Of these, almost one million reside in New York City, about the same number as live in the island's capital, San Juan, and its greater metropolitan area.

The historical interplay of Spanish and American involvement in Puerto Rico has resulted in a population that shares many cultural attributes with Latin America yet is heavily influenced by American social and economic forces. Nowhere else in Puerto Rico are the close ties between the island and the United States in greater evidence than the Luis Muñoz Marín International Airport in San Juan. From this bustling compound there are daily departures of Puerto Ricans to all parts of the mainland United States. During holidays, the airport bursts with Puerto Ricans arriving from all parts of the continental United States.

Despite the heavy influence of the United States on the Puerto Rican population, its Latin American and Caribbean heritage is still evident. The Hispanic and Afro-Caribbean cultures are deeply embedded. Spanish remains the primary language of nearly the entire population. San Juan reminds the visitor of other Latin American cities in the Caribbean—of Santo Domingo or Cartagena—not Boston or Chicago.

Puerto Rico has maintained its cultural contacts with other Latin American nations, and with Spain. The proximity of Puerto Rico and the Dominican Republic, for example, has resulted in a long history of migratory movements between the two nations, movements that continue to the present. Currently, thousands of undocumented Dominican immigrants arrive on the deserted beaches of Puerto Rico's west coast every year. Most of them make the perilous trip in flimsy boats. Some stay in Puerto Rico, part of a growing community of undocumented immigrants. Many, however, end up at the Muñoz Marín airport, where the ease of movement between Puerto Rico and the mainland allows safe travel to the United States (see Rivera-Batiz 1995).

Nearly fifty years have passed since Puerto Rico and the United States entered into their present political and economic relationship. What fundamental demographic shifts have occurred during this period? How has the integration of Puerto Rico's small, developing economy to the much larger and economically industrialized economy of the United States affected social and economic conditions on the island? Despite having made substantial socioeconomic progress, Puerto Rico currently confronts serious social and economic problems. How have the intimate social, economic, and political ties of Puerto Rico to the United States contributed to the crisis confronting the island in the 1990s?

The information presented in this volume is based largely on U.S. census data, primarily from the 1970, 1980, and 1990 censuses of population and housing. The decennial census represents the most exhaustive count of the Puerto Rican population and the most detailed survey of its characteristics. The margin of error of the data provided by the census is much smaller than for other surveys on the Puerto Rican population carried out by the Puerto Rican government. (See appendix 1 for information on the design of the census for Puerto Rico and how this census differs from the one for the mainland United States.)

This monograph focuses on the demographic and social changes that occurred in Puerto Rico during the decade of the 1980s and the early 1990s, when the sustained decline of a series of socioeconomic indicators reached alarming levels. A disturbing rise in the unemployment rate, high poverty rates, sustained social inequities, and a sharp increase in substance abuse and crime were characteristic of the period. These transformations and their policy implications can only be understood in their historical context.

The Tarnished Showcase

In the early 1970s, Puerto Rico was held up as a showcase of economic development, as a shining example of how political stability, democracy, and open-market economic policies lead to economic growth. This image has been tarnished by the island's disappointing and painful social and economic experiences of the last twenty years. What happened? What accounts for the sharp turnaround of the Puerto Rican economy and the accompanying breakdown of social structures?

By any measure, Puerto Rico has undergone dramatic changes in the last fifty years. From a largely rural, agricultural economy, it has become a nation of urban dwellers mostly employed in manufacturing and service activities. In 1940, two-thirds of all Puerto Ricans resided in rural areas; now, two-thirds live in urban areas. In the 1940s, close to 45 percent of the labor force was engaged in agricultural activities; by 1990, this number had dwindled to 3.7 percent.

These changes were accompanied by substantial economic growth and social gains. In 1948, gross national product per capita in Puerto Rico was $1,478, in 1990 dollars; by 1994, GNP per capita had increased more than four times, to $6,361, in 1990 dollars (see figure 1.1). Associated with these improvements in income were impressive advances in the standard of living. Consider the area of health, for example. In 1940, there was one physician for every 3,763 persons in Puerto Rico; by 1990,

Figure 1.1   Economic Growth in Puerto Rico, 1948–94

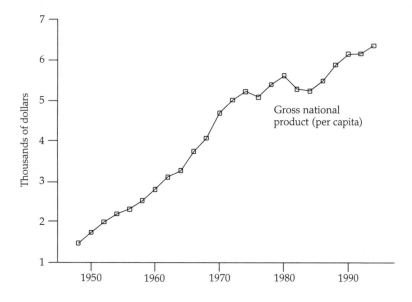

Gross national
product (per capita)

Source: Puerto Rico Planning Board, *Economic Report of the Governor,* various years.

there was one physician for approximately every 350 persons. The improvement in health facilities has led to sharp increases in life expectancy. In 1940, life expectancy was 46 years; by 1990 it was 75 years. The infant mortality rate has been drastically curtailed, from 109.1 infant deaths per thousand births in 1940, to 14.3 in 1990. Educational attainment is another area of major progress. In 1950, only 7 percent of the Puerto Rican population 25 years of age or older had a high school diploma; by 1990, this proportion had risen to approximately 50 percent. While in 1940, 31.5 percent of the population 10 years of age or older were able to read and write in any language, by 1990, this proportion had risen to well over 90 percent (Rivera-Batiz 1992a).

The substantial economic growth of Puerto Rico over the last fifty years is also reflected in the island's per capita GNP, which is higher than that of any other Latin American nation. This was not the case fifty years ago. Indeed, in 1940, per capita income was significantly lower in Puerto Rico than in Argentina, Chile, and Panama (Puerto Rico's per capita income was a third of Argentina's). By 1993, the Latin American nation with the highest per capita GNP relative to Puerto Rico's was Chile, whose per capita GNP was 79 percent of Puerto Rico's

Figure 1.2   Per Capita GNP in Latin America Relative to Puerto Rico, 1993

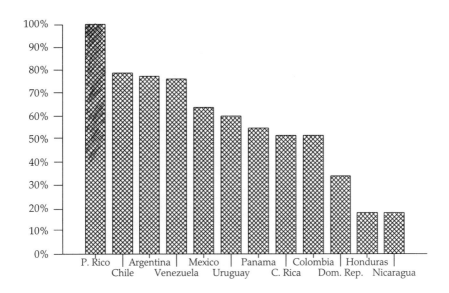

Source: World Bank (1995).
Note: GNP adjusted for purchasing power differences between countries.

(see figure 1.2). The per capita GNP of the poorest countries in Latin America, Nicaragua and Honduras, was less than 20 percent of Puerto Rico's. The World Bank ranks Puerto Rico among the middle-income countries worldwide. Within this group of countries, Puerto Rico's per capita GNP ranks slightly higher than that of Greece and South Korea, but somewhat below that of Ireland, Portugal, and Spain.

This glittering image of economic growth has an ugly underside, however. Although by some measures Puerto Rico has shown great progress since the 1940s, in recent years it has suffered from the effects of deep economic and social malaise. The unemployment rate, which had declined steadily during the 1950s and 1960s—the golden age of Puerto Rican economic development—to a low of under 6 percent, began to rise sharply after 1970 (see figure 1.3). By 1990, the unemployment rate had increased, to over 20 percent, nearly double what it was in 1940.

The crash of the labor market in Puerto Rico since the 1970s has had severe repercussions, particularly in the young. According to census data, in 1970, young men between the ages of 16 and 19 had an

Figure 1.3   Unemployment Rate in Puerto Rico, 1940–90

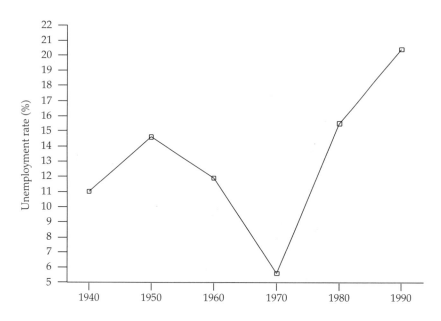

Source: U.S. Census of Population, Puerto Rico: Detailed Characteristics, various years.

unemployment rate of 17 percent. By 1990, the unemployment rate for this group was 54 percent. The unemployment rate for men aged 20 to 29 rose from 7 percent to 24 percent during this same period. Among young women, the rise in unemployment was just as dramatic. In 1970, females aged 16 to 19 had an unemployment rate of 21 percent; by 1990, the rate was 62 percent. Among women aged 20 to 29, unemployment went from 8 percent in 1970 to 29 percent in 1990.

Unemployment rates of 30 to 60 percent are indicative of a severely depressed labor market: consider that, in 1933, at the height of the Great Depression, unemployment in the United States was 25 percent. The social distress such a situation causes is bound to be severe. Indeed, the rising unemployment rate in Puerto Rico has been accompanied by disturbing social trends, the rise in the crime rate being the most visible. As the statistics on murder, rape, robbery, and theft show, crime in Puerto Rico has reached crisis levels. In the early 1990s, carjacking became a dangerously common crime all over the island. In 1992, there were 8,669 carjackings in Puerto Rico, or 2.4 carjackings per one thousand persons, the highest rate in the world at the time (Navarro 1994). By comparison, the rate in Los Angeles was 2.0 carjack-

Figure 1.4 Murder Rate in Puerto Rico, 1941–91

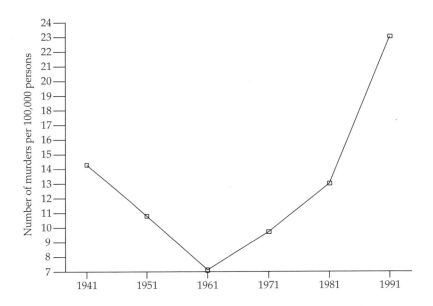

Sources: Data for 1941 through 1971 are from Silvestrini de Pacheco (1980), 273. Data for 1981 and 1991 are from U.S. Federal Bureau of Investigation, *Crime in the United States,* various issues.

ings per thousand. Although carjackings declined sharply after the taking of a vehicle with the use of a firearm became a federal crime in 1992—with penalties ranging up to life in prison—the paranoia caused by this crime spree persists. Expressing the feeling of powerlessness present in most of the population, one San Juan resident admitted, "My wife and I don't go out at night, out of fear. . . . We don't even like to go to the shopping center any more. The only place you can feel safe is where entry is controlled and there are guards there. It's an absurd situation" (Rohter 1993a, A13).

The murder rate, which had declined sharply between 1941 and 1961, started to go back up in the 1960s and early 1970s, rising gradually thereafter until it began to skyrocket in the early 1990s (see figure 1.4). In 1990, there were 17 murders per 100,000 persons; by 1992, the murder rate had climbed to 24.1. By comparison, the average murder rate in the United States in 1991 was 9.8. Only in large urban centers was the murder rate in the United States equal to or higher than the murder rate in Puerto Rico. In New York City, for example, in 1991 it was 29.3.

The rising level of crime on the island led Governor Pedro J. Rossello in 1993 to the unprecedented use of the national guard in raids on public housing projects and to patrol beaches and high crime areas. Although there was some worry about the possible militarization of the island and civil rights violations, most of the residents in areas ravaged by crime welcomed the initiative. One woman, who lived with her four children in the Vista Hermosa housing project in San Juan, said, "Now we can finally enjoy some peace. . . . Before the Guard came in, there were gun battles all over the place and you didn't dare stick your head out the window. But now I can let my kids play outside after dark. God bless them! As far as I am concerned, they can stay here forever" (Rohter 1993b, A10).

The rise of unemployment and its associated social ills occurred during a period of slowdown in economic growth. On average, real per capita GNP grew by 1.6 percent each year between 1970 and 1990. This constitutes a sharp drop from the 1950s and 1960s, when it grew by an average of 8.4 percent per year. What caused the deceleration of economic growth and the fourfold rise of unemployment in Puerto Rico between 1970 and 1990? How has the island's population adjusted to these changes? And, what is in store for Puerto Ricans in the coming years? In order to answer these questions, we must first consider Puerto Rico's economic history of the last fifty years.

Public Policy and Economic Change from 1947 to 1995

There have been three stages in Puerto Rico's development strategy over the last fifty years.[1] The first stage—Operation Bootstrap—lasted from 1947 to the early 1960s. The economic strategy pursued during this period led to the industrialization of the island.

Operation Bootstrap

Operation Bootstrap, a set of government policies aimed at fostering private-sector investment by U.S. firms in Puerto Rico, essentially replaced earlier initiatives to expand local employment through public investment. A new government agency, the Economic Development Administration (FOMENTO) was created. According to the economist Harvey Perloff, an early architect of this development strategy, "promoting industrial development . . . centered on the attempt to attract mainland industries and capital to the island through tax exemption,

---

1. On Puerto Rico's economic history, see Santiago (1992a), Pantojas-García (1990a), Dietz (1986), DeJesús Toro (1982), and Ruíz (1982).

industrial services, the provision of factory buildings, loans, and special assistance in various forms" (1950, 51).

Such incentives were necessary to attract U.S. capital to the island, even though manufacturing wages were four or five times lower than those on the mainland United States and the island enjoyed political stability and the free movement of goods, capital, and people with the United States. This was because the comparatively lower productivity of labor in Puerto Rico and the island's lack of infrastructure offset any cost advantages of locating there.[2] As a result, the government decided to undertake massive public investments in infrastructure, including the construction of physical plant facilities tailored to foreign investors. A "tax holiday" law was passed in 1947, and later amended in 1963, that provided income and property tax exemptions for U.S. investments in new manufacturing establishments. This, in combination with section 931 of the Internal Revenue Code of 1954, under which income earned by U.S. manufacturing firms in Puerto Rico was exempt from federal taxes, gave these firms a strong incentive to locate on the island.

Operation Bootstrap generated rapid growth of manufacturing production and employment. In 1950, there were 96 manufacturing plants promoted by the government. By 1963, there were 910. Most of these were in light manufacturing, many in the garment and small consumer-goods industries. The plants were labor-intensive and relied on unskilled, low-wage labor. They were also comparatively small (with an average of 80 or fewer employees per establishment). Many of them were assembly operations: raw materials and parts were shipped from the mainland, and the assembled goods were exported back to the mainland. The absence of tariffs or other barriers to trade between Puerto Rico and the mainland was critical to the success of these operations and gave Puerto Rico a cost advantage over other low-wage locations outside the United States.

Despite the island's rapid economic growth during this period, the situation was not entirely rosy. Puerto Rico's almost total dependence on the U.S. market for its exports left it hostage to sustained U.S. economic growth. This, combined with the *enclave* nature of its budding manufacturing industry, was worrisome. As economists Lloyd Reynolds and Peter Gregory noted: "Should the processing op-

2.   The lack of foreign investment in Puerto Rico may also have been related to a failure of single investors to recognize the potential profits of a coordinated, large-scale investment on the island. As Rodrik (1994, 80) observes: "Market prices reflect the profitability of different activities as they are currently undertaken; they do not provide any signals about the profitability of activities that would require a large-scale reallocation of resources within the economy (which, after all, is what economic development is all about)."

erations performed by these plants ever become unprofitable, they can be closed down at little cost to the parent company. Workers can be dismissed, the rented factory building turned back to FOMENTO, and the simple machinery in use shipped home or abandoned" (Reynolds and Gregory 1965, 23).

The Rise and Fall of Petrochemical Development

The potentially disastrous cyclical sensitivity of the employment generated by American capital in Puerto Rico moved the government to support the diversification of production. As a result, in the mid-1960s a new development strategy—the so-called petrochemical (capital-intensive) development strategy—emerged. Based on the theories of the economist Albert Hirschman (1958), the idea was to attract industries to the island whose output could be used as an input by other industries. These industries were also expected to make considerable capital investments in Puerto Rico and to be able to withstand a downturn in the business cycle. The government promoted huge petrochemical complexes, for example, in the hope that pharmaceuticals and other chemical companies, which use derivatives of the oil refining process, would also locate in Puerto Rico. The public sector's large subsidies for capital-intensive production engendered optimism and hopes that, in combination, the labor-intensive and capital-intensive industries would lead to astounding growth rates.

The boom of the 1950s and 1960s, however, became a bust in the 1970s and 1980s. In 1973, the sharp increase in the price of oil was associated with the start of a major recession in the United States. The old saying, "when the United States sneezes, the rest of the world catches cold," applied only too well to Puerto Rico. The demand for Puerto Rican manufactures collapsed and, as a result, between 1972 and 1976 unemployment almost doubled.

The U.S. economy recovered in the late 1970s, but Puerto Rico's did not. The island's GNP increased at a sluggish rate and the unemployment level, which stood at 5.6 percent in 1970, reached 15.5 percent in 1980. The increases in international oil prices had signaled the demise of the local petroleum refining industry. Puerto Rico had been importing cheap crude from Venezuela for processing on the island. As Venezuelan oil prices rose according to the guidelines set by the Organization of Petroleum Exporting Countries (OPEC), importers began to seek other, less expensive, sources of refined oil and to circumvent Puerto Rico's refineries, many of which closed their doors. The abandoned facilities can be seen today throughout the island, a ghostly reminder of this failed development strategy.

However, the crash of Puerto Rico's petrochemical industry was not the only reason its labor market failed to recover in the 1970s and 1980s. Under Operation Bootstrap, Puerto Rico had been at the forefront of a worldwide movement to open local markets to direct foreign investment. But by the 1970s and 1980s, many other industrializing and newly industrialized nations had begun to follow suit. This meant that U.S. firms now had a wide array of alternative sites in Asia and Latin America—where wages were as low or lower than those in Puerto Rico—from which to choose. At the same time, a worldwide movement to reduce tariff and nontariff barriers to trade meant that Puerto Rico lost its advantage in this area as well. Many U.S. firms were now locating their assembly plants in these low-tariff countries or in duty-free zones elsewhere.

The Expansion of Tax Breaks as Industrial Policy

The reaction of policymakers to the crisis of the 1970s was to generate a new round of tax breaks that would keep U.S. firms from leaving Puerto Rican soil and revive the incentives for greater foreign investment in the island.[3] This strategy, which began in 1976, constitutes the third, and latest, stage of industrial policymaking in Puerto Rico over the last fifty years. The legislative basis for the new strategy was section 936 of the U.S. Internal Revenue Code, as amended by the Tax Reform Act of 1976. Section 936, which superseded the previously mentioned section 931 of the U.S. tax code, in essence allowed subsidiaries of U.S. companies located on the island to repatriate income generated from their investments in Puerto Rico to their parent companies on the mainland free of federal taxes, but only if these funds were deposited in Puerto Rico for at least six months before repatriation. Such funds had to be used for investment purposes on the island or in the other countries of the Caribbean Basin. The so-called 936 funds in Puerto Rico's financial system grew quickly—from $7.4 billion in 1980, to close to $10 billion in 1992. These funds (which accounted for 18.6 percent of all commercial bank deposits in 1992) have become one of Puerto Rico's most important sources of private investment. Most of the money has been used to finance commercial loans, mortgages, and government loans (Daubón 1989; Escobar 1982).

The new tax laws perpetuated the tradition of relying on American direct investment to stimulate the local economy. In 1970, close to 80

---

3. Puerto Rico's development strategies are discussed by Bofil (1987), del Valle-Caballero (1994), Dietz and Pantojas-García (1993), Meléndez (1988), Curet (1986), Villamil (1983), Heine and Passalacqua (1983), Long (1988), and Freyre (1979).

percent of all manufacturing employment in Puerto Rico was in plants operating under the governmental incentive program; by 1989, this number had risen to 87 percent. The strategy suffered from two major shortcomings, both of which had surfaced under the previous strategies in the early 1970s. First, the tax and other incentives offered by Puerto Rico to American employers were aimed at reducing the relative cost of investing capital on the island, and they thus led to capital-intensive, rather than labor-intensive, investments. As a result, they were not able to generate a sustained boom in employment (Gutiérrez 1977). Indeed, the firms that were attracted under the 936 incentives plan produce capital-intensive pharmaceuticals, electronics equipment, and scientific instruments (Colón 1994; Marqués Velasco 1993). Second, the export-oriented plants established as a result of this strategy are highly sensitive to U.S. business cycles, and this contributed to increased variability of employment (Meléndez 1988; Alameda 1979; Baer 1960). The pattern of economic activity in Puerto Rico during the last three decades mirrors that of the United States, except that the booms and busts are magnified. As a result, recessions in the United States lead to massive social and economic dislocations on the island. This pattern was very evident in the 1980s and early 1990s.

A Time of Turbulence

The 1980s and early 1990s were a tempestuous period in Puerto Rico's history, and the sharp economic fluctuations of these years hit the island with the impact of a hurricane. Not even the hugely destructive hurricane Hugo, which blasted the island in September 1989, left such devastation in its wake as the economic turbulence of this period.

In 1982, the U.S. economy moved into a sharp recession, which led to American unemployment rates of close to 10 percent. The recession's repercussions in Puerto Rico were severe. By 1986, as many as 282 plants that had operated under government incentive programs had closed, with a loss of over 13,000 jobs. Unemployment soared to over 22 percent in 1986.

The U.S. economy rebounded quickly from this recession, and its recovery was strong and sustained. By 1989, the average unemployment rate in the United States had dropped to about 5 percent. In some states, unemployment fell below 4 percent. Although Puerto Rico also experienced brisk increases in production in the second half of the decade, unemployment rates remained high, exceeding 20 percent in 1990.

Economic activity in the United States slowed down once more between 1991 and 1993, with unemployment rising to over 7 percent in 1992. Again, Puerto Rico felt the impact of the U.S. economic slowdown. According to government figures, the unemployment rate on the island climbed an additional four percentage points between 1989 and 1993. Only in 1995 did the high unemployment levels in Puerto Rico begin to subside, a turnaround associated with the increased U.S. economic growth of the mid-1990s.

This economic hurricane did not affect Puerto Rico's population uniformly, however. Just as an actual hurricane may leave in its wake some areas less damaged than others, the effects of the economic and social crises of the last fifteen years have not been felt equally by all. While part of the population was becoming immiserized, part of it was substantially improving its socioeconomic status.

The divergent fortunes of different groups in the Puerto Rican economy are seen most clearly in the labor market. Although the average unemployment rate in Puerto Rico in 1990 was over 20 percent, the overall unemployment picture was uneven. In urban San Juan, for example, the unemployment rate was 15.5 percent, and in the urbanized *municipio* (county) of Guaynabo, located next to San Juan, unemployment was under 13 percent. On the other hand, in the *municipio* of Guayama on the sparsely populated southern coast of Puerto Rico, the unemployment rate exceeded 38 percent. In Jayuya and Utuado, located in the mountainous center of the island, the unemployment rates were 34 percent and 29 percent, respectively.

These regional differences in unemployment rates are reproduced in income levels. The *municipios* with the highest per capita income in Puerto Rico are Guaynabo, San Juan, and the bordering *municipios* of Carolina, Bayamón, and Trujillo Alto. Among the *municipios* with the lowest per capita income are Jayuya, Utuado, and others in the rural, central region of the island.

In addition to regional inequities, Puerto Rico's economic landscape is uneven in other respects as well. While unemployment rose to alarming proportions between 1980 and 1990, the earnings of those who were employed grew significantly (by close to 20 percent) during the same time period, especially in the second half of the decade. This suggests that the recessionary periods in the economy left a more lasting imprint on unemployment than on the pay of those who were employed. This was particularly devastating for young workers entering the labor market for the first time. Older, experienced workers and highly educated employees made substantial economic gains. What caused these inequities?

A significant part of the employment generated by the Puerto Rican economy in the 1980s was associated with U.S. direct investment. As we have noted, these investments were capital-intensive and provided comparatively high-paying jobs, but did not supply a boost to employment relative to the growing labor force (Santiago 1987a).

A second explanation for the rising average pay—and the growing unemployment—is the sharp increase in minimum wages during the period. Minimum wages in Puerto Rico are established under a combination of federal and Puerto Rican statutes. The 1938 Fair Labor Standards Act (FLSA) first set minimum wages both for the mainland and for Puerto Rico. However, a few years later, the U.S. government allowed Puerto Rico's minimum wages to be set below the federal standards. In addition, the minimum wage covered only limited sectors of the island's economy. This changed in the late 1970s and the 1980s, when amendments to the FLSA extended coverage widely in Puerto Rico.

One of the ideas behind a minimum wage is to make sure that unwitting workers are not exploited by unscrupulous employers who offer wages much below the prevailing market rate. In Puerto Rico, however, prevailing market wages have traditionally been much below those on the mainland. The federal minimum wage has thus often exceeded the wages offered by many employers. Although some firms have been able to raise their salaries to the federal minimum wage level, becoming more productive in the process, others have found it extremely difficult to do so. Puerto Rico first felt the full force of the federal minimum wage in the 1980s. As this study shows, the widespread application of the minimum wage contributed significantly to the higher earnings obtained by employed Puerto Ricans in the 1980s but, at the same time, by making it more expensive to employ labor, it also contributed to the island's unemployment problem.[4]

Shifts in U.S. Government Policies

The federal government has made itself increasingly felt in the Puerto Rican labor market and in other areas as well. Federal transfers to Puerto Rico increased sharply between 1970 and 1990. Payments made by the U.S. government to persons in Puerto Rico rose from just over $500 million to over $6 billion annually, and the proportion of personal income accounted for by these transfer payments nearly doubled, from 15 percent to 29 percent (see figure 1.5).

The increase in federal transfer payments ameliorated the social impact of the climbing unemployment rate and the sluggish economy. Many of the poor in the population were able to sustain minimum consumption levels and maintain their living standards in spite of the economic crisis. Since a large share of the transfer payments was spent on local consumer goods and services, the rise in federal entitlements led to a surge in the service and commerce sectors of the economy.

---

4. Our findings are consistent with those of Castillo-Freeman and Freeman (1992). See also Santiago (1987a, 1989).

Figure 1.5 Federal Transfer Payments as a Fraction of Personal Income in Puerto Rico, 1940–90

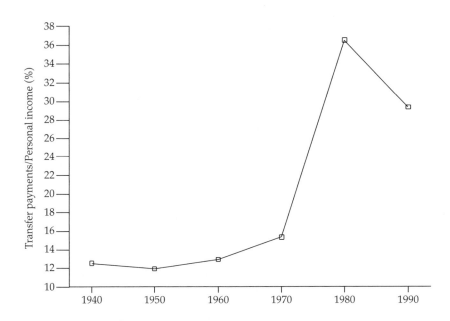

Source: Puerto Rico Planning Board, *Economic Report of the Governor,* various years.

Indeed, in the economy as a whole, services and commerce were the only two sectors to show a substantial gain in employment between 1970 and 1990, by which time they accounted for close to half of the employment on the island.

One of the most important federal welfare programs applied to Puerto Rico in the 1970s was the Food Stamp Program, which was extended to the island in 1971 but effectively introduced only in 1974. The following year, $388 million in food stamps were issued to the population (Choudhury 1977, 1978). In 1982, the program was phased out and replaced by the Nutritional Assistance Grant (NAG) program, under which individuals receive checks instead of coupons. In 1993, grants to Puerto Rico under this program amounted to $1 billion.

The broad participation of Puerto Rico's population in the food stamp and NAG programs has had a double-edged impact on the island's economy. On the one hand, the program has clearly succeeded in ensuring minimum nutritional levels for the poor. As the economist Richard Weisskoff (1985, 60) notes: "The largest single federal program ever directed to the people of Puerto Rico, food stamps were introduced quickly throughout the island from September 1974 to January 1975, 'like a hurricane relief expedition,' according to one federal official. Seen in historical perspective, the food stamp program in Puerto Rico arrived at a critical juncture in the island's development. . . . Food stamps have served as the rescue operation for the entire Commonwealth economy."

At the same time, some social scientists believe that the wide application of the food stamp and NAG programs to the low-income economy of Puerto Rico has created a ghetto-style economy there. They argue that the easily available transfer payments encourage labor market participants to scale upward the wage offers at which they are willing to accept employment. They are thus more likely to remain unemployed, searching for high-paying job offers that may never surface. This generates a vicious cycle in which the programs that were intended to alleviate a short-term problem discourage work, promote long-term dependency on transfer payments, and create long-term poverty. As the Puerto Rican economist Elías Gutiérrez (1983, 127) points out, "The problem with the level and nature of the welfare system, or the transfer payments system, is that payments are such that it keeps the recipients in poverty. Their poverty in turn tends to reinforce itself because of the social and psychological impact of poverty on the poor or the dependent" (see also, Weisskoff 1985). Some critics (Murray 1985; Chavez 1991) of public assistance programs in the United States have further claimed that such welfare programs as food stamps and Aid to Families with Dependent Children (AFDC), increase poverty among women by inducing them to have more children out of wedlock and to form single-headed households in order to qualify for higher benefits.

After the Reagan administration tightened eligibility requirements for welfare programs and lowered benefits, food stamp/NAG transfers to Puerto Rico declined, from $896 million in 1982, to $780 million in 1985. However, this drop was only temporary and, by the early 1990s, NAG transfers exceeded $1 billion annually.

There have also been significant changes in federal policies with respect to 936 funds. In 1982, the Reagan administration changed the rules so that half of the income generated by U.S. firms in Puerto Rico would be subject to the 46 percent federal corporate income tax. Up to that point, all such income had been exempt from federal corporate taxes under section 936. The resulting increase in tax revenues collected by the U.S. Treasury did not end the controversy surrounding these tax breaks, however. Periodically, both the U.S. Treasury and Congress threaten to eliminate section 936. In May 1992, the General Accounting Office released a report documenting the huge tax benefits received by some U.S. corporations in Puerto Rico, feeding speculation that the tax breaks would soon be gone. Moreover, the periodic plebiscites to determine Puerto Rico's political status have eroded investor confidence, which undermines section 936's effectiveness. The outcome of the latest plebiscite, in 1994, favored continued commonwealth status, but this did little to remove the underlying uncertainty, especially given the general antagonism among the American public toward any form of "corporate welfare."

Island Paradox

The relationships between Puerto Rico and the United States have led to a paradoxical situation. Overall, the integration of Puerto Rico into the U.S. economy has been associated with substantial income growth in the island. At the same time, the tight links with the United States have led to increased economic volatility, and, during the last twenty years, to growing unemployment and widespread social malaise. In some ways, Puerto Rico is no different from any other economic region of the United States. But there is one major difference between Puerto Rico and almost all other regions of the United States: by comparison with almost any part of the United States, Puerto Rico has much lower per capita income. Disposable income per capita in the United States in 1990 was $14,948, while in Puerto Rico it was $5,215 (see figure 1.6). Even the state with the lowest per capita income, Mississippi, had close to twice that of Puerto Rico. Richer states, like New Jersey and Connecticut, had per capita incomes close to four times that of Puerto Rico. Furthermore, the per capita income of every ethnic and racial group within the United States—including mainland Puerto Ricans—was substantially above the average for Puerto Ricans living in Puerto Rico. On this account, Puerto Rico remains a developing economy, more akin the rest of Latin America than the United States.

The differences in standard of living between Puerto Rico and the United States, combined with the freedom of movement between them, have given rise to massive migration flows. There were over a million persons who were born in Puerto Rico residing in the mainland United States in 1990. This constituted 26 percent of all native-born Puerto Ricans. In terms of its impact on the source country, Mexican migration to the United States pales in comparison. In 1990, only about 5 percent of all persons born in Mexico were residing in the United States.

The impact of migration flows on Puerto Rico's economy and society runs deep. Historically, emigration has served as a safety valve for the island, as evidenced by the Commonwealth's own policies, which fostered migration to the mainland by aiding in the recruitment of Puerto Rican labor. Between 1940 and 1970, 835,000 Puerto Ricans emigrated to the mainland United States on a net basis, constituting one of the

Figure 1.6   Per Capita Personal Income in Puerto Rico and the United States, 1990

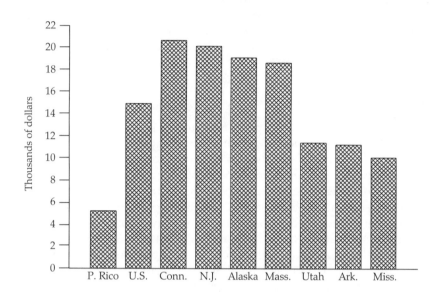

Sources: For Puerto Rico, the data are from Commonwealth of Puerto Rico, Planning Board, *Informe Económico al Gobernador, 1991,* statistical appendix, table 1. For the United States, the data are from U.S. Bureau of the Census, *Statistical Abstract of the United States, 1991.*

most massive emigration flows occurring anywhere in this century. Although most of this population settled in New York City, in recent years, Puerto Rican migration to the United States has become more geographically dispersed. From California to Connecticut, from Florida to Massachusetts, Puerto Rican communities now exist all over the country. This other Puerto Rico maintains its intimate ties with the island. Reinforced by constant flows back and forth between the two communities, the Puerto Rican population on the mainland continues to exert a serious political, economic, and social influence on Puerto Ricans on the island.

The fact that migration flows between Puerto Rico and the mainland are not just one-way flows to the mainland is significant. Between 1980 and 1990, there was a net emigration of 116,571 persons from Puerto Rico, but this number hides the massive gross flows of people moving back and forth between the two places. In the 1980s, 432,744 persons left the island to reside in the mainland and 316,172 persons emigrated from the mainland to reside in Puerto Rico. Many of the latter were return migrants, although a significant number were Puerto Ricans born and raised in the United States. In fact, close to one in ten Puerto Ricans residing on the island in 1990 had moved from the mainland to Puerto Rico in the 1980s. The Puerto Rican migration process is studied carefully in this book since it embodies the paradoxical nature and consequences of the relationships between Puerto Rico and the United States.

Outline of the Book

This book maps the socioeconomic status of the Puerto Rican population in the 1990s. In a territory of 3,420 square miles, population growth and population density have long been a matter of concern in Puerto Rico. The number of people residing in Puerto Rico boomed during this century. Between 1900 and 1980, the population more than tripled. The 1980s, however, were witness to a significant slowdown in population growth. Between 1980 and 1990, the population of Puerto Rico increased from 3,196,500 to 3,522,000, representing an annual change of about 1 percent a year. This constitutes a sharp drop compared with the rate of increase of the population in the 1970s. Chapter 2 addresses the nature of this drop in population growth, focusing on the role played by decreases in fertility. The chapter examines trends in fertility, age structure, marriage, and household composition in Puerto Rico during the 1980s. These trends are compared with those for the Puerto Rican population in the mainland. The questions we examine include: Does a drop in birth rates explain the declining population growth of the island in the 1980s? Is the average age in Puerto Rico rising? And how has household composition changed in the past decade? Did divorce rates increase among Puerto Ricans in the 1980s? Did single parenthood rise as much as it did in the mainland during the decade?

Migration to the United States also has had a major impact on the Puerto Rican population. Emigration to the mainland serves as a safety valve, releasing the local labor market from the pressures of a bulging labor force. For example, in the 1950s, when close to half a million Puerto Ricans emigrated to the United States, population growth in the island slowed down to a trickle. Chapter 3 examines the patterns of Puerto Rican migration in the 1980s, comparing them with those prevailing in earlier decades. The characteristics of the out-migrants from Puerto Rico are examined in detail in this chapter, since they have been a matter of controversy. Some analysts have argued that recent emigrants have been mostly highly educated professional and technical workers, altering the composition of the island's migratory contingent from unskilled to highly skilled. Is Puerto Rico suffering from a "brain drain" phenomenon? Chapter 3 answers this question using 1980 and 1990 census data. Other questions examined in this chapter include: How much return migration is occurring in the island, and what are the characteristics of these migrants? Is migration between Puerto Rico and the mainland becoming circular or commuter-like, with people moving back and forth instead of staying at their place of destination for a long period of time?

In the second half of the 1980s, more than a decade of stagnant income growth came to an end, as per capita income in Puerto Rico again grew rapidly, pulled by a strong upswing in American economic activity. Chapter 4 discusses the changes in the level and distribution of income in Puerto Rico occurring in the 1980s. Household income and poverty rates are examined for the island overall, for demographic groups, and for regions of the island. The issue of whether inequality has increased or decreased is also analyzed in detail, including a discussion of how public assistance has influenced poverty and income distribution. Educational attainment is a major determinant of individual income and it is given close attention in this chapter. Other questions discussed include: Why did the increase in educational levels slow down in the 1980s? How did the educational attainment of women change relative to that of men in Puerto Rico? Has the gender gap in education declined in the island, as it did in the United States in the 1970s and early 1980s?

The Puerto Rican labor market has been the subject of tremendous turbulence during the last twenty-five years. There is, however, a disturbing long-term trend of rising unemployment rates. Chapter 5 examines changes in the Puerto Rican labor market during the 1980s. The chapter studies the changes in the unemployment rate and labor force participation rate between 1980 and 1990, by age and gender. The analysis examines the determinants of the rising unemployment rate, including a thorough discussion of the role played by the minimum wage. In addition, the chapter dissects the changes in the earnings of men and women during the 1980s, as well as the determinants of those changes. Given that earnings inequality increased substantially in the United States during the 1980s, the research presented in chapter 5 seeks to determine whether there has been a similar shift in the wage structure in Puerto Rico. Other questions examined include: Has labor market inequality on the basis of gender decreased in Puerto Rico? Have the returns to education increased in Puerto Rico, as they did in the United States over the past twenty years? And what role does labor market segmentation play in the economy?

The population of Puerto Rico in 1990 included 321,097 people born outside the island. This constitutes 9.1 percent of the population in the island, a proportion almost identical to the proportion of the population in the United States born outside the nation. Thus, Puerto Rico hosts a foreign-born population approximately equal in proportion to that in the United States, a country famed for absorbing great numbers of immigrants. Chapter 6 examines the characteristics of persons born outside Puerto Rico, supplying a comparative profile of their socioeconomic status in 1990. The intermediate economic position of Puerto Rico, between less developed Latin America and the highly developed United States, has generated a distinct pattern of labor migration, in which Puerto Ricans emigrate to the United States as other Caribbeans (mostly from Cuba and the Dominican Republic) migrate to Puerto Rico. Chapter 6 describes the population of immigrants settling in Puerto Rico and their characteristics.

There are close to three million Puerto Ricans residing in the mainland, making it the second largest Latino population in the continental United States. This population has become increasingly dispersed over the years. While in 1960 close to two-thirds of all Puerto Ricans in the United States lived in New York City, by 1990 only one-third resided there. Substantial populations have emerged in smaller urban areas. For example, Puerto Ricans account for close to one-quarter of the population in cities such as Hartford and Bridgeport. Chapter 7 describes changes in the socioeconomic status of Puerto Ricans living in the United States during the 1980s. The chapter also describes shifts in where Puerto Ricans settle in the mainland and analyzes the geography of Puerto Rican poverty. Questions examined in this chapter include: Are Puerto Ricans the worst-off ethnic group in the United States? Is there a substantial Puerto Rican middle class sprouting in America? How has the educational attainment of Puerto Ricans changed in recent years and what impact has this had on the economic outcomes of Puerto Ricans in the United States?

Puerto Rico's experiences under Commonwealth political status provide a rich background for evaluating the consequences of the economic policies followed by Commonwealth policymakers. They also set the stage for the design of new policies that can move the island toward the twenty-first century. Chapter 8 summarizes various demographic and economic trends discussed in the book and examines the policy agenda facing the 1990s. The experience of Puerto Rico is highly relevant to countries moving toward more open trade and investment policies. The application of federal legislation in Puerto Rico also constitutes a virtual experiment into the consequences of political and economic integration of countries with widely divergent levels of development. One can only hope that the analysis provided in this book will help inform future policymaking in Puerto Rico and other developing nations.

CHAPTER 2

Population Growth and Demographic Changes

T HE ISLAND of Puerto Rico is only 100 miles long by 34 miles wide. In such close quarters, the congestion and agglomeration associated with sustained population growth are a matter of serious concern. Puerto Rico's population density has increased at an astounding rate, rising from 545 persons per square mile in 1940, to 1,059 persons per square mile in 1993. For comparison, average population density in the mainland United States currently hovers around 10 persons per square mile. No state has a higher population density than Puerto Rico, and only the large U.S. metropolitan areas are more congested.

The number of people in Puerto Rico has risen rapidly since the turn of the century when the island had approximately one million residents; by 1980, the population had broken the three million mark. Population growth slowed considerably in the 1980s, however. Between 1980 and 1990, the population of Puerto Rico grew by about 325,000, an increase of 10.2 percent. This represents one of the slowest periods of population growth on the island this century. There was certainly a sharp slowdown from the rate of expansion during the decades of the 1970s and 1960s (see table 2.1). What explains this decline in population growth?

Changes in population can be accounted for by differences between births and deaths (the *natural* increase of the population) or by net migration flows (the net balance of people moving in and out of a jurisdiction). As shown in table 2.2, the natural increase of the population between 1980 and 1990 was equal to 442,108 persons. This represents a significant drop relative to the previous decade, when the natural in-

Table 2.1   Population Growth in Puerto Rico, 1899–1990

	Total Population	Increase in Population from Preceding Census	
		Number	Percentage
1899	953,243	154,678	19.4
1910	1,118,012	164,769	17.3
1920	1,299,809	181,797	16.3
1930	1,543,913	244,104	18.8
1940	1,869,255	325,342	21.1
1950	2,210,703	341,448	18.3
1960	2,349,544	138,841	6.3
1970	2,712,033	362,489	15.4
1980	3,196,500	484,487	17.9
1990	3,522,037	325,537	10.2

Sources: 1980 U.S. Census of Population and Housing: Characteristics of the Population, Number of Inhabitants: Puerto Rico, table 1; and 1990 U.S. Census of Population and Housing: Summary Social, Economic, and Housing Characteristics, table 1.

Table 2.2   Population Growth in Puerto Rico: Natural Increase versus Net Migration

Component of Population Change	1970–80	1980–90
Total change in population	484,487	325,537
Natural increase of the population	550,300	442,108
Net migration	−65,813	−116,571

Sources: Figures for population change are as determined by the decennial census of Puerto Rico (see table 2.1). Data for births and deaths in Puerto Rico are as supplied by the U.S. Bureau of the Census (quoted in *Statistical Abstract of the United States, 1992,* supplemented with information from Planning Board of Puerto Rico, *Informe Económico del Gobernador, 1992.*
Note: The natural increase of the population is the difference between births and deaths, as determined by the Demographic Register of the Puerto Rico Department of Health. Net migration figures are calculated as a residual.

crease of the population was equal to 550,300 persons. At the same time, it is clear that net migration also accounted for some of the population growth slowdown in the 1980s.

However, the sharp reduction in the rate of natural increase is the more important factor. If the net emigration from the island in the 1980s had remained at the lower rate prevailing in the 1970s, population growth between 1980 and 1990 would still have been only 11.1 percent, close to its actual value of 10.2 percent. On the other hand, if the natural increase of the population in the 1980s had remained at the high level prevailing in the 1970s, population growth between 1980 and 1990 would have been a substantially higher 16.6 percent.

Population Growth and Demographic Transition

The changes in population growth associated with economic develop-ment have been found to follow certain empirical regularities that are referred to collectively as *demographic transition* (Coale 1987; World Bank 1994). The beginning of the process of demographic transition in a developing country is typically characterized by slow population growth. This slow growth is associated with offsetting high birth and mortality rates. Very low levels of economic development are associ-ated with high infant mortality rates, which means that few infants make it into adulthood. As economic development proceeds and health delivery systems, sanitation facilities, and nutrition improve, mortality declines. This drop in mortality occurs rapidly, with fertility staying constant or even increasing. Population growth booms during this sec-ond stage of the demographic transition. A third stage of the demo-graphic transition occurs when the economic, social, and cultural changes linked to economic development reduce birth rates, thus low-ering population growth. In this last stage, as families in industrial, urban societies choose to have a smaller number of children, the lower birth rates converge with death rates and population growth sharply decreases (Easterlin 1968; Rivera-Batiz 1984).

Mortality rates started to drop precipitously in Puerto Rico in the 1930s. Between 1930 and 1950, the number of persons who died each year dropped from 20 per thousand to fewer than 10 per thousand (see figure 2.1). This reduced death rate was linked to improved health conditions and better nutrition. During the same time period, the birth rate stayed more or less constant, fluctuating around 40 births per thou-sand.[1] The stable birth rate, combined with the sharply declining death rate, led to booming population growth.

Puerto Rico's birth rate declined steadily after the beginning of the 1950s, and in 1990, there were 18.8 births per thousand. (The birth rate in the United States in 1990 was 16.7 births per thousand.) Puerto Rico's death rate continued to decline between 1950 and 1980. However, the 1980s witnessed a sharp turnaround in the death rate, which *rose* from 6.6 deaths per thousand in 1980, to 7.4 in 1990. The fall in the birth rate

1. The birth rate edged up in the late 1940s, an increase associated with the "baby boom" that followed the Second World War. The official records of births are incomplete, however, and the actual birth rate for the period before 1950 may be higher (Vázquez Calzada 1980 and 1988, 119).

Figure 2.1   Birth and Death Rates in Puerto Rico, 1930–90

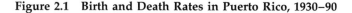

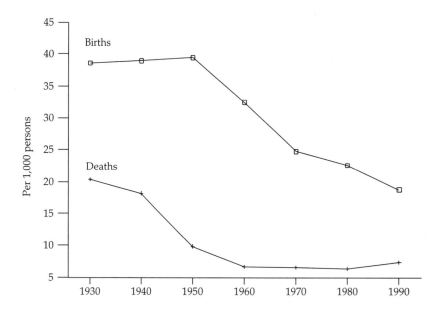

Source: Planning Board of Puerto Rico, *Informe Económico al Gobernador,* various issues.

and the rise in the death rate in the 1980s together account for the significant slowdown in the natural increase of the population during this decade.

The Rise of Death Rates and the Graying of the Population in the 1980s

What accounts for the rise in mortality rates in Puerto Rico in recent years? Sudden changes in death rates are sometimes associated with increases in the death rates of children or older people due to their greater vulnerability to disease. However, the recent increase in the death rate in Puerto Rico is not related to changes in infant mortality: the rate of infant deaths continued its downward trend during the 1980s. The infant death rate (deaths per 1,000 live births) dropped from 109.1 in 1940, to 18.5 in 1980, to 12.5 in 1988. Moreover, the mortality rate among the elderly also fell in the 1980s: the mortality rate for those aged 70 to 74, for example, decreased from 34 deaths per thousand in 1980, to about 30 per thousand in 1990.

Mortality rates did rise for persons 25 to 44 years of age, especially men. Men between the ages of 30 and 34 suffered the highest increase in mortality rates, from 2.7 deaths per thousand in 1980, to approximately 4 per thousand in 1990. The rise in the mortality rates of adults aged 25 to 44 is partly related to a higher incidence of homicide and traffic accidents, which were among the top three causes of death for the age group in 1990. However, the top cause of death within this age group in 1990 was Acquired Immune Deficiency Syndrome (AIDS), a disease that was virtually absent from the Puerto Rican landscape in 1980 (Cunningham, Ramos Bellido, and Ortiz Colón 1991).

AIDS now constitutes the fourth most important cause of death in Puerto Rico overall, according to official statistics released in 1995. According to the government, by December 1995, 16,669 persons had been diagnosed with AIDS, of which 60 percent had died. But the real mortality rate due to AIDS may be even higher, since deaths from AIDS often go unreported as such. It is not a coincidence that deaths from diseases often associated with AIDS grew sharply during the 1980s and early 1990s. For instance, the mortality rate due to pneumonia rose from 25.3 per thousand deaths in 1980, to 41.8 in 1990. It is likely that most, if not all, of this increase was the result of AIDS-related pneumonia.

The increased mortality rates of the 1980s were also related to the aging of the population. As the proportion of the population 65 years of age or over increases, overall mortality rises (Vázquez Calzada 1988, ch. 9). The median age in Puerto Rico climbed from 18.4 years in 1950, to 28.4 years in 1990. (The median age in the United States in 1990 was 32.9 years.)

Table 2.3 details the changing age structure in Puerto Rico between

Table 2.3   **Age Distribution of the Puerto Rican Population, 1980–90**

Age	1980	1990
Younger than 16	34.3%	29.1%
16–19	8.2	7.4
20–24	8.4	8.1
25–34	14.5	14.7
35–44	11.2	13.2
45–54	8.5	10.2
55–64	7.0	7.6
65 and older	7.9	9.7
Median age of the population	24.6	28.5
Male	23.7	27.2
Female	25.5	29.6

Sources: 1980 and 1990 U.S. Census of Population and Housing: Puerto Rico, 5% PUMS.

Figure 2.2   Population of Puerto Rico in 1980 and 1990

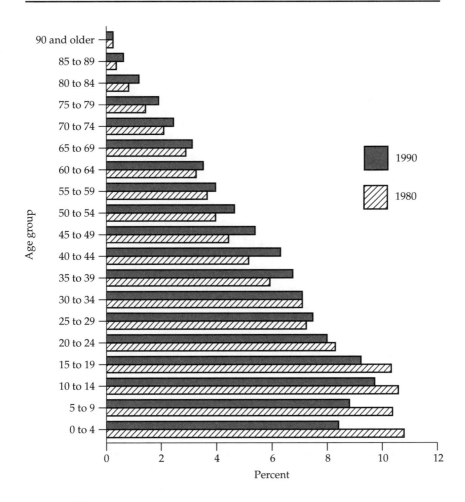

1980 and 1990, and figure 2.2 reproduces the data from this table diagrammatically. The fraction of the total population over 24 years of age increased by 6.3 percentage points between 1980 and 1990. By 1990, youth dependency (persons 0–10 years old as percent of those 15 to 64) had declined below 50 percent, while old-age dependency had increased to over 15 percent. This is in sharp contrast to the structure of the Puerto Rican population forty years ago, when youth dependency reached 80 percent and old-age dependency was under 10 percent.

Table 2.4   Changes in Fertility, 1980–90

Measure of Fertility	1980	1990
Average number of children ever born to women aged 15 to 44	1.7	1.5
General fertility rate[a]	98.7	66.9
Total fertility rate[b]	3.6	3.0

Sources: 1980 and 1990 U.S. Census of Population and Housing: Puerto Rico, 5% PUMS.
[a]The general fertility rate is calculated by multiplying the number of births of both sexes in a given year by 1,000 and dividing the result by the number of women in the 15–44 age group.
[b]The total fertility rate represents the estimated number of children that would be born to a woman, if she were to live to the end of her child-bearing years and bear children at each age in accordance with the prevailing age-specific birth rates.

The overall aging of the Puerto Rican population has been influenced by declining birth rates and by the net migration of Puerto Ricans to the mainland United States. Between 1980 and 1990, the proportion of children in the population fell by more than 5 percent. Migration has also left the island with an older population because out-migrants from Puerto Rico are generally younger than the average. Between 1985 and 1990, when the median age of the overall population was 28.4 years, Puerto Ricans migrating to the United States had a median age of 24 years. Since close to 110,000 persons emigrated from Puerto Rico to the mainland during the 1980s on a net basis, this exodus means that a substantial number of young Puerto Ricans have left the island.

The Decline in the Birth Rates

Although the rising death rate explains some of the recent population growth slowdown exhibited in Puerto Rico, a more significant factor is the steep drop in the birth rate, as reflected in the sharply falling measures of fertility.

Recent Changes in Fertility

Table 2.4 illustrates the changes that occurred in fertility rates between 1980 and 1990 using three alternative measures. The first measure is the mean number of children ever born to women in the prime child-bearing years between ages 15 and 44. This decline in the average number of children ever born in Puerto Rico, from 1.7 in 1980 to 1.5 in 1990, brought the island's average closer to that of the United States, where the corresponding figure in 1990 was 1.2 children.

Note that the average number of children ever born is not sharply affected by recent changes in fertility since it is a measure of the total number of children that women aged 15 to 44 years have had over time. Over a period of ten years, this measure changes slowly, so demographers often turn to alternative measures of fertility that reflect recent changes in fertility more clearly. One alternative measure of fertility is calculated by dividing the number of births in any given year multiplied by 1,000, by the number of women of child-bearing age in the population. This is referred to as the general fertility rate (GFR). Between 1980 and 1990, Puerto Rico's GFR dropped by a third.

Another measure of fertility commonly used in demographic analysis is the total fertility rate (TFR), or the average estimated number of children that would be born to a woman if she were to live to the end of her child-bearing years and bear children at each age according to the prevailing birth rates at various ages. Puerto Rico's TFR fell from 3.6 to 3.0 children between 1980 and 1990, meaning that, on average, a woman entering her child-bearing period in 1990 would have three children over her lifetime. By comparison, a woman who entered her child-bearing years in 1980 would likely have closer to four children in her lifetime.

Teenage Pregnancy and Single Parenthood

The fertility drop in Puerto Rico in the 1980s occurred in all age groups, but especially among the older cohorts. As a comparison of the two curves presented in figure 2.3—which illustrate the relationship between age and the mean number of children ever born in Puerto Rico in 1980 and in 1990—reveals at any given age, the number of children ever born in 1990 was below the level prevailing in 1980. For instance, in 1980, the average number of children ever born to women aged 35 to 44 was 3.3. By 1990, the corresponding number was 2.5 children. This constitutes a sharp drop in so short a period. The mean number of children ever born declined more sharply among older women; it hardly declined at all among teenagers. The proportion of Puerto Rican women 15 to 19 years of age who had given birth to one or more children (11 percent) remained unchanged between 1980 and 1990. This contrasts sharply with the mainland United States, where the birth rate for women in this age group climbed by close to 20 percent between 1980 and 1991 (Roberts 1993, 51).

Marital status is another key variable linked to fertility. Since it is through marriage that child-bearing is traditionally sanctioned by religion and society, the likelihood that a woman will have children is much greater among married women than among women who have

**Figure 2.3   Mean Number of Children Ever Born in Puerto Rico, 1980 and
1990**

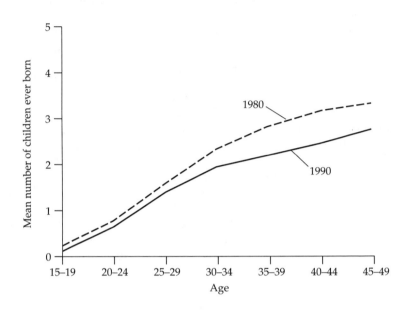

Sources: 1980 and 1990 U.S. Census of Population and Housing: Puerto Rico, 5% PUMS.

never married. In the United States, in 1992, for example, the average
number of children ever born to married women was six times that
for women who had never married. Nevertheless, one of the most significant demographic changes in the United States over the last ten
years has been the rapid rise of single parenthood among women, either as the result of divorce or of bearing children out of wedlock
(McLanahan and Casper 1995, 10–12). The birth rate among unmarried
women in the Unted States rose from 29.4 children per thousand
women in 1980, to 45.2 children per thousand in 1991. Single parenthood increased among all age groups in the U.S. population during
this period: among unmarried women aged 15 to 19 years, the birth
rate climbed from 27.6 to 44.8 children per thousand; among unmarried
women aged 30 to 34, the increase was from 21.1 to 38.1.

The census questionnaire for the mainland United States lists four
choices under marital status: *never married, married, divorced,* or *widowed.*
In the census of Puerto Rico, however, there are five choices, the additional one being *consensually married,* that is, persons living together in
a marital union without a civil or religious matrimonial contract. For

the purposes of this analysis, married persons include the consensually married. Although some may consider consensual marriages to be more unstable than formal marriages, the fact is that, in Puerto Rico, a high proportion of these marriages are stable and many are eventually legalized (Vázquez Calzada 1988, 55).[2]

As in the mainland United States, in Puerto Rico married women are much more likely to have children than unmarried women (Hill, Black, and Stycos 1957). In 1990, the number of children ever born to married women 15 to 44 years old was 2.23, while among never-married women, the average was 0.21. But, as in the United States, the average number of children born to never-married women in Puerto Rico in the 1980s rose, doubling during the decade. This increase in the birth rate of never-married women runs against the general decline of fertility in Puerto Rico in the 1980s: for married women aged 15 to 44, the average number of children ever born dropped from 2.5 to 2.2.

Single parenthood has also increased in Puerto Rico. As figure 2.4 shows, between 1980 and 1990, the proportion of women aged 18 to 55 who were single parents rose from under 16 percent to nearly 19 percent, about twice that of the U.S. mainland.[3] Because single parenthood in America varies widely, figure 2.4 presents the data for the mainland United States decomposed by race and ethnicity.

The Determinants of Declining Fertility

Despite the rising fertility among women who are not married, the overall drop in fertility in Puerto Rico in the last fifty years has been remarkable. Changes in fertility are related to a complex interplay of biological, socioeconomic, and institutional forces. Declining fertility is usually the result of a decision by women, their families, or society to reduce family size by limiting births (Schultz 1973). The shifting roles of women in society play a big role in this decision. Higher educational attainment, rising labor force participation, and increased earnings among women are major contributing factors in fertility reduction because they raise the opportunity cost of having children. Rural-to-urban migration is also associated with reduced fertility. Since all of these factors have come into play in Puerto Rico since the 1950s, its declining fertility rate is not surprising.

2. Fewer than 5 percent of all persons declaring marriage as their marital status in the 1990 census stated that they were consensually married.
3. The definition of single women adopted here includes divorced, separated, and widowed women, in addition to never-married women.

Figure 2.4   Single Parenthood among Women Aged 18 to 55 Years

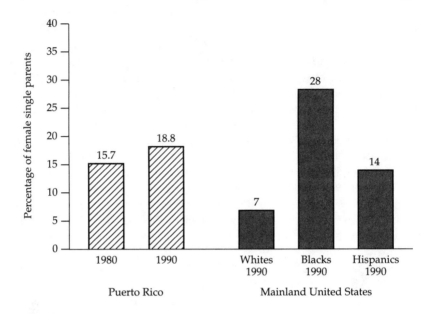

Sources: The data for the mainland United States are from McLanahan and Casper (1995), 14; data for Puerto Rico are from 1990 U.S. Census of Population and Housing: Puerto Rico, 5% PUMS.

Public Policy toward Birth Control

Public policy also plays an important role in birth control. The increased awareness and availability of contraceptive methods is clearly associated with lower birth rates. By supplying birth control information and services, governments can act to lower fertility rates. Public policy toward birth control in Puerto Rico has ranged from aggressive support to benign neglect. In the 1930s and 1940s, the government took aggressive measures in providing contraceptives to the population. It later shifted its approach to one of supplying information and family planning services and has vigorously pursued this policy from the 1970s to the present. The swings in government policy correlate with the effectiveness of the Catholic Church in lobbying against birth control. As Luis Aponte Martínez, the archbishop of Puerto Rico, noted in 1966: "To put an end to the conflict between the Church and the Commonwealth of Puerto Rico, the Government has decided to be neutral and to let private organizations promote birth control . . . the Church has made known its position. There is no doubt that we were opposed and continue to be opposed to government promotion of birth control" (Earnhardt 1982, 62).

Whenever the government's policy has shifted from proactive to passive support for birth control, nongovernmental organizations have taken up the slack, aggressively supplying birth control information and services through a network of clinics and volunteers. In the 1950s, for example, the Family Planning Association widely promoted oral contraceptives as well as male and female sterilization. Both public and private efforts to control the birth rate have been controversial at times, as, for example, when the Family Planning Association participated in organizing human trials of experimental oral contraceptives, or in the wake of reports of involuntary sterilizations (Presser 1973; Mass 1977).

In any event, the widespread dissemination of birth control information and services by both the public sector and nongovernmental organizations has contributed to a reduction in the birth rate. The sociologist Joseph Mayone Stycos found that, as early as 1955, 100 percent of men and 84 percent of women in Puerto Rico knew about at least one method of birth control and that female sterilization was the most common method of birth control (Stycos 1955). Of the women he surveyed, 43 percent of those using birth control methods were sterilized. Sterilization operations were performed in both public and private health clinics. The popularity of sterilization as a method of birth control, especially among older women, has continued to increase. By 1976, over 35 percent of all women aged 15 to 49 were sterilized (Vázquez Calzada and Morales del Valle 1982). By 1982, this proportion had risen to 39 percent, the highest of any nation in the world (Vázquez Calzada 1988).

Fertility and Socioeconomic Factors

Although birth control initiatives have certainly contributed to the decline in fertility in Puerto Rico over the past fifty years, the socioeconomic changes that have occurred on the island during this period had an even greater impact on the declining birth rate. The development of Puerto Rico into a semi-industrialized, urban economy with a highly literate population has irrevocably changed attitudes toward childbearing.

Higher educational attainment among women has been found to be strongly correlated with reduced fertility. According to the economist Nancy Birdsall (1988, 514), "female education above four years . . . bears one of the strongest and most consistent negative relationships to fertility." There are a number of reasons why increased educational attainment is a fertility-reducing force.[4] First, the opportunity cost of time rises with educational attainment, making each additional child relatively more costly for highly educated women. Second, more-educated households tend to have a desire for more-educated children, and a substitution effect leads to fewer but more educated children. Third, increased education among women leads to a delay in marriage that in turn reduces the number of children ever born. Fourth, educated women have greater access to birth control information and are thus better able to have their desired number of children.

The number of children ever born in Puerto Rico to women aged 25 to 55 years in 1990 is decomposed by educational attainment in figure 2.5. In 1950, the average woman 25 years of age or older in Puerto Rico had completed 3.3 years of schooling; by 1990, this figure had more than tripled, to over 10 years of schooling. However, between 1980 and 1990, the proportion of women 25 years of age or older who had completed at least one year of college increased from 19 percent to 30 percent. The negative association between educational attainment and fertility is therefore a likely explanation for a significant part of the reduction in fertility in Puerto Rico during the last fifty years.

There are other socioeconomic factors associated with declining fertility. Fertility rates tend to be substantially higher in rural than in urban areas. In part, this is because child labor has traditionally been employed in agriculture, especially during harvesting periods. The use of children in urban production is much more limited. The economic value of children is thus much higher in rural areas than in urban areas, resulting in higher fertility rates in the former (Rivera-Batiz 1984). In 1960, for example, the fertility rate in Puerto Rico among women aged 20 to 24 residing in urban areas was 236 children per thousand; among rural women in this age group the fertility rate was 342 children per thousand (Vázquez Calzada 1966, 269). Among women aged 25 to 29 years, the urban fertility rate was 204 children per thousand, while the rural fertility rate was 290 children per thousand. The same relationship holds for other age groups. Given Puerto Rico's transformation from a largely rural to a mostly urban society over the last fifty years, a drop in fertility during this period was to be expected.

The age structure of the female population also has a significant impact on fertility. As women reach 30 years of age, birth rates begin to drop, and in Puerto Rico the median age of women has risen noticeably

4. The causality between educational attainment and fertility can run both ways. For instance, teenage pregnancy is one of the major factors given by female school dropouts for their leaving school. In this case, greater fertility may cause lower educational attainment. Despite this connection, there is some research suggesting that higher educational attainment does cause lower fertility (Birdsall 1988).

Figure 2.5   Female Education and the Average Number of Children Ever Born to Women in Puerto Rico, 1990

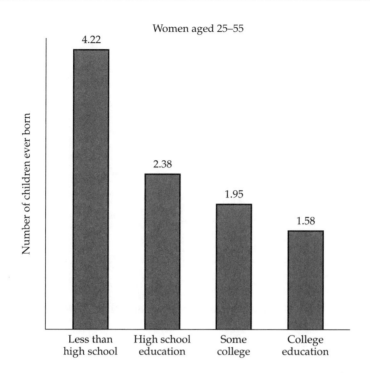

Women aged 25–55

Source: 1990 Census of Population and Housing: Puerto Rico, 5% PUMS.

over the last fifty years. In 1950, it was 18.6 years. By 1990, it was 29.6. Furthermore, the proportion of women aged 50 and over has risen in recent years.

Changes in Marital Status

Evidence from a variety of countries suggests that, as women increase their educational attainment and labor force participation, the average age at which they first marry increases. Since the birth rate among never-married women is sharply lower than among married women, when women delay marriage, overall birth rates decline. The crucial question here is whether marriage delay has taken place in Puerto Rico.

The category of people who have ever married includes those who

Figure 2.6   Proportion of Men and Women in the Population Who Have Ever Married, 1910–90

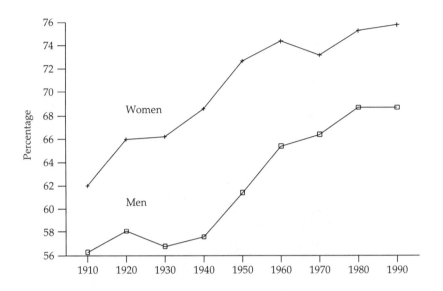

Sources: For 1910–70: Vázquez Calzada (1988), 56; for 1980 and 1990: U.S. Census of Population for Puerto Rico, 5% PUMS.

are currently married, plus those who are divorced, separated, or widowed. The proportion of the population of Puerto Rico 15 years of age or older that has ever married since the beginning of the century is decomposed by gender in figure 2.6. The proportion has sharply increased over the years, for both men and women. In 1910, 56 percent of men and 62 percent of women had married at least once. By 1990, 69 percent of men and 76 percent of women had ever married, although the rise in the proportion of ever-married persons reached a plateau in the 1980s.

Trends in Marriage and Marriage Delay

The great majority of any population marries for the first time before the age of 40. Although less than 20 percent of women in Puerto Rico marry for the first time before the age of 20, by the age of 40, close to 90 percent of the female population has been married at least once (see table 2.5). The overall aging of the Puerto Rican population over the

Table 2.5   Proportion of Puerto Rican Women Who Have Ever Married

Age Group	1960	1980	1990
15 and older	74.4%	75.3%	76.0%
15–19	17.7	17.0	14.4
20–29	76.0	67.6	60.4
30–39	92.8	90.5	87.1
40–49	94.5	94.0	92.0
50–59	94.1	93.9	94.4
60 and older	94.1	93.7	94.1

Sources: For 1960: Vázquez Calzada (1988), 366; for 1980 and 1990: U.S. Census of Population and Housing: Puerto Rico, 5% PUMS.

last fifty years thus explains the generally upward trend of the proportion of people on the island who are, or have been, married. As table 2.5 also shows, in 1990 women were marrying for the first time at a substantially older age than in earlier decades. Moreover, the proportion of women in each age group under the age of 50 who ever married fell between 1960 and 1990, particularly among those aged 20 to 29. In 1960, 76 percent of the women in this age cohort had ever married; by 1990, only 60 percent had ever married.

The increase in the proportion of women who have never married, especially among the younger cohorts, may be linked to higher educational attainment and the greater participation of women in the labor force. For instance, in 1990 among women between the ages of 25 and 29 with less than a high school diploma, 18 percent had not married. In contrast, 42 percent of college graduates in this age group had never married.

The increase in marriage delay in Puerto Rico parallels the trend toward later marriage in the United States. However, marriage delay occurs among a greater proportion of women in the United States than in Puerto Rico. For example, in 1990, 47 percent of women on the mainland aged 20 to 29 had never married, compared to less than 40 percent of women in this age group on the island. Among women in the United States aged 40 to 49, over 15 percent had never married, compared to nearly 13 percent in Puerto Rico.

The Increasing Divorce Rate

The trend toward delayed marriage in Puerto Rico has been accompanied by another significant social trend: marriages on average are lasting shorter periods of time. This is reflected in a rapidly rising divorce

Table 2.6   Married, Divorced, and Widowed Population of Puerto Rico, 1910–90

Marital Status	1910	1940	1970	1980	1990
	Women Aged 15 or Older				
Ever married	62.0%	68.6%	73.2%	75.3%	76.0%
Married	51.1	55.4	60.0	58.7	56.9
Divorced	0.2	1.6	3.9	7.3	9.2
Widowed	10.7	11.6	9.3	9.3	9.9
	Men Aged 15 or Older				
Ever married	56.3%	57.6%	66.4%	68.7%	68.6%
Married	52.3	53.3	61.7	62.5	60.9
Divorced	0.1	0.5	1.8	3.5	5.1
Widowed	3.9	3.8	2.9	2.7	2.6

Sources: For 1910 to 1970: Vázquez Calzada (1988), 56; for 1980 and 1990: U.S. Census of Population and Housing: Puerto Rico, 5% PUMS.

rate. Table 2.6 details the marital status of those in Puerto Rico who have ever been married—which includes married, divorced, and widowed persons—from 1910 to 1990. The percentage of married women aged 15 or older rose until 1970, partly in response to the aging of the population. Since 1970, the proportion of married people in the population has declined.

For most of the century, only a small proportion of the population was divorced. In 1910, a mere 0.2 percent of females 15 years of age or older were divorced. This percentage rose slowly thereafter, to 1.6 percent in 1940, to 3.9 percent in 1970. Between 1970 and 1990, however, the proportion of divorced women jumped to 9.2 percent. Divorce among men follows a similar pattern, the proportion rising from 1.8 percent in 1970, to 5.1 percent in 1990.

The rising divorce rate is linked to social and cultural changes that

Table 2.7   Proportion of Divorced Women by Age, 1990

Age Cohort	Puerto Rico	United States
18–19	1.0%	0.4%
20–29	6.0	5.2
30–39	12.2	11.5
40–54	14.3	15.8
Over 54	9.0	7.4

Sources: For Puerto Rico: 1990 U.S. Census of Population and Housing: Puerto Rico, 5% PUMS; for the mainland United States: U.S. Bureau of the Census, Current Population Reports, P-20, no. 461 (Washington: U.S. Department of Commerce, 1991).

makes it more socially acceptable to end marriages (Muñoz Vázquez and Fernández Banzó 1988; Muñoz Vázquez 1987). It is also linked to the aging of the population, as table 2.7 illustrates. The data show this to be the case for the mainland United States as well. Moreover, there are only slight overall differences in the proportions of divorced women in Puerto Rico and the United States. This is significant, because the United States has one of the highest divorce rates in the world. Puerto Rico, with 9.5 percent of its female population aged 25–44 divorced, has by far the highest divorce rate in Latin America and the Caribbean, with the exception of Cuba, which has approximately the same proportion of divorced women. In comparison, only about 2 percent of women in Argentina in the 25–44 age cohort are divorced; in Guatemala, the proportion is 4.2 percent, in Uruguay, 2.9 percent, and in Venezuela, 2.5 percent (United Nations 1991, table 2).

The Changing Puerto Rican Household

Nearly 99 percent of all persons in Puerto Rico live in households. A household is made up of all the persons who live and eat together in

Figure 2.7   Declining Household Size in Puerto Rico, 1910–90

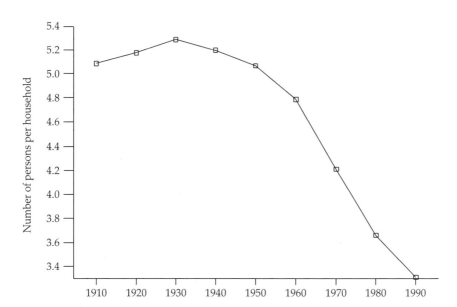

Sources: For 1910–70: Vázquez Calzada (1988), 62; for 1980 and 1990: U.S. Census of Population for Puerto Rico, 5% PUMS.

Table 2.8   Types of Families in Puerto Rico

Type of Family	1970	1980	1990
Married Couple	78.8%	77.1%	71.6%
Female householder with no spouse present	15.6	18.8	23.2
Male householder with no spouse present	5.6	4.1	5.2

Sources: 1970, 1980, and 1990 U.S. Census of Population and Housing: Puerto Rico, 5% PUMS.

a housing unit with separate living quarters (which includes houses, apartments, mobile homes, a group of rooms, or a single room). Persons who reside in what the Bureau of the Census calls group quarters (such as homeless shelters or shelters for abused women) or who are institutionalized persons (in prisons or nursing homes, for example) are not included in the statistics on households.

The declining birth rate and the slowing down of population growth have sharply reduced the average number of people living in a single household in Puerto Rico, as figure 2.7 illustrates. The average number dropped from 5.1 in 1910, to 3.3 in 1990. Despite this fall, the number of persons per household continues to be higher in Puerto Rico than in the mainland United States, where it was 2.6 in 1990.

Households may encompass one or more families living together, groups of related or unrelated individuals, or persons living alone. Families, according to the Bureau of the Census definition, include only persons who are related to each other—spouses, single parents living with children, or people with other kinship relationships. In 1990, 84 percent of all households in Puerto Rico were families. The role of the family as a unit of organization is on average stronger in Puerto Rico than in the mainland United States, where, according to the 1990 census, only 71 percent were also families.

However, the proportion of married couples constituting families has been declining sharply. Between 1970 and 1990, the proportion of married-couple families dropped from nearly 79 percent to under 72 percent. As table 2.8 shows, this fall in married-couple families is matched by a significant rise of the percentage of families headed by a female with no spouse present, from under 16 percent in 1970, to over 23 percent in 1990. This can be compared to 16.5 percent in the mainland United States in 1990. (In the United States, though, the proportion of families headed by women varies greatly by ethnicity. In 1990, female-headed families with no spouse present accounted for almost 44 percent of all black families, 23 percent of all Hispanic families, and 12.5 percent of all white families.) The growth in the proportion of families headed by women with no spouse present, both in the United States and Puerto Rico, has gained substantial attention in the press and among policymakers, particularly since these families have the highest poverty rates.

Summary: Population Growth and Demographic Changes in Puerto Rico

1. Between 1980 and 1990, the population of Puerto Rico rose from 3,196,500 to 3,522,037, an increase of 10.2 percent. This was one of the slowest periods of population growth on the island during this century.
2. Most of the decline in population growth during the 1980s was due to a reduction in the natural growth of the population. Net migration was also a factor. There was a net outflow of 116,571 persons during the decade.
3. The drop in the natural growth of the population in Puerto Rico was due to a fall in the birth rate and to an increase in the death rate during the decade. The Puerto Rican birth rate has systematically declined since the 1950s, from 38.9 births per one thousand persons in 1950, to 23.8 births per thousand in 1980, to 18.8 per thousand in 1990. Death rates declined from 9.9 to 6.6 deaths per thousand persons between 1950 and 1980. But in contrast to the birth rate, the death rate *rose* sharply during the 1980s, from 6.4 deaths per thousand persons in 1980, to 7.4 in 1990.
4. The increased mortality rate was related, in part, to the aging of the population and the consequent increased proportion of people aged 65 or over. The age of the average person in Puerto Rico climbed from 18.4 years in 1950, to 21.6 years in 1970, to 28.4 years in 1990. The overall aging of the Puerto Rican population has been partly influenced by the migratory movements of Puerto Ricans to and from the Island. Out-migrants are generally younger than the average population.
5. The rising death rate in the island is also associated with increased mortality among the 25–44 age group. This is due to the rise of AIDS-related deaths and the growing incidence of accidents and homicides. For persons in the 25–44 age group, AIDS constitutes the most important cause of death, followed by accidents and homicides.
6. The drop in the birth rate is closely associated with increased educational attainment among women. More-educated women tend to have lower birth rates. In 1990, the number of children ever born to women between 25 and 55 years of age who had not completed a high school education was 4.2. To those with a college degree, it was 1.6. Since educational attainment increased sharply in Puerto Rico during the 1980s, this accounts for a significant part of the drop in fertility. Fertility has also declined because of rising urbanization, marriage delay, and other social and demographic trends. Birth control initiatives have had an impact by providing information and the means to those who desired smaller families.
7. Teenage pregnancy does not appear to be on the rise in Puerto Rico. On the other hand, single parenthood increased rapidly in the 1980s.

In 1990, 18.8 percent of all women aged 18–55 were single parents, up from 15.7 percent in 1980.

8. The proportion of people ever married has generally risen in Puerto Rico. However, among the younger cohorts in the population, the 1980s saw a drop in the proportion of people getting married. Among women aged 20–29, the proportion ever married fell from 67.6 percent in 1980, to 60.6 percent in 1990. This suggests the presence of a substantial number of women who are delaying marriage until their thirties. Higher educational attainment and the greater participation of women in the labor force were the main causes of marriage delay.

9. Divorce rates have been climbing since the 1960s. The proportion of men who were divorced rose from 3.5 percent in 1980, to 5.1 percent in 1990. For women, the proportion rose from 7.3 percent in 1980, to 9.4 percent in 1990, with the result that Puerto Rico now has one of the highest divorce rates in the world.

10. The role of the family is on average stronger in Puerto Rico than in the mainland United States. In 1990, the proportion of all households in the mainland United States that were also families was 70.8 percent, compared to 84 percent in Puerto Rico.

11. Between 1970 and 1990, the proportion of married-couple families dropped from 78.8 percent to 71.6 percent. This fall was matched by a rise in the proportion of families headed by a female with no spouse present, from 15.6 percent in 1970, to 23.2 percent in 1990.

CHAPTER 3

Migration between Puerto Rico and the United States

B Y ANY measure, the migration between Puerto Rico and the United States during the last fifty years has been remarkable: 835,000 people emigrated from Puerto Rico to the mainland United States on a net basis between 1940 and 1970 alone. This represents approximately *half* of the natural increase of the population of Puerto Rico during this period—that is, for every two persons added to the population of the island, one left to reside in the mainland. This makes Puerto Rico the site of one of the most massive emigration flows of this century.

The migration of Puerto Ricans to the United States slowed considerably in the 1970s but picked up again in the 1980s, when close to 120,000 people left the island on a net basis. This resurgence of out-migration differed from previous migration flows in that the emigrants dispersed more widely than in the past. As a result, substantial Puerto Rican communities now exist throughout the United States, from southern California and Texas, to upstate New York and western Massachusetts.

Although it is the migration to the mainland United States that is more visible and more often commented upon, hundreds of thousands of Puerto Rican emigrants have returned to their place of birth over the years, as have many of their children. Over 200,000 persons born in the mainland United States of Puerto Rican parents were residing on the island in 1990. This comparatively young population undergoes a difficult adjustment when it arrives in Puerto Rico. In addition to the hardships experienced by migrants everywhere, its members suffer from culture shock and a loss of identity. As a character in Pedro Juan Soto's novel, *Ardiente Suelo, Fría Estación* (1961), exclaims: "We are not Americans because in New York we are considered Puerto Ricans. Yet, we are not Puerto Ricans because here [in Puerto Rico] we are considered Americans."

It has been argued that the migration between Puerto Rico and the United States is different from most other migratory movements in that there are significant numbers of circular migrants, that is, persons who move back and forth between the two nations without putting down permanent roots in either one. Tienda and Díaz (1987) contend that this circular migration "separates them [Puerto Ricans] from other inner-city minority groups . . . [and] severely disrupts families and schooling, leading inevitably to a loss of income." Hernández Cruz (1985), argues that circular migration is a reflection of the high unemployment rate of Puerto Ricans both in the island and in the mainland. The pool of unemployed move back and forth between Puerto Rico and the United States seeking employment wherever there is a greater likelihood of employment at any given time. Despite the popularity of the concept of circular or "commuter" migration, there is relatively little reliable information available on the extent to which Puerto Rican migrants are circular migrants.

The data on Puerto Rican migration to the United States presented in this chapter are based on information provided by the decennial U.S. Census of Population and Housing. An alternative set of migration estimates is constructed by the Planning Board of the Commonwealth of Puerto Rico based on the number of passengers arriving and departing by air annually to and from Puerto Rico. The net balance of these passenger flows represents the net in- or out-migration during a given period of time. We believe that the planning board data are subject to serious measurement errors, however, and for this reason we rely exclusively on census-based data. (The measurement problems associated with the planning board data are discussed in appendix 2.)

The Migration of Puerto Ricans to the United States

Migration between Puerto Rico and the United States was inevitably altered by the annexation of Puerto Rico to the United States in 1898, although during the first decades of this century, the number of Puerto Rican emigrants to the United States was not significant. The largest flow consisted of an estimated 10,000 Puerto Ricans recruited to work in sugarcane fields in Hawaii (Rosario Natal 1983; Maldonado Denis 1980, 61; Mintz 1955). Migration did receive a boost in 1917 with the passage of the Jones Act, which granted American citizenship to Puerto Ricans. This facilitated the movement of labor to the mainland and, as table 3.1 shows, net emigration rose significantly in the 1920s. The

Table 3.1   Net Emigration from Puerto Rico, 1900–90

Year	Net Number of Out-Migrants
1900–10	2,000
1910–20	11,000
1920–30	42,000
1930–40	18,000
1940–50	151,000
1950–60	470,000
1960–70	214,000
1970–80	65,817
1980–90	116,571

Sources: The data for 1900–70 are from Vázquez Calzada (1988), 286; the data for 1970–80 and 1980–90 are from the 1980 and 1990 U.S. Census of Population and Housing: Puerto Rico.

Great Depression produced a sharp cut in the flow, however, as employment opportunities on the mainland dried up during the 1930s. Between 1900 and 1940, there was a net outflow of 73,000 persons from the island, an average of only 1,825 emigrants per year. Migration accelerated in the late 1940s, and during the 1950s the average annual net outflow was 47,000.

The massive emigration of Puerto Ricans to the United States after the Second World War can be traced to a booming U.S. economy, lower travel costs between Puerto Rico and the mainland, and governmental policies fostering emigration. Facing acute labor shortages, American employers greatly expanded their recruitment of Puerto Rican workers in the late 1940s and 1950s, with Puerto Rico's Department of Labor arranging contracts between workers and employers (Nieves Falcón 1975, 40–41). The department's Migration Division in New York City served as a rich source of information about employment in the city. Most of these emigrants intended to return home, as one such migrant, Bernardo Vega, later wrote in his *Memoirs:* "The topic of conversation, of course, was what lay ahead: life in New York. First savings would be for sending for close relatives. Years later the time would come to return home with pots of money. Everyone's mind was on the farm they'd be buying or the business they'd set up in town. . . . All of us were building our own little castles in the air" (1984, 6). Despite their original intentions, many migrants eventually remained in the United States, living in neighborhoods in large cities, such as *El Barrio* in New York City (Sánchez Korrol 1983).

Emigration from Puerto Rico to the United States peaked in the 1950s, when the net outflow was 470,000 persons. Migration slowed

Table 3.2   **Net Migration from Puerto Rico in the 1980s**

	1970–80	1980–90
Net migration	−65,813	−116,571
In-migration	391,280	316,173
Out-migration	457,093	432,744

Sources: 1980 and 1990 U.S. Census of Population and Housing.

thereafter, especially in the 1970s, when the net outflow was under 66,000. Forecasts made at the time projected a continued slowdown and greater numbers of return migrants, but there was a new surge of emigration in the 1980s, when the net outflow was close to double that of the 1970s.

The Exodus Continues: Out-Migration in the 1980s

Net migration represents the difference between the number of people moving into an area, the in-migrants, and the persons emigrating from that area, the out-migrants. The increased net out-migration from Puerto Rico in the 1980s might have been the result of a larger outflow from the island or a reduced inflow, or a combination of the two.

Table 3.2 disaggregates the net migration flow in Puerto Rico during the 1970s and 1980s into its out-migration and in-migration components. Note that the increased net emigration from the island during the 1980s is closely related to a sharp drop in the number of in-migrants. The in-migration declined by 75,000 in the 1980s. Out-migration also declined, but not by as much, with approximately 24,000 fewer people leaving the island in the 1980s than in the 1970s. Still, with over 400,000 people exiting the island in the 1980s, emigration was sustained at a fairly high level: 12.3 percent of the Puerto Rican population that had resided on the island in 1980 was no longer living there in 1990.

One of the distinguishing features of Puerto Rican migration to the United States is the relative ease of movement between the island and the mainland, due to the absence of legal impediments to travel between the two places and the relatively low cost of transportation, itself associated with the proximity of the island to the mainland United States. Immigration restrictions and the cost of transportation no longer play a significant role in determining Puerto Rican migration.

Early empirical research on the determinants of Puerto Rican migration to the United States supported the proposition that economic factors are important determinants of Puerto Rican migration, particularly wages and employment conditions in the United States and Puerto

Rico (Fleisher 1963; Friedlander 1965; Maldonado 1976). This is confirmed by more recent research, which shows that Puerto Rican migration to the United States is significantly linked to changes in both wages and unemployment differentials between Puerto Rico and New York City (Santiago and Basu 1993); that the emigration of particular groups of workers from the island (nurses, engineers) is closely linked to higher wages and improved employment opportunities for those occupations in the United States (Rivera-Batiz 1989, 10); and that Puerto Rican migration is sensitive to variations in the island's minimum wages (Santiago 1991, 1993). Changes in the U.S. statutory minimum wage, when extended to Puerto Rico, have had considerable impact on the Puerto Rican labor market, slowing employment growth, in particular, which has the effect of keeping unemployment rates high and dampening labor force participation (Castillo-Freeman and Freeman 1992; Santiago 1992b).

Based on these findings, it is clear that nonconverging wage and unemployment differentials between the island and the mainland may explain the continuation of mass Puerto Rican migration to the United States in the 1980s. Overall, the 1980s constituted a period of brisk economic growth in the United States, which was not matched by the growth of the Puerto Rican economy. Although the Puerto Rican economy expanded rapidly in the second half of the decade, which raised real wages and reduced unemployment, this economic expansion followed, both in time and in strength, the boom of the U.S. economy after 1983. As a result, wage and unemployment differentials between the island and the mainland generally increased in the 1980s. For instance, in 1980, the annual earnings of male workers in New York City were on average 2.5 times those of male workers in Puerto Rico, and the earnings of female workers in New York City were 1.9 times those of female workers in Puerto Rico. This earnings gap widened during the decade, and by 1990, the average annual earnings of New York City male workers had risen to 2.8 times those of Puerto Rican workers; the earnings of New York City female workers were 2.4 times higher than those of female workers in Puerto Rico. A gap in unemployment rates also persisted. In 1980, the unemployment rate in Puerto Rico was twice that in New York City for both men and women. This gulf widened during the decade. While the unemployment rate dropped to below 5 percent in some areas of the United States in the late 1980s, especially in the Northeast, Puerto Rico's unemployment rate hovered around 20 percent.

The Characteristics of Recent Puerto Rican Emigrants to the United States

The Puerto Rican public and some members of the Puerto Rican academic community have become increasingly concerned about the emigration of Puerto Rican professional and technical workers, and fears of a "brain drain" in the direction of the United States are openly expressed. The Puerto Rican press provides a window onto these fears. *Caribbean Business* sounded the alarm in 1990: "Puerto Ricans are going west, east, north and south. . . . This is the second largest migration of Puerto Ricans since the 1940s and 1950s . . . but this migration is different: those leaving now are primarily professionals and highly-trained white collar workers. . . . The exodus of thousands of Puerto Ricans is adversely thinning the island's talent" (Blasor 1990). Some are also worried that more women than men are leaving the island, which, if true, could have a variety of demographic as well as socioeconomic effects.[1] Moreover, a widespread perception exists that a disproportionate number of young Puerto Ricans are emigrating. If true, this could have serious repercussions for public finance: an older population means that the demand for health and other social services, and social insurance benefits, will increase. On the other hand, a reduction in the number of children on the island could eventually lead to lower overall school expenditures.

Data from the 1990 U.S. Census of Population and Housing give us a clear picture of the characteristics of persons who migrated from Puerto Rico to the mainland United States between April 1, 1985, and April 1, 1990. Of the 202,868 people in this category, the great majority—72 percent—were born on the island. The next largest group of out-migrants—or 20 percent of the total—were born in the mainland United States but were residing in Puerto Rico in 1985. Most of the latter were of Puerto Rican ancestry, one or both of their parents having been born in Puerto Rico. The remaining out-migrants were persons born in Cuba, the Dominican Republic, and other foreign countries who were residing in Puerto Rico in 1985.

Table 3.3 shows the broad demographics of those who were born in Puerto Rico and emigrated to the United States during the 1985–90 period. For comparison purposes, table 3.3 also presents the corresponding characteristics for the overall population residing in Puerto Rico in 1990. Fifty-three percent of the out-migrants were women, a number slightly higher than the proportion of women in the non-migrant population. However, the out-migrants were disproportionately young. In 1990, 85 percent of out-migrants were under the age of 45; in contrast, only 72.5 percent of the non-migrant population was under the age of 45. This pattern of out-migration of young Puerto

1.   As Vázquez Calzada (1988, 57) notes: "It is likely that the massive emigration that occurred to the United States during the 1950–1970 period, in which males predominated, may have been an important factor in the rise of women never married during these years."

Table 3.3   Demographic Characteristics of Recent Out-Migrants Born in
Puerto Rico

	Out-Migrants 1985–90	Population Residing in Puerto Rico, 1990
Total population	202,868	3,522,037
Male	47.4%	48.5%
Female	52.6	51.5
Age		
Younger than 16	26.1	29.1
16–44	58.5	43.4
45–64	11.2	17.8
65 and older	4.2	9.7

Sources: 1990 U.S. Census of Population and Housing, 5% PUMS; 1990 U.S. Census of Population and Housing: Puerto Rico, 5% PUMS.

Ricans is typical of most emigration flows, which are often spear-headed by young workers with little to lose and much to gain.

Is There a Puerto Rican "Brain Drain"?

There is a widespread perception among the public in both Puerto Rico and the mainland United States that the educational characteristics of out-migrating Puerto Ricans to the mainland changed drastically in the late 1970s and 1980s. During the 1950s and 1960s, emigrants were thought to be predominantly young, unskilled laborers with relatively low levels of education. In the 1980s, some experts and the public came to believe that the majority of the new emigrants over the previous fifteen years were college-educated professional and technical workers, constituting an irreplaceable loss of human capital that was depriving the island of its most able and best-trained people (Beardsley 1980; Gutiérrez 1983; Gomez 1988; Román 1990; Viglucci 1994).

    At first glance, the census data on the educational attainment of Puerto Rican emigrants from the 1950s to the 1980s appear to confirm these perceptions. Of the Puerto Rican emigrants between 1955 and 1960, approximately 86 percent had not completed high school. The figure declined to about 80 percent for the emigrant cohort of 1965–70, and to approximately 60 percent for the 1975–80 cohort. According to the 1990 census, the proportion of Puerto Rican emigrants between 1985 and 1990 without a high school degree was slightly above 40 percent. So, indeed, Puerto Rican emigrants have become increasingly more educated. However, the population of the island has also become more educated over time. To prove that there is a brain drain from

Puerto Rico, it is not enough to show that emigrants are becoming more educated; it must be demonstrated that the emigrant outflow is significantly more educated and more skilled than the Puerto Rican population in general. The emigrant outflow must be observed to have had an educational distribution that shifted over time *relative to* the overall population of the island.

There is a second significant methodological issue when the educational attainment of emigrants is compared with that of the non-migrant population of Puerto Rico. As we have seen, the out-migrants are disproportionately young, and since younger cohorts of Puerto Ricans have higher educational attainment than older cohorts, on this demographic basis alone the emigrant cohorts would appear to be more educated than Puerto Ricans in general. Indeed, it is possible for the data to show that, overall, emigrants are more educated than the general population even though, for every given age group, the emigrants are less educated. To test the hypothesis that the emigrants are more educated than non-migrants, therefore, the data must be adjusted to take into account the different demographics of the two groups. One way to do this is by standardizing the out-migrant population by age. This amounts to computing the educational attainment of the out-migrants as if they had the same age structure as the Puerto Rican population in general. In a comparison of the age-standardized educational attainment of the emigrants with that of the Puerto Rican population, the demographic influence on educational differences dissipates.

Previous studies using this methodology indicated that educated, skilled Puerto Ricans were not overrepresented in the out-migrant flow. Examining the data from the 1980 census, Ortiz (1987, 625) concluded that "Puerto Rican migrants have not been, nor are increasingly becoming, a select portion of the Puerto Rican population. Rather, Puerto Rican migrants are of similar or lower socioeconomic level than nonemigrants." Similarly, Rivera-Batiz (1989, 10), in a study based on a survey of migrants carried out by the Puerto Rico Planning Board during the 1983–84 fiscal year, concluded that "in contrast to popular beliefs, recent Puerto Rican out-migrants do not appear to be predominantly college-educated, white-collar workers. The largest component of the sample of 1984 out-migrants is blue-collar, with more than 90 percent of those migrants 25 years of age or older having no college degree."[2]

Figure 3.1 illustrates the outcome when the educational attainment of the out-migrant population, as reported in the 1990 census, is standardized relative to the non-migrant population. The census data indicate that of the out-migrants 25 years of age or older who moved from

2. See also Rivera-Batiz (1987); and Estado Libre Asociado de Puerto Rico (1984).

**Figure 3.1   Educational Attainment of Out-Migrants 25 Years of
Age or Older**

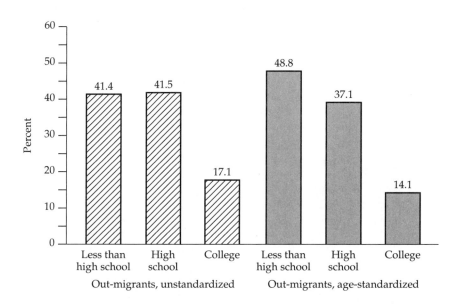

Sources: 1990 U.S. Census of Population, 5% PUMS; 1990 U.S. Census of Population:
Puerto Rico, 5% PUMS.
Note: The age-standardized educational distribution represents the educational distribution of the out-migrants as if they had the same age distribution of the population residing in Puerto Rico in 1990.

Puerto Rico to the mainland United States between 1985 and 1990, 17
percent had a college degree, while 41 percent lacked a high school
diploma. When the data is age-standardized, the distribution, as antici-
pated, shifts toward lower educational levels. The proportion of migrants with less than a high school education jumps to 49 percent, while
the proportion with a college degree drops to 14 percent.

Figure 3.2 compares the adjusted educational distribution of out-
migrants who moved between 1985 and 1990, with the educational attainment of non-migrants in the Puerto Rican population in 1990, as
well as of those who emigrated between 1975 and 1980 in relation to
the Puerto Rican population in 1980. It is apparent that the educational
attainment of both out-migrants and non-migrants rose significantly
during the 1980s. The proportion of non-migrant Puerto Ricans 25
years of age or older who had not completed high school dropped from
60 percent in 1980, to 50 percent in 1990. The proportion of out-
migrants with less than a high school education declined from 63 per-

Figure 3.2   Is There a Brain Drain of Puerto Ricans to the United States? Educational Distribution of Out-Migrants and Non-Migrants for Persons 25 Years of Age or Older[a]

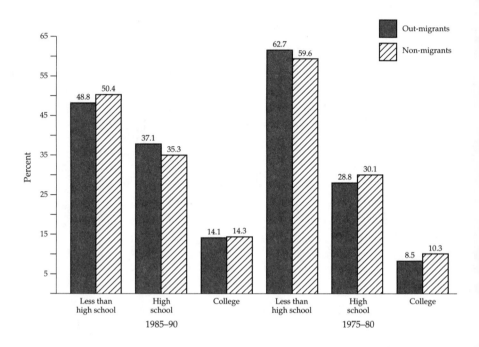

Sources: 1980 and 1990 U.S. Census of Population for Puerto Rico, 5% PUMS; 1980 and 1990 U.S. Census of Population, 5% PUMS.
[a]The educational attainment distribution for out-migrants has been age-standardized for greater comparability with the population residing in Puerto Rico.

cent for the 1975–80 contingent, to 49 percent for the 1985–90 group. At the same time, the proportion of both out-migrants and non-migrants with a college education rose. Among non-migrants, the proportion of college graduates increased from 10 percent in 1980 to 14 percent in 1990. Among out-migrants, the proportion of college graduates rose from 8.5 percent for the 1975–80 cohort, to 14 percent for the 1985–90 contingent.

The data presented in figure 3.2 suggest that persons who migrated from Puerto Rico to the mainland United States during the 1985–90 window had an age-standardized educational distribution almost identical to that of the Puerto Rican population. This means that, in terms of educational attainment, the recent emigrants represent a near cross-section of the Puerto Rican population. There is certainly not an

Table 3.4   Occupational Distribution of Out-Migrants and Non-Migrants

	Out-Migrants (1985–90)	Non-Migrants (1990)
White-collar	44.0%	51.3%
Executive, administrative, and managerial	5.7	9.6
Professional specialty	11.9	12.3
Technical and related	2.6	2.7
Sales	9.2	11.3
Administrative support	14.6	15.4
Blue-collar	56.0	48.7
Private household service occupations	0.4	0.6
Protection services	1.3	3.2
Health and other services	15.3	10.7
Farming, forestry, and fishing	2.6	2.8
Precision production, craft and repair occupations	11.3	11.7
Machine operators, assemblers, and inspectors	15.8	9.3
Transportation workers	3.1	4.3
Handler/Laborers	6.2	6.2

Sources: 1980 and 1990 U.S. Census of Population and Housing, 5% PUMS; 1980 and 1990 U.S. Census of Population and Housing: Puerto Rico, 5% PUMS.
Note: Data for all employed persons 16 years or older.

overrepresentation of highly educated people. On the other hand, the migrants who left during the 1975–80 period included a greater proportion of less-educated persons.

Aside from comparing the educational attainment of migrants and non-migrants, the question of whether there is a brain drain of Puerto Ricans to the United States can be examined by comparing the occupational distribution of the out-migrants with that of the non-migrants. Table 3.4 displays the occupational distribution of out-migrants 16 years of age or older who emigrated from Puerto Rico to the United States between 1985 and 1990, compared to that of the non-migrant population of Puerto Rico in 1990. Forty-four percent of all employed out-migrants had a white-collar occupation, compared to 51 percent of the employed workforce in Puerto Rico. The occupations overrepresented among emigrants—health and other services, and machine operators, assemblers, and inspectors—fall in the blue-collar category.

Although it is doubtful that there has been a Puerto Rican brain drain, the emigration rates for certain occupations requiring special-

Figure 3.3   Categories of In-Migrants Moving to Puerto Rico in the 1980s

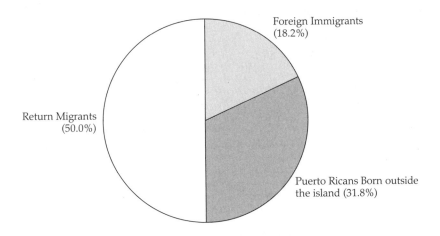

Foreign Immigrants
(18.2%)

Return Migrants
(50.0%)

Puerto Ricans Born outside
the island (31.8%)

Source: 1990 U.S. Census of Population and Housing: Puerto Rico, 5% PUMS.

ized training, such as engineers and physicians, are high (Alameda and Ruiz Oliveras 1985; Aura 1988). Within the 1985–90 out-migrant contingent, for example, the fraction who declared engineering as their occupation was twice as large as that in the Puerto Rican workforce. Indeed, surveys of graduates from the Mayagüez campus of the University of Puerto Rico (the major institution granting engineering degrees) show that over a third are recruited to work in the mainland United States. Within the chemical engineering specialty, more graduates are employed in the United States than in Puerto Rico (Rivera-Batiz 1989, 10).

The Island-Seekers: In-Migrants to Puerto Rico

The cultural and ethnic formation of Puerto Rico throughout the centuries has been molded by successive in-migration flows (González 1980). In this century, the number of people moving onto the island was comparatively small until the 1960s (Hernández Alvarez 1967). Since then in-migration has boomed, bolstered by return migrants, Puerto Ricans born in the United States, and foreign-born immigrants. Between 1980 and 1990, 316,173 took up residence in Puerto Rico. Half of these were return migrants—individuals born in Puerto Rico who were returning to the island after a period of residence in the United States or other countries (see figure 3.3). A third were persons born in the United States of Puerto Rican parentage, meaning that at least one parent was

Figure 3.4 Return Migration to Puerto Rico for Persons 5 Years of Age or Older

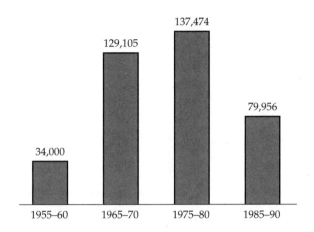

Source: U.S. Census of Population and Housing, table on selected social and economic characteristics, various years.
Note: The return migrants counted here are persons born in Puerto Rico who changed their residence from the U.S. mainland to Puerto Rico during the five-year period before the decennial census count.

born in Puerto Rico. The remaining 18 percent of in-migrants came from the Dominican Republic, the continental United States (with no Puerto Rican parentage), Cuba, and other countries.

The Characteristics of Return Migrants

The decennial census looks closely at Puerto Ricans who returned to the island from the United States during the five years previous to the census. Return migration to Puerto Rico peaked in the 1970s, as shown in figure 3.4, which presents the number of return migrants according to each decennial census since 1960. During the 1975–80 period alone, over 137,000 Puerto Ricans returned from the United States. It is estimated that for a few years in the 1970s the usually negative net flow of migrants to and from the island suddenly turned positive, meaning that more people were moving into Puerto Rico than were moving out. Return migration slowed in the 1980s, but the flow remained substantial, with 80,000 Puerto Ricans returning to the island during the 1985–90 period.

The characteristics of return migrants have long been a matter of controversy in Puerto Rico. Some have argued that the return migrants are mostly unskilled workers who have met with little success in the

Table 3.5   Demographic Characteristics of Recent Return Migrants

	Return Migrants, 1985–90	Non-Migrant Population Residing in Puerto Rico, 1990
Total population in category	79,956	3,220,179
Male	49.4%	48.3%
Female	50.6	51.7
Age		
Younger than 16	15.5	22.6
16–24	12.5	16.8
25–44	41.8	30.5
45–64	22.1	19.5
65 and older	8.1	10.6

Source: 1990 U.S. Census of Population and Housing: Puerto Rico, 5% PUMS.
Note: Data for persons 5 years or older.

mainland labor market. This view is based on research showing that migrants, including return migrants, respond swiftly to shifting earnings differentials (Reyes 1994). Unskilled workers in the United States suffered a sharp drop in real earnings during the 1970s and 1980s, triggering, so the argument goes, the return migration of unskilled Puerto Ricans back to the island, where unskilled labor did not experience such a deep deterioration in economic status. Some believe that the return migration consists of those former Puerto Rican emigrants who were successful in the United States, and who are returning to the island after accumulating a target amount of savings. In this case, skilled workers, who benefited from unprecedented gains in real earnings during the 1980s, should be overrepresented in the return migration flow. And others think that the flow is unrelated to labor market outcomes or skills because it consists mostly of retirees, who are coming back to the island after lengthy stays in the United States.

Table 3.5 displays the basic demographic characteristics of Puerto Rican migrants who returned to the island between 1985 and 1990, compared to those of the overall population in Puerto Rico in 1990. The distribution by gender is similar, with the percentages of men and women returning almost equal to the percentages of men and women in the population. However, the age structure of returning migrants is quite different from that of the overall population. First, there is no evidence that people aged 65 or older are overrepresented in the emigrant flow: only 8 percent of return migrants fit into this category. The majority are therefore not typical retirees going back to Puerto Rico

Figure 3.5   Educational Distribution of Return Migrants and Non-Migrants for Persons 25 Years of Age or Older

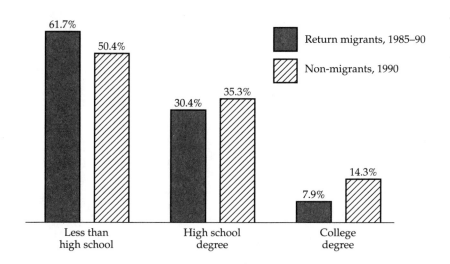

Sources: 1980 and 1990 U.S. Census of Population for Puerto Rico, 5% PUMS; 1980 and 1990 U.S. Census of Population, 5% PUMS.
Note: The educational attainment for return migrants has been age-standardized for greater comparability with the population residing in Puerto Rico.

after a long stay in the mainland. It is also apparent that the proportion of young people (below age 25) among the return migrants (28 percent) is lower than among the general population (40 percent). Sixty-four percent of the return migrant population was made up of adults in prime working age, compared to 50 percent of the population as a whole.

The recent return migrants also appear to have substantially lower educational attainment than the overall population.[3] In figure 3.5, the educational distribution of return migrants is compared with that of the Puerto Rican population (the figures for return migrants have been age-standardized). Close to 62 percent of the return migrants aged 25 or older did not have a high school diploma in 1990, compared to 50 percent of the island's population. The proportion of the general population with a college degree was nearly twice that of the return migrants.

There is also a predominance of blue-collar workers among the return migrants. Among return migrants aged 16 or older who were em-

---

3.   Ramos (1992) noted this pattern for return migrants in the 1970s. See also Zell (1976).

Table 3.6   Occupational Distribution of Return Migrants and Non-Migrants

	Return Migrants (1985–90)	Non-Migrants (1990)
White-collar	43.0%	51.3%
Executive, administrative, and managerial	6.9	9.6
Professional specialty	10.3	12.3
Technical and related	2.3	2.7
Sales	10.5	11.3
Administrative support	13.0	15.4
Blue-collar	57.0	48.7
Private household service occupations	0.3	0.6
Protection services	4.0	3.2
Health and other services	10.3	10.7
Farming, forestry, and fishing	2.8	2.8
Precision production, craft and repair occupations	13.9	11.7
Machine operators, assemblers, and inspectors	13.3	9.3
Transportation workers	4.7	4.3
Handler/Laborers	7.7	6.2

Sources: 1980 and 1990 U.S. Census of Population and Housing, 5% PUMS; 1980 and 1990 U.S. Census of Population and Housing: Puerto Rico, 5% PUMS.
Note: Data for all employed persons 16 years or older.

ployed in 1990, 57 percent were blue-collar workers, compared to 49 percent of non-migrant workers (see table 3.6). Occupations overrepresented among the return migrant workers—compared to all workers—include those of machine operator, assembler, and inspector as well as jobs in the precision production, craft, and repair area.

The picture that emerges of the return migration of the 1980s from the 1990 census data is that of a population with a greater proportion of less-educated, blue-collar workers relative to the general population. This is consistent with the view that the deterioration of the market for unskilled labor in the United States in the 1970s and 1980s pushed blue-collar, unskilled Puerto Rican laborers back to the island.

Back and Forth: Circular Migration in Puerto Rico

Return migrants are defined as those people who were living in the United States at the beginning of any given period and moved to Puerto Rico sometime during the interval of time under consideration.

Table 3.7   Distribution of Migrants to the United States, by Length of Stay

Length of Last Stay in the United States	1980	1990
6 months–1 year	19.9%	24.3%
1–2 years	16.3	22.1
3–4 years	10.7	15.3
5–9 years	14.5	14.8
10 or more years	38.6	23.5

Source: 1990 U.S. Census of Population and Housing: Puerto Rico, 5% PUMS.

Between 1980 and 1990, there were an estimated 158,175 such migrants. However, these are not the only Puerto Ricans who moved to the United States during the 1980s and returned to the island during the decade. There is a substantial group of *circular migrants,* or persons who resided in Puerto Rico in 1980, subsequently moved to the mainland United States for at least six months, and returned to live in Puerto Rico by 1990. These individuals do not appear as return migrants during the 1980 to 1990 period since they resided in Puerto Rico in both 1980 and 1990. Census data suggest that circular migration is a significant phenomenon among Puerto Ricans, and that there were as many as 130,335 circular migrants in the 1980s—a number of people almost as large as that of return migrants.

Circular migrants account for a large fraction of migrants who stay for short periods of time in the United States. Table 3.7 shows the length of stay in the United States of all persons residing in Puerto Rico in 1990 who had lived in the United States for at least six months between 1980 and 1990. The greatest proportion of Puerto Rican migrants who resided in the mainland United States in the 1980s—over 46 percent—did so for a period of only between six months and two years. Moreover, the length of stay in the United States of the Puerto Rican migrants who go back to the island appears to be getting shorter over time. Only 36 percent of the Puerto Rican migrants returning to the island in the 1970s had lived in the mainland for as short a time as two years.

These numbers support the research of those scholars who suggest that the migration of Puerto Ricans between the island and the United States has become increasingly circular, particularly as it involves New York City and other parts of the Northeast. Some fear that circular migration, with its disruptive effect on human lives, may be dampening investment in human capital among Puerto Ricans (Rodríguez 1988, 1989; Tienda and Díaz 1987). Short-term circular migrants may be workers caught in a poverty trap, unable to find stable employment on the island or the mainland. This view is consistent with the occupational distribution of the migrants. The 1990 census data suggest that Puerto Ricans who stayed for the shortest period of time in the United States were largely unskilled and blue-collar—operators, fabricators, and laborers. Such workers are often those subject to the greatest employment instability. They are the "last hired, first fired."

Other than the census-based estimates provided in this monograph, the incidence of circular migration among Puerto Ricans is not well documented. Hence, the extent to which it is characteristic of the island's population cannot be independently confirmed. Despite the widespread belief that circular migration is a fundamental characteristic of Puerto Rican migration, there has been only one published attempt to estimate its magnitude to date (Hernández Cruz 1985). The results of this study cannot be considered to be definitive since it was based on a small sample (100 migrants). Nonetheless, Hernández Cruz concludes that circular migration is highly characteristic of Puerto Rican migration. Sixty-four percent of his sample were circular migrants. The typical pattern (41 percent of the sample) was for a migrant to leave Puerto Rico for New York City in search of employment, return to Puerto Rico after a period of at least three months, only to return

Summary: Migration between Puerto Rico and the United States

1. Puerto Rico experienced one of the most massive emigration flows of any country this century. Net migration from Puerto Rico to the United States peaked in the 1950s, when 470,000 persons left the island. Emigration slowed in the 1960s, fell sharply in the 1970s, and surged again in the 1980s. The net outflow from Puerto Rico during the 1980s was equal to 116,571 persons.
2. Net migration represents the difference between in-migrants and out-migrants. Reduced in-migration accounts for most of the increase in net out-migration in the 1980s. The number of in-migrants declined from 391,280 in the 1970s, to 316,173 in the 1980s. During the same period, the number of out-migrants dropped only slightly, from 457,093 to 432,744.
3. Nonconverging wage and unemployment differentials between the island and the mainland United States may explain the continuation of mass Puerto Rican migration to the United States in the 1980s.
4. Worries about a Puerto Rican "brain drain" appear to be unfounded. Census data suggest that the out-migrants moving between Puerto Rico and the mainland United States during the 1985 to 1990 window had an age-standardized educational distribution almost identical to that of the Puerto Rican population. This means that in terms of educational

to New York City later. The remaining 23 percent of circular migrants followed a similar pattern of migration between Puerto Rico and states in the Northeast other than New York. The work history of most of these circular migrants was one of extended unemployment or low-wage jobs.

Recent unpublished research on circular migration attests to the increasing importance being given to this topic by scholars. New data sources are being sought, but the evidence is so far somewhat mixed and few conclusions can be drawn. One such study combines two surveys, the Puerto Rico Fertility and Family Planning Assessment (PRFFPA) survey of 1982 and the New York Fertility, Employment and Migration (NYFEM) survey of 1985 (Ortiz 1992). Altogether, a sample of 3,405 Puerto Rican women, aged 15 to 49, were interviewed to determine their employment and migration history. Ortiz found that, among all interviewees, 35 percent had migrated at some time in their life and, of these, 18.5 percent exhibited patterns of circular migration. This means that only 6 percent of the entire sample were circular migrants.

   attainment the recent emigrants represent almost a cross-section of the Puerto Rican population. Similarly, the occupational distribution of the emigrants is similar to that of the Puerto Rican workforce, although certain occupations, such as nursing and engineering, are overrepresented in the out-migrant labor force.

5. Between 1980 and 1990, 316,173 persons entered Puerto Rico intending to reside there. Of these, 50 percent were born in Puerto Rico and were returning to the island after a period of residence in the United States or other countries. The remaining 50 percent were born outside of Puerto Rico and were mostly persons with some Puerto Rican parentage.

6. Return migration peaked in the 1970s, although there were still close to 150,000 return migrants in the 1980s. Recent return migrants to Puerto Rico have substantially lower educational attainment than the overall population in the island and are predominantly blue-collar workers.

7. Census-based measurements suggest that circular migration is a significant phenomenon among Puerto Ricans. There were as many as 130,335 circular migrants in the 1980s, almost as many as the number of return migrants.

8. Circular migration accounts for a large fraction of migrants who stay for short periods of time in the United States. In the 1980s, 46 percent of the Puerto Rican migrants who moved to the mainland United States resided there for only between six months and two years. Furthermore, the length of stay in the United States of the Puerto Rican migrants who return to the island is getting shorter over time. Only 36 percent of return migrants in the 1970s lived in the mainland between six months and two years, compared to 46 percent in the 1980s.

Another study uses the Migration Survey of the Puerto Rico Planning Board—in which travelers passing through the Luis Muñoz Marín International Airport in San Juan during the period 1982–87 were interviewed—to examine the circular migration thesis (Meléndez 1991). Focusing on interviews conducted during 1986–87, and merging data to capture at least one full migratory cycle, Meléndez finds that two-thirds of those leaving the island in 1987–88 had resided at least once before in the United States and that return migration to Puerto Rico is more characteristic of circular migration than corrective migration—in which unsuccessful migrants return permanently to their area of origin.

A more extreme migratory process prevails among some sectors of the Puerto Rican population. This is *commuter* migration, in which individuals repeatedly move between given areas of origin and destination (Torre, Rodríguez, and Burgos 1994). This phenomenon, with its potential links to poverty, may have significant policy implications, but it does not show up clearly in conventional migration models. Commuter migration should not be dismissed as a simple form of human capital investment, since it often leads to interruptions of schooling and job training for all members of a household. It would therefore be useful to have a broader behavioral conception in which the household is viewed as making frequent migratory decisions in response to constantly changing labor market conditions. Such decision making is more likely to occur among low-income households with unstable earnings opportunities and relatively flat age / earnings profiles. Unfortunately, the available census data do not provide us with a picture of the extent or nature of commuter migration since respondents were not asked questions about the number or frequency of their moves. On the other hand, the census-based evidence of circular migration—and of the comparatively large number of people moving to the United States for short periods or time—supports the notion that this type of migration may be an increasingly significant phenomenon among Puerto Ricans.

CHAPTER 4

The Socioeconomic Transformation: Income, Poverty, and Education

W HEN *Time* magazine ran a cover story on Puerto Rico in June 1958, it portrayed the island as a "laboratory of democracy in Latin America" and as a showcase for economic development. *Time* praised Governor Luis Muñoz Marín and his economic development strategy, which relied heavily on attracting American investment with the goal of expanding production for export to American markets and was associated with a sharp growth in per capita income. Puerto Rico's strong economic growth continued unabated in the 1960s and early 1970s. Between 1948 and 1978, the island's per capita gross national product (GNP), adjusted for inflation, more than tripled.

However, the picture of Puerto Rico as a showcase did not survive the 1970s. By mid decade, the island had entered a period of stagnation that would last for more than ten years. Economic growth resumed in the mid-1980s, only to be stopped on its tracks by the recession of the early 1990s.

Puerto Rico's economic development since the late 1940s is now seen in much less benign terms than previously. The transformation of the island in a few decades from a largely rural, agricultural nation with few links to the United States, into an urban, industrial economy highly integrated with the U.S. economy produced painful socioeconomic changes. For many among the population, the average economic gains achieved during this period did little to raise them from poverty. The high unemployment rates that persisted during the 1970s and 1980s exacerbated an array of social ills, from crime and violence, to alcohol and substance abuse.

Puerto Rico's wrenching transformations—the plight of families

63

Table 4.1   Changes in Mean Household Income in Puerto Rico, 1979–89

	Mean Household Income (in 1989 dollars)[a]	Persons in Household	Mean Per Capita Household Income (in 1989 dollars)
1979	$13,205	4.67	$3,353
1989	$14,843	4.15	$4,099
Proportional change, 1979–89	12.4%	−11.1%	22.2%

Sources: 1980 and 1990 U.S. Census of Population and Housing: Puerto Rico, 5% PUMS.
[a]The income data for 1979 have been converted into 1989 dollars, adjusted by the gross national product price deflator index between 1979 and 1989.

from the coffee, tobacco, or sugar-producing areas who migrated to San Juan and other cities, the deterioration of employment opportunities and the associated social disruption in rural communities, the growth of urban slums and ghettoes, the budding expansion of a metropolitan middle class in sprawling suburban complexes—have been vividly depicted by Puerto Rican writers of fiction and nonfiction alike.[1] This chapter focuses on what the census data reveal about the major socioeconomic changes that occurred during the 1980s.

Recent Changes in the Income Level

When the accelerated income growth that the Puerto Rican economy had sustained for more than twenty years since the late 1940s ran out of gas in 1973, a deep recession took hold that lasted a decade and resulted in a reduction of real income. Sustained income growth resumed after 1983, and the economic recovery of the mid-1980s was brisk. In order to show the change in mean household income between 1979 and 1989, the 1979 figure in table 4.1 is expressed in 1989 dollars.

1. This body of literature, too vast to detail here, includes the work of social scientists Acosta-Belén (1986), Azize Vargas (1987), Buitrago Ortiz (1980), Fernández Méndez (1972), Lewis (1969), Maldonado Denis (1969, 1980), Nieves Falcón (1972, 1975), Quintero Rivera (1985), Ramírez (1980), Safa (1980), Seda Bonilla (1985), Steward (1956), Torre, Vecchini, and Burgos (1994), Torruellas and Vázquez (1976), Tumin and Feldman (1961), and Vázquez Calzada (1988). Puerto Rican fiction writers whose writings reflect the social and cultural transformation of Puerto Rico in the last fifty years include Abelardo Díaz Alfaro (*Terrazo*), Rosario Ferré (*Papeles de Pandora, La Batalla de las Vírgenes*), José Luis González (*Paisa, Mambrú se fue a la Guerra, En Nueva York y Otras Desgracias*), Edgardo Rodriguez Juliá (*Las Tribulaciones de Jonás*), Enrique Laguerre (*Cauce sin Rio*), Ana Lydia Vega (*Encancaranublado y Otros Cuentos, Pasión de Historia*), Luis Rafael Sánchez (*La Guaracha del Macho Camacho, En Cuerpo de Camisa, La Guagua Aerea*), Pedro Juan Soto (*Ardiente Suelo, Fría Estacion, Spiks, Usmail*), and Emilio Dìaz Valcarcel (*Harlem Todos los Dias*).

Table 4.2   Mean Per Capita Household Income in Puerto Rico and the
             United States, 1979 and 1989

	Mean Per Capita Household Income (in 1989 dollars)		Proportional Change
	1979	1989	1979–89
Puerto Rico	$3,353	$4,099	22.2%
United States, average	11,928	14,052	17.8
Non-Hispanic white	12,954	15,593	20.4
Non-Hispanic black	7,489	8,779	17.2
Hispanic	7,771	8,397	8.1
Puerto Rican	6,490	8,370	29.0
Asian	11,692	13,519	15.6

Sources: 1980 and 1990 U.S. Census of Population and Housing, 5% PUMS; 1980 and
1990 U.S. Census of Population and Housing: Puerto Rico, 5% PUMS.
Note: The U.S. income data for 1979 have been converted into 1989 dollars, adjusted by
the rate of inflation of the consumer price index between 1979 and 1989. The income
data for Puerto Rico for 1979 have been converted into 1989 dollars, adjusted by the
gross national product price deflator index between 1979 and 1989.

Thus, the 12 percent rise in income between 1979 and 1989—from an
average of $13,205, to $14,843—represents the change in real income.[2]

In assessing economic growth on the basis of household income, it
is critical to take into account the number of people residing in a household, since even if household income remains steady over a period of
time, the standard of living of its members may shift widely if the number of persons living within the household changes. For instance, if a
household with a fixed income has two persons living in it at one point,
and five persons at a later time, its standard of living will decline significantly. In order to adjust for differences in household size, economists usually compute household income on a per capita basis.

The gains in mean household income per capita in the 1980s are
magnified because the average size of Puerto Rican households declined during the decade, from 4.67 persons per household in 1979, to
4.15 in 1989. This contributed to the 22 percent rise in the mean per
capita household income in Puerto Rico, from $3,353 in 1979, to $4,099
in 1989 (table 4.1).

The economic recovery in Puerto Rico during the 1980s paralleled
the economic boom in the mainland United States during the decade.
Per capita household income in the United States rose 18 percent, from
$11,928 in 1979, to $14,052 in 1989, as indicated in table 4.2. This table

2. Except where noted otherwise, income data for 1979 throughout this chapter
are expressed in 1989 dollars.

also shows that the non-Hispanic white population of the United States had the highest per capita household income of all groups in the population and that the Hispanic and black populations had the lowest. The Hispanic population in general also had the lowest increase—8 percent—in per capita income during the 1980s. However, among Puerto Ricans residing in the United States, per capita household income increased by close to 30 percent.

Notice that there is a wide income gap between Puerto Ricans residing in the mainland and the non-Hispanic white population of the United States. In 1990, the per capita household income of Puerto Ricans in the United States was just 59 percent of that of non-Hispanic whites. Consequently, despite the substantial growth in their income in the 1980s, the per capita household income of Puerto Ricans on the mainland in 1989 was on average approximately the same as that of blacks and Hispanics in general.

The data in table 4.2 also illustrate the substantial gap in per capita income between Puerto Rico and the mainland United States. The per capita household income of the population of Puerto Rico was less than a third of that of the United States in 1989. Puerto Ricans living on the island had slightly less than half the per capita household income of Puerto Ricans living on the mainland. However, since the cost of living in Puerto Rico is generally less than that in the United States, the income differentials between the two places are overstated. When adjusted for the variation in the cost of living, the per capita household income of Puerto Rico in 1989 was 44 percent of that of the United States—compared to 29 percent when purchasing power differences are not taken into account (World Bank 1995, 221). Furthermore, the per capita household income of Puerto Ricans on the island as a proportion of that of Puerto Ricans on the mainland in 1989 was 74 percent when adjusted for cost of living differences, much higher than the 49 percent computed with unadjusted income figures.

The Distribution of Income

The mean level of income tells us something about the overall economic status of the population. However, individuals and groups within society usually have income substantially below or above the average. In general, income inequality leads to the presence of a few who have a substantially larger share of an economy's income than the majority of the population.

Table 4.3 presents a profile of family income distribution in Puerto Rico in 1989, in comparison with that in the United States. The poorest 20 percent (quintile) of all families in Puerto Rico received 3 percent of all family income, while the richest quintile received 54 percent.

Table 4.3   **Family Income Distribution: Puerto Rico and the United States in 1989**

Share of All Income for Each Quintile	Puerto Rico	United States
Quintile 1 (bottom)	2.8	4.6
Quintile 2	4.7	10.6
Quintile 3	13.4	16.5
Quintile 4	22.3	23.7
Quintile 5 (top)	53.6	44.6

Sources: For Puerto Rico: 1990 U.S. Census of Population and Housing: Puerto Rico, 5% PUMS. For the United States: Levy (1995), 25.

Moreover, the poorest 40 percent of all families in the island received only 7.5 percent of all family income. In contrast, the poorest 40 percent of all families in the United States received 15 percent of the nation's family income. The extent of inequality in Puerto Rico in 1989 was closer to that of developing countries such as Brazil, where the poorest 40 percent of the population in 1989 received only 7.8 percent of all income, or Panama, where the corresponding figure in 1989 was 8.3 percent.

Income inequality appears to have risen sharply in Puerto Rico since the island's initial period of economic growth in the 1950s and 1960s, according to earlier studies, which found that the poorest 40 percent of families received 16.5 percent of total family income in 1953, and 13 percent in 1963 (Castañeda and Herrero 1965, 1966; Weisskoff 1970; Andic 1964, 1965). These studies were based on Puerto Rican Department of Labor data, rather than on U.S. census data, which means that their findings are not strictly comparable to ours. More recent research (Mann 1985, Sotomayor 1994, 1996) suggests a narrowing of income inequality in the 1970s and 1980s, largely due to the growth of transfer payments to the island.

Differentials in Household Income by Sex and Age

There are wide differences in the income of various demographically defined groups in the population of Puerto Rico. According to the census, persons residing in non-family households had the highest per capita household income—$6,479—in 1989 (figure 4.1). Next came persons living in married-couple households, who constituted the great majority of the population, with an average per capita household income of $4,370. The population living in households headed by women (no spouse present) confronted the worse economic conditions, with an average per capita household income of $2,846. With 30 percent of

Figure 4.1   Gaps in Mean Per Capita Household Income by Type of Household, 1989

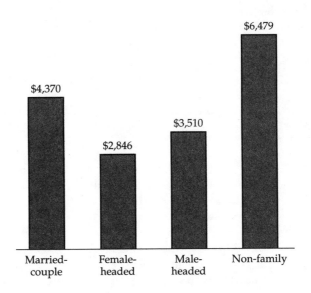

Source: 1990 U.S. Census of Population and Housing: Puerto Rico, 5% PUMS.

all women fifteen years of age or older living in female-headed house-holds, gender is a significant factor in the island's income distribution.

Age is another demographic variable intimately related to income. As persons mature and their labor market experience—as well as their spouses'—grows, their household income climbs. After a certain age, however, as persons retire, household income tends to decline relative to younger cohorts (figure 4.2). In 1989, the average per capita household income for persons under 25 years of age was $3,163. This rises to a peak of $5,231 for persons aged 45 to 64. However, for persons over the age of 65, the average per capita household income declines to $4,678.

Race and Socioeconomic Status in Puerto Rico

In studies addressing the differences in socioeconomic status among various groups in the United States, race and ethnicity usually occupy a prominent place. Most studies on Puerto Rico, however, ignore race and ethnicity as a variable. The reason for this is that the U.S. Census of Population and Housing for Puerto Rico has not included a race/

Figure 4.2 Age/Income Profile of the Puerto Rican Population, 1989

Per Capita Household Income of All Persons in the Population

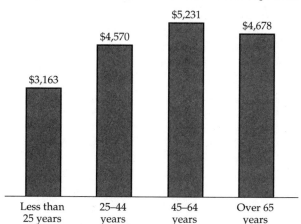

| Less than 25 years | 25–44 years | 45–64 years | Over 65 years |

Source: 1990 U.S. Census of Population and Housing: Puerto Rico, 5% PUMS.

ethnicity question in its decennial survey questionnaire since 1950. As a result, racial or ethnic income differentials for Puerto Rico cannot be determined from census data.[3]

U.S. census data on race is available for Puerto Rico from 1910 until 1940, and prior to 1940, the Spanish government also conducted censuses in which the population was classified according to race. From 1812 to 1940, the term *colored* was used broadly to denote non-whites, including blacks and mixed-race persons. Individuals were counted as white or *colored* on the basis of the visual identification of the persons doing the counting or administering the census surveys. According to these census data, in 1812, 53 percent of the population was *colored*. By 1910, however, close to two-thirds of the population was counted as white. In general, changes in the racial composition of the population in Puerto Rico can be accounted for by racial mixing and by shifts in the cultural construction of racial labels. However, the changes during the nineteenth century were primarily the result of an influx of white European, mostly Spanish, immigrants. This migration was encouraged by the *Cédula de Gracias* of 1815, which was aimed at stimulating

3. The census does provide data on race/ethnicity and the socioeconomic status of immigrants and their children. (See chapter 6.)

Spanish population growth in the Caribbean through the provision of land grants to persons moving to the island.[4]

According to the U.S. census, the share of the *colored* population in the island declined further between 1910 and 1940, from 34.5 percent to 23.5 percent. This drop did not correspond to any massive immigration flow. Rather, it reflected the continued racial mixing of the population, which tended to cloud racial identity and induced census-counters to include as *colored* only those persons with skin color of the deepest shades. According to the 1940 U.S. census, the *colored* population was concentrated in the eastern half of the island in the coastal areas. The *municipios* with the greatest concentration were Dorado, whose popula-tion was 60.5 percent *colored*, and Carolina, with 58.8 percent (Bartlett and Howell 1944, 71). These are the areas to which African slaves were brought in large numbers during the eighteenth and nineteenth centu-ries to work in agricultural ventures (slavery was abolished in 1873).

The elimination of racial identification questions in the census for Puerto Rico came about because Puerto Ricans increasingly refused to identify themselves in strict racial terms. The substantial mixing of the various racial populations in the island has moved Puerto Ricans away from a dichotomous, white-black conception of race (Rodríguez 1989, chap. 3). The population in the island sees itself as a mixture of races, with most people lying in some shade of the gradient, not at the ex-tremes. This is reflected in the popular culture and in the answers that Puerto Rican emigrants in the United States give when asked the race question: most respond by writing "other" or "Spanish."

The absence of a dichotomous racial identity in Puerto Rico does not mean that racial prejudice is nonexistent, but it does suggest that discrimination has a more limited social role and operates in much more subtle ways than in the United States. After examining a broad sample of Puerto Ricans Tumin and Feldman (1961, 239, 245) stated: "The evidence urges upon us the conclusion that skin color is consider-ably less important in Puerto Rico than in the United States; that it is virtually of no significance whatsoever in many important areas of life; that the majority feel that people of darker color are not blocked from major opportunities by their color; that only on job opportunity is there any serious question. . . . [But] by any objective measure, there is only a small and relatively insignificant relationship between skin color and education, income, occupation, or any of the other indices of social and economic position." Whether or not this conclusion holds true today

---

4. The *Cédula de Gracias* also exempted colonists from taxes for ten years (Dietz 1986, 22–23). The role of the massive European immigration to Puerto Rico in the nineteenth century in altering the racial makeup of the population has been examined by González (1980).

for the Puerto Rican economy as a whole is—in the absence of the relevant data—not known.

The Geography of Income Inequality

As the geography of production in an economy changes, deep geographical inequities emerge. In a little over forty years, as Puerto Rico's productivity base shifted from agriculture to industry and services, its mostly rural population became a predominantly urban one. Between 1960 and 1980, the urban population of the island rose from 44 percent to 67 percent of the total population, and by 1990, 72 percent of the population lived in urban areas. Furthermore, the metropolitan areas, which may include contiguous rural areas with a certain degree of population density, have greatly expanded in recent years. The metropolitan population of Puerto Rico rose from 62 percent of the total population in 1980, to 89.5 percent in 1990.

The maps in figure 4.3 illustrate this phenomenon. It is apparent that the metropolitan areas cover a substantially greater number of *municipios* (counties) in 1990 than in 1980. In fact, by 1990, *municipios* forming part of metropolitan areas dominated the western, eastern, and northern coasts of the island. Only the *municipios* in the interior and in the south remained nonmetropolitan in 1990.

The San Juan metropolitan area is the largest, followed by the contiguous Caguas metropolitan area. Of the four other metropolitan areas— Ponce, Mayagüez, Arecibo, and Aguadilla—the last was not a metropolitan area in 1980 (see table 4.4). Almost all *municipios* increased in population between 1980 and 1990 (see appendix 3), with areas in the fringes of San Juan experiencing the highest rates of growth during the decade.

There is substantial regional inequality in Puerto Rico, and the gap between the income of the *municipios* with the highest and lowest per capita income is substantial. As table 4.5 illustrates, Guaynabo, which is located in the San Juan metropolitan area, had close to four times the per capita income of Adjuntas in 1989—$8,321, as opposed to $2,196. This inequity follows closely metropolitan/nonmetropolitan lines. Most of the *municipios* with the lowest per capita incomes were in nonmetropolitan areas of the island. Faced with declining economic conditions, these *municipios* also had comparatively high unemployment rates (table 4.5). While the unemployment rates in the top ten *municipios* by per capita income range in the teens and are mostly below the average for Puerto Rico, in all but one of the bottom ten *municipios*, the unemployment rate is sharply above the average. With its low per capita income, and a 30 percent unemployment rate, a great part of the population in Adjuntas—and in the other *municipios* like it—must live in poverty.

Figure 4.3 *Municipios*, Metropolitan Areas, and Cities in Puerto Rico 1980 and 1990

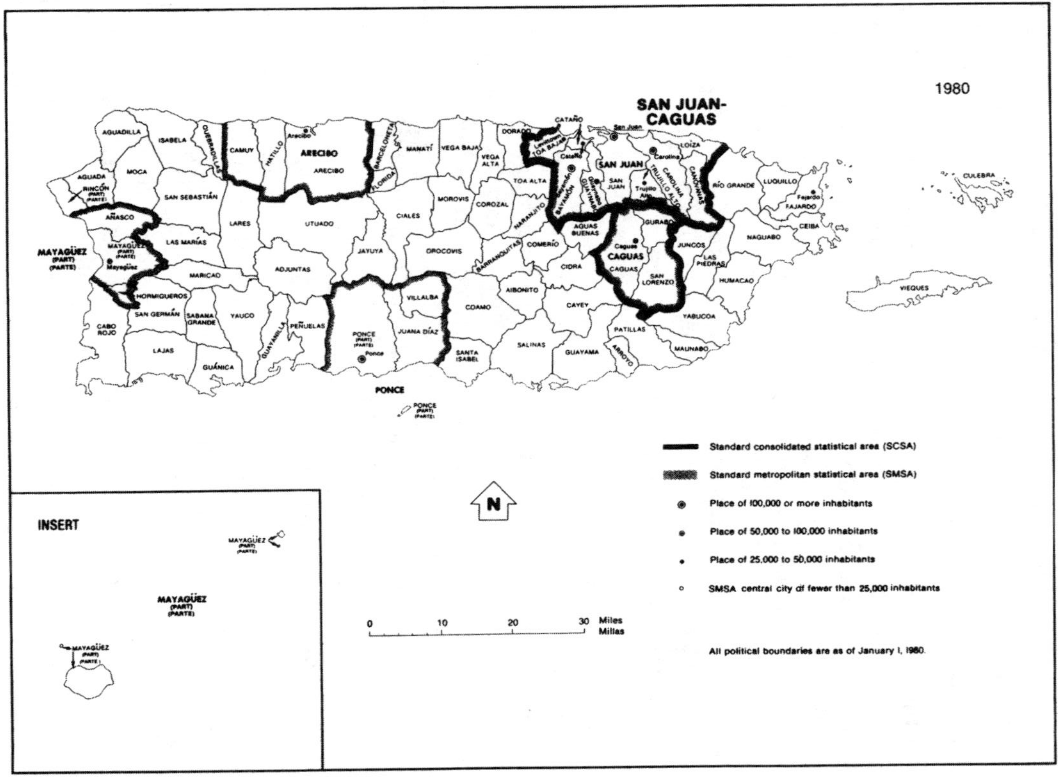

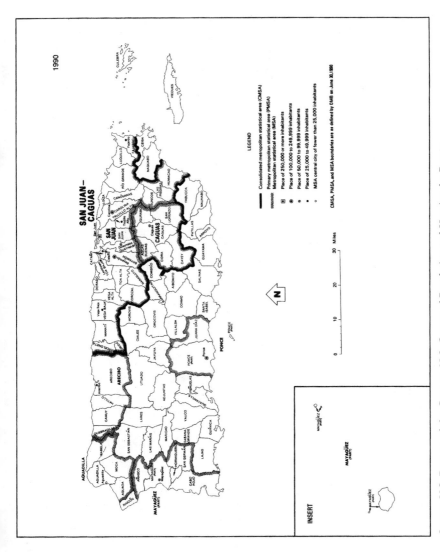

1990

LEGEND

▬ Consolidated metropolitan statistical area (CMSA)
▭ Primary metropolitan statistical area (PMSA)
▬ Metropolitan statistical area (MSA)

▣ Place of 250,000 or more inhabitants
● Place of 100,000 to 249,999 inhabitants
◉ Place of 50,000 to 99,999 inhabitants
● Place of 25,000 to 49,999 inhabitants
○ MSA central city of fewer than 25,000 inhabitants

CMSA, PMSA, and MSA boundaries are as defined by OMB on June 30,1990

0   10   20   30 Miles

INSERT

Source: U.S. Bureau of the Census, *U.S. Census of Population and Housing for Puerto Rico, 1980 and 1990: General Population Characteristics*

73

Table 4.4   **Metropolitan Population of Puerto Rico, 1980 and 1990**

	1980		1990	
	Population	Percent	Population	Percent
Total population	3,196,500	100.0%	3,522,037	100.0%
Outside metropolitan statistical areas	1,192,294	37.3	369,814	10.5
Within metropolitan statistical areas	2,004,206	62.3	3,152,223	89.5
San Juan MSA	1,302,855	40.7	2,056,302	58.4
Caguas MSA	173,961	5.4	304,925	8.6
Ponce MSA	253,285	7.9	232,947	6.6
Mayagüez MSA	133,497	4.2	214,300	6.1
Arecibo MSA	140,608	4.4	176,430	5.0
Aguadilla MSA	. . .	. . .	167,319	4.7

Sources: 1980 and 1990 U.S. Census of Population and Housing: Puerto Rico.

Poverty in Puerto Rico

A family is said to be "below the poverty level" when its income does not reach a certain threshold, which condemns it to a substandard of living for a family in the United States. The poverty thresholds established by the Bureau of the Census, which are applied uniformly throughout the mainland United States and Puerto Rico, vary according to family size and number of children. They are revised annually to reflect changes in the cost of living, as measured by the Consumer Price Index (CPI). The poverty threshold for a family of four persons (two adults and two related children) in 1989 was $12,674.[5]

Although Puerto Ricans achieved substantial gains in income in the 1980s, it is important to understand how these gains affected the poorest Puerto Ricans. One would expect the decline of economic activity in the 1970s and the recovery of the 1980s to have been associated in the first instance with an increase and in the second with a decrease in

---

5. These thresholds do not take into account the differences in the cost of living between the mainland and Puerto Rico. For this reason, the incidence of poverty in Puerto Rico may not be accurately measured by the census data. On the other hand, changes in poverty rates are more likely to reflect actual changes in the unobserved, underlying poverty levels of the population. For more details on the poverty thresholds used by the 1990 census, see U.S. Department of Commerce, *1990 Census of Population and Housing Public-Use Microdata Samples for Puerto Rico: Technical Documentation* (Washington: U.S. Bureau of the Census, 1993), p. B-23.

Table 4.5   **Distribution of Mean Per Capita Family Income and Unemployment among *Municipios*, 1989**

	Mean Per Capita Income, 1989	Unemployment Rate
Puerto Rico	4,177	20.4%
Wealthiest ten		
Guaynabo	8,321	12.7
San Juan	6,383	15.5
Carolina	5,524	14.7
Bayamón	5,134	14.1
Ceiba	5,119	18.4
Trujillo Alto	4,868	13.5
Cataño	4,644	17.8
Caguas	4,547	17.4
Culebra	4,488	6.7
Mayagüez	4,380	20.1
Poorest ten		
Adjuntas	2,196	28.4
Orocovis	2,308	30.0
Villalba	2,416	29.7
Jayuya	2,446	34.0
Comerío	2,505	25.8
Utuado	2,505	29.1
Maunabo	2,528	27.1
Morovis	2,541	19.2
Guánica	2,575	38.3
Juana Diaz	2,582	30.0

Source: 1990 U.S. Census of Population and Housing: Puerto Rico.

poverty rates. However, the overall poverty rate declined both between 1970 and 1980, and between 1980 and 1990 (table 4.6). In 1970, 63 percent of the population lived in families with income below the poverty level. In 1980, 60 percent of the population was below the poverty level. By 1990, the poverty rate had dropped to 57 percent. Yet, the poverty rate in Puerto Rico remains dismally high. The overall poverty rate in the United States in 1990 was 13 percent. Puerto Ricans living in the United States suffered a significantly higher poverty rate of 30 percent, but this was still much lower than the prevailing poverty rate in Puerto Rico.

There is the lingering question of why the poverty level dropped between 1970 and 1980, during a period when the economy of Puerto Rico had collapsed and per capita household income declined in real

Table 4.6   **Poverty Rates in Puerto Rico for All Families, 1970–90**

	1970	1980	1990
Total family income below poverty line	62.8%	59.8%	57.3%
Income excluding transfer payments below poverty line	64.4	65.1	64.9

Source: Sotomayor (1994).

Table 4.7   **Transfers from the Federal Government to Residents of Puerto Rico, 1992**

Federal Government Assistance Program	Receipts in 1992 (in millions of dollars)
Total	$5,025.2
Transfers to individuals	4,944.8
Veteran's benefits	382.4
Medicare benefits	480.6
Social Security benefits	2,414.1
Scholarships	331.0
Student loan subsidies	6.3
U.S. civil service pensions	100.2
Housing assistance	232.8
Nutritional assistance	956.7
Transfers to private nonprofit institutions	396.1
Other transfers to persons	1.1
Subsidies to industries	80.4

Source: Estado Libre Asociado de Puerto Rico, *Informe Económico al Gobernador, 1992* (San Juan: Planning Board of Puerto Rico, 1993).
Note: Data are for fiscal year 1992.

terms. Residents of Puerto Rico are entitled to participate in many of the U.S. federal government programs for public assistance to individuals and families. Puerto Rican residents received over $5 billion in transfer payments during the 1992 fiscal year (table 4.7). Most of the transfers are in the form of payments to individuals, primarily social security benefits and from the Nutritional Assistance Program (which until 1982 corresponded to the Food Stamp Program). The $5 billion distributed to the island's residents in transfer payments in 1992 corresponds to about $1,429 per person. Clearly, transfers can make a major difference in allowing individuals to sustain an income level above the poverty line.

The role played by public assistance programs in reducing poverty on the island is illustrated in table 4.6. When *monies from public assistance* are subtracted from the incomes of Puerto Ricans the overall poverty rates rise. In 1970, the poverty rate *excluding public assistance income* was 64.4 percent, in 1980, it was 65.1 percent, and in 1990, it was 64.9 percent—a remarkably stable path over a span of thirty years. The implication is that rising levels of public assistance explain to a large extent the downward trend in overall poverty since 1970.

Other Correlates of Poverty

There are various demographic and household characteristics associated with poverty. The age structure of a population, for instance, makes a significant difference in poverty levels: up to a certain age, as persons get older, their incomes tend to increase. As a result, if the average age of a population rises, average income may rise and poverty decline even in the absence of any other economic change. Another key variable associated with poverty is the proportion of all households headed by women with no husband present. As Danziger and Gottschalk (1993, 14) observe: "Since these [female-headed households] have much lower income than married-couple families, this demographic shift places more families in the lower tail of the distribution and is clearly poverty-increasing." There are also differences in poverty levels related to gender, age, and educational attainment, among other variables.

Poverty rates in Puerto Rico between 1980 and 1990 according to age, gender, and educational attainment are delineated in table 4.8. Poverty rates in both years were significantly higher than the average among the youngest and oldest populations, women in general, and persons with less than a high school education.

Generally, women earn less income than men in the labor market and tend to have higher poverty rates. Poverty is especially high among households headed by one adult female, with no spouse present. As Wilson and Neckerman (1986, 240) have noted with respect to the United States, "The rise of female-headed families has had dire social and economic consequences because these families are far more vulnerable to poverty than other types of families. Indeed, sex and marital status of the head [of household] are the most important determinants of poverty status for families, especially in urban areas." Poverty rates among Puerto Rican women in 1990 were substantially higher than among men, with close to 70 percent of women in Puerto Rico living in poverty in 1990, compared to 52 percent of men (table 4.8). This is linked to the growing proportion of female-headed households in Puerto Rico.

Table 4.8   Poverty Rates in Puerto Rico, by Age, Gender, and Education

Demographic Group	1980	1990
Total population	59.8%	57.3%
Age		
25 and younger	65.0	70.0
26–35	54.0	59.0
36–45	60.0	54.0
46–55	56.0	49.0
56–65	62.0	55.0
66–75	66.0	61.0
Older than 75	69.0	69.0
Gender		
Male	56.0	52.0
Female	71.0	68.0
Education		
Less than high school	65.0	64.0
High school	48.0	52.0
College or more	21.0	19.0

Sources: 1980 and 1990 U.S. Census of Population and Housing, 5% PUMS; 1980 and 1990 U.S. Census of Population and Housing: Puerto Rico, 5% PUMS.
Note: Percentage below the poverty line for all persons living in households.

The highest poverty rates by age in Puerto Rico occur among the youngest and oldest populations. In 1990, the poverty rate for those 25 years of age or less was 70 percent (table 4.8). For those over 75, it was 69 percent. In contrast, the poverty rate for those aged 46–55 was 49 percent. Due to these differences in poverty rates by age group, demographic changes can deeply influence the overall poverty rates of a population. Among Puerto Ricans, the age distribution has shifted significantly toward the middle. This may have reduced overall poverty rates in Puerto Rico in the 1970s and 1980s.

The impact of educational attainment on poverty is clear-cut and dramatic. The poverty rate among persons who graduated from college is three times lower than the poverty rate among persons without a high school diploma. This result generally extends to other economic variables, since income, employment, and occupational status tend to improve with educational attainment.[6] And, in general, as the level of education increases overall, so does the level of income. Human capital accumulation is one of the factors most closely linked to increased eco-

6. For a survey of the connections among literacy, education, and various economic outcomes, see Schultz (1989), Ehrenberg and Smith (1994), and Rivera-Batiz (1991, 1992b).

Figure 4.4   Student Enrollment in Elementary and Secondary Education, 1940–90

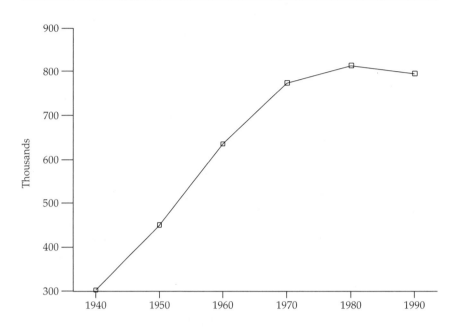

Source: Rivera-Batiz (1994).

nomic growth among nations (Mankiw, Romer, and Weil 1992; Barro and Sala-i-Martin 1995; Rivera-Batiz 1996b).

Educational Attainment

Elementary and secondary school enrollment boomed in Puerto Rico between 1940 and 1980, after which it began to decline (figure 4.4). Between the 1939–40 and the 1979–80 school years, enrollment rose from 302,000 to 815,500. Enrollment declined to 777,886 for the 1990–91 school year. The increasing enrollment up to 1980 was partly the result of the population explosion of the first half of the century. A drop in the school-age population in the 1980s resulted in the turnaround in enrollment (Rivera-Batiz 1992a).

The shifting school rolls were also linked to shifts in public school expenditures. The public sector dominates elementary and secondary education in Puerto Rico. In the 1950s, over 90 percent of all students enrolled in elementary and secondary schools were in public schools.

Although this proportion has declined to around 80 percent at the present time, public schools still account for the great majority of the student population. A massive investment in the educational system beginning in the late 1940s and 1950s provided the teachers, classrooms, and materials that enabled the rising school-age population to go to school, many for the first time in their families. The number of classroom teachers rose from 8,062 in the 1944–45 school year, to 21,492 in 1969–70, and 32,000 in 1979–80.

The 1980s saw a retrenchment in the public investment in education. Between 1979 and 1991, the share of the budget of the Department of Education in Puerto Rico as a proportion of GNP declined from 6 percent to about 4.7 percent. Real spending on education by the Commonwealth government declined during this time period. The number of teachers barely increased, if at all. The decline in educational expenditures during the decade was linked to the declining enrollments in public schools and associated with a reduction in the number of students per teacher. However, a consensus emerged among the public and policymakers in the late 1980s that the reduced investment in education was partly to blame for an inability of the public school system to meet the technological and skill requirements of many of the new workplaces on the island. As former labor secretary Ruy Delgado Zayas put it at the time, "The Puerto Rican economy is now going at the speed of a racecar, but education is going at the speed of a Volkswagen Bug" (Valdivia 1992, 6).

The consensus on the crisis of public education led to an educational reform movement whose climax was the signing into law of a comprehensive public school reform act in August 1990 (Rivera-Batiz 1996a). The *Ley Orgánica* sharply raised public spending for education. Teacher salaries, which by 1990 had dropped in real terms to the levels of the late 1960s, were increased. And between 1991 and 1995, spending by the Department of Education calculated as a fraction of GNP rose to the levels of the 1970s. In addition, the new law called for major changes in the curriculum and administration of the public school system. A decentralized, school-based system of administration is now being implemented. The impact of these drastic changes on educational outcomes is not likely to be observed immediately.

Rising Educational Attainment

In 1950, 93 percent of the population of Puerto Rico 25 years of age or older lacked a high school diploma (table 4.9). This proportion dropped to 59.5 percent in 1980, and to 50 percent in 1990. Meanwhile, the proportion of the population 25 years of age or older with a college degree or more rose from 2 percent in 1950, to 10 percent in 1980, to 14 percent in 1990.

Table 4.9   Educational Status of the Population of Puerto Rico, 1950–90,
for Persons 25 Years of Age or Older

Group, by Educational Attainment	1950	1960	1970	1980	1990
Less than high school	92.9%	85.0%	72.9%	59.5%	50.4%
High school graduate	3.6	7.5	15.0	21.3	21.0
Some college	1.7	4.0	6.0	8.9	14.3
College graduate	1.8	3.5	6.1	10.3	14.3

Sources: For 1950 to 1970: Vázquez Calzada (1988), 75; for 1980 and 1990: 1980 and 1990 U.S. Census of Population and Housing: Puerto Rico, 5% PUMS.

Table 4.10   Educational Status of the Population of Puerto Rico, by Sex,
for Persons 25 Years or Older

Group, by Educational Attainment		1980	1990
Less than high school	Men	59.0%	51.0%
	Women	60.0	49.8
High school graduate	Men	21.6	21.9
	Women	21.0	20.2
Some college	Men	8.4	13.7
	Women	9.2	14.9
College graduate	Men	11.1	13.4
	Women	9.8	15.1

Sources: 1980 and 1990 U.S. Census of Population and Housing: Puerto Rico, 5% PUMS.

Women in particular have exhibited substantial growth in educational attainment in recent years. The number of women with a college degree or more (as a proportion of all women 25 years of age or older) grew from less than 10 percent in 1980 to over 15 percent in 1990 (table 4.10). In 1990, a greater proportion of women than men in Puerto Rico graduated from college (Rivera-Batiz 1994b).

The growing role of women in higher education is reflected in the number of college degrees granted to women during the 1989–90 academic year. During that year, 7,922 women received college degrees in the island, compared to 4,171 for men. There remains, however, a substantial gender gap in the areas of study that men and women pursue while in college. Men continue to be drawn to higher-paying occupations and women to lower-paying occupations. Teaching, for in-

Table 4.11   **Women as a Proportion of All Degrees Granted, by Field of Study (University of Puerto Rico)**

Field of Study	Proportion Female, 1983–84	Proportion Female, 1989–90
Medicine	31.5%	43.9%
Law	39.0	57.5
Engineering	15.5	28.5

Source: Consejo de Educación Superior, *Compendio Estadístico de las Instituciones de Educación Superior en Puerto Rico,* various years.

stance, continues to be a major career choice for women on the island, despite the lower wages in education compared to other professions. During the 1989–90 academic year, 1,810 women received college degrees in education, compared to 440 men (Rivera-Batiz 1996a).

However, the 1980s saw a breakthrough in the number of women graduating with degrees pertaining to traditionally male occupations. Among those receiving law degrees, the proportion of women grew from 39 percent in the 1983–84 academic year, to 57.5 percent in 1989–90 (table 4.11). Women received 31.5 percent of the medical degrees awarded in 1983–84, and 44 percent in 1989–90. The proportion of women receiving degrees in engineering, a traditionally male occupation, rose from 15.5 percent, to 28.5 percent. These are hopeful signs that the serious economic disparities that now exist between men and women in Puerto Rico will diminish in the near future.

Summary: The Socioeconomic Transformation

1. After decades of accelerated economic growth, the Puerto Rican economy came to a standstill in the mid-1970s through the mid-1980s. Brisk economic growth returned in the second half of the 1980s, and per capita income surged. Mean household income per person rose 22.2 percent, from $3,353 in 1979, to $4,099 in 1989.
2. There is a substantial gap in per capita income between Puerto Rico and the mainland United States. Adjusted for variations in the cost of living between the two, the per capita household income of Puerto Rico in 1990 was 44.3 percent that of the United States. The per capita household income adjusted for cost of living differences of Puerto Ricans on the island was 74.4 percent of that of Puerto Ricans on the mainland in 1990.
3. The degree of income inequality in Puerto Rico is very high. The poorest 40 percent of all families on the island received only 7.5 percent of all family income in the island in 1989. In contrast, in the United States, the poorest 40 percent of all families received 15.2 percent of the nation's family income. The extent of inequality in Puerto Rico in 1989 was closer to that of developing countries like Brazil, where the poorest

40 percent of the population received only 7.8 percent of all income, or Panama, where the corresponding figure was 8.3 percent. Inequality also appears to have risen sharply in Puerto Rico since the island's early period of economic growth in the 1950s and 1960s.

4. Socioeconomic status is affected by the type of household a person lives in. The population living in households headed by women (no spouse present) confronted the worse economic conditions, having an average per capita household income of $2,846 in 1990. With 30 percent of all women 15 years of age or older living in female-headed households, gender constitutes a significant force in the island's income distribution. Indeed, poverty rates in 1990 were substantially higher for women than men: close to 70 percent of Puerto Rican women were living in poverty in 1990, compared to 52 percent of men.

5. The absence of racial polarization in Puerto Rico suggests that racial discrimination has a more limited social role and operates in much more subtle ways than in the United States.

6. Puerto Rico's productive base has shifted from agriculture to industry and services. This has been associated with massive rural to urban migration. In just over 40 years, the population of Puerto Rico changed from mostly rural to predominantly urban. Between 1960 and 1980, the urban population of the island rose from 44.2 percent to 66.8 percent. By 1990, the percentage of the population in urban areas was 71.2 percent.

7. The metropolitanization of Puerto Rico has boomed in recent years. Since metropolitan areas may include contiguous rural areas with a certain degree of population density, the portion of the population residing in metropolitan areas is much larger than the urban population. The metropolitan population rose from 62.3 percent of the total population in 1980, to 89.5 percent in 1990.

8. There is deep regional inequality in Puerto Rico. The gap between the income of the *municipios* with the highest and lowest per capita income in 1989 was substantial: Guaynabo had close to four times the income per capita of Adjuntas. This inequity follows closely along metropolitan/nonmetropolitan lines. Most of the *municipios* with the lowest per capita income were in nonmetropolitan areas. The economic conditions in these *municipios* are declining and they have comparatively high unemployment rates.

9. The proportion of persons living below the poverty income line (the poverty rate) declined both between 1970 and 1980, and between 1980 and 1990. In 1970, 62.8 percent of the population lived in families with income below the poverty level. In 1980, 59.8 percent was below the poverty level. By 1990, the poverty rate had dropped to 57.3 percent.

10. Rising federal transfer payments to Puerto Rico explain to a large extent the decline in poverty between 1970 and 1990.

11. The highest poverty rates in Puerto Rico are observed among the youngest and oldest populations. For those under 25 years of age, the poverty rate in 1990 was 70 percent. In contrast, among persons aged 46–55, the poverty rate was 49 percent. For persons over 75, it was 69 percent. Because of these differences in poverty rates by age group, demographic changes can strongly influence the overall poverty rate. Among Puerto Ricans, the age distribution has shifted significantly toward the middle range of the age distribution. This may have contributed to a drop in overall poverty rates in the 1970s and 1980s.

Millie

12. Elementary and secondary school enrollment boomed in Puerto Rico between the 1950s and the late 1970s, then declined in the 1980s. The expansion of enrollment was linked to an increased school-age population, as well as to rising public sector investments in elementary and secondary education. The drop in school enrollments in the 1980s was related to a decrease in the school-age cohort. At the same time, public sector investments in education dropped sharply, recovering in the 1990s as a result of sweeping public school reform efforts.

13. Educational attainment has greatly increased in Puerto Rico over the last forty years. In 1950, 92.9 percent of the population 25 years of age or older did not have a high school diploma. This proportion dropped to 50.4 percent by 1990. Similarly, the proportion of the population 25 years of age or older with a college degree or more rose from 1.8 percent in 1950, to 14.3 percent in 1990.

14. Women have exhibited substantial growth in educational attainment. By 1990, women in Puerto Rico had a greater likelihood of completing college than men did: 15.1 percent of women had a college degree or more, compared to 13.4 percent of men.

CHAPTER 5

The Labor Market and the Unemployment Crisis

T HE PUERTO RICAN labor market has changed dramatically over the last forty years. In 1950, 35 percent of the 600,000 workers in the labor force was employed in agriculture. By 1990, the workforce of close to one million was mostly employed in other sectors—trade, services, and manufacturing—with only 3.7 percent left in agriculture. This economic restructuring was associated with a period of rapid economic growth that lasted until the early 1970s and reduced unemployment rates from close to 15 percent in 1950, to less than 5 percent in 1970. However, this picture of economic expansion very soon turned bleak. Precipitated by a sharp increase in oil prices and a depressed U.S. economy, a deep recession enveloped the island in the middle of the 1970s. The result was a rapidly climbing unemployment rate, which by 1980 had risen to 14 percent for men and 16 percent for women. The 1980s saw unemployment rise even further. By 1990, the average unemployment rate among men was almost 19 percent, and among women it was 22 percent. In some rural areas of the island, the unemployment rate was substantially higher. In the *municipio* of Jayuya, for instance, the unemployment rate in 1990 was 34 percent, and in the *municipio* of Guánica it exceeded 38 percent.

Shifts in Puerto Rico's Labor Force since 1950

One of the most fundamental changes in the Puerto Rican labor force over the past forty years is the decline in the proportion of the population employed in agriculture. What is most remarkable about this decline is the speed at which it occurred. By virtually any international standard, the rate of reduction of the labor force dedicated to agricultural activities was almost without precedent. This was exactly what

85

Table 5.1   Distribution of Puerto Rican Labor Force by Employment Sector, 1950–90

	1950	1960	1970	1980	1990
Agriculture	35.0%	24.1%	9.9%	4.5%	3.7%
Manufacturing	19.0	17.0	20.2	21.0	17.4
Construction	5.7	9.8	12.2	8.3	8.3
Trade	14.4	16.6	18.2	17.5	20.6
Finance, insurance, and real estate	0.7	1.3	2.0	3.2	3.5
Transportation, communications, and public utilities	5.0	7.2	6.6	6.7	6.0
Services	13.0	13.4	16.4	26.2	26.5
Public administration	7.2	10.6	14.5	12.6	14.0

Sources: For 1950 and 1960: Puerto Rico Department of Labor and Human Resources, Bureau of Labor Statistics, *Household Survey;* for 1970–90: 1980 and 1990 U.S. Census of Population and Housing: Puerto Rico, 5% PUMS.

Operation Bootstrap and the development strategy pursued by the Commonwealth government were meant to achieve, and it is fair to characterize Puerto Rico's postwar development strategy as "industrialization first."[1]

The Shifting Industrial Structure

In 1950, 35 percent of the Puerto Rican labor force was employed in agriculture. By 1990, the agricultural workforce had declined to 3.7 percent of the island's labor force (table 5.1). This drastic transformation was associated with the decline of agriculture as an income-generating sector in the economy. In 1950, exports based on sugar production, coffee, and tobacco made up a substantial portion of the island's external trade, with agricultural production accounting for close to a third of national income. As policymakers pursued their urban-based, industrialization-first strategy of development, however, the rural labor force was rapidly siphoned off into the expanding urban areas, and by 1990, agriculture accounted for only 1.9 percent of Puerto Rico's national income.

The shifting labor force was absorbed at first by an expanding trade sector, a booming construction industry, and a ballooning government sector spurred by social investments in education, health, and other areas. In the late 1970s, construction slowed down considerably, as a

1. The term is used by Pyatt and Thorbecke (1974), and has been applied to Puerto Rico by Santiago (1992a).

result of higher interest rates and a drop in some federal housing subsidy programs (DeJesús Toro 1982, chap. 28). At the same time, the service sector began to expand rapidly, supported by tourism and expenditures financed by growing transfer payments from the United States. As the data in table 5.1 illustrate, services constituted the fastest-growing sector during the period 1950–90, rising from 13 percent of the labor force in 1950, to 26.5 percent in 1990. Trade rose from 14.4 percent of the island's workforce in 1950 to 21 percent in 1990. The public administration sector also grew, from 7 percent of the labor force in 1950, to 14 percent in 1990. By 1990, the trade, services, and public administration sectors together accounted for almost 50 percent of the 963,000 persons employed on the island.

The manufacturing sector's share of the labor force has been approximately stable since 1950. However, Puerto Rican industry in 1990 was a very different animal than it was in 1960. The transformation of manufacturing in Puerto Rico occurred in three stages. The first stage, 1950–63, was associated with the development of light, labor-intensive manufacturing. This gave way in the second stage, 1964–76, to an influx of American, capital-intensive industries, many of which were drawn to Puerto Rico by tax incentives, particularly the petrochemical industry. The third stage, which began in 1977 and continues to the present, has been oriented toward the production of high-technology manufactures, including electronics, scientific instruments, pharmaceutical products, chemicals and derivatives, and other relatively capital-intensive goods.

These changes in the type of manufacturing production on the island were not only the result of shifts in federal and Commonwealth policies toward American investment but were also partly associated with shifts in comparative advantage that led labor-intensive industries to move elsewhere in Latin America and Asia as well. During the 1980s, however, manufacturing employment contracted, dropping from 21 percent of the labor force in 1980, to 17 percent in 1990. Linked to this fall was a period of reduced tax incentives for American investment in the island and increased uncertainty about the sustainability of those incentives over time.

Women have been heavily employed in manufacturing in Puerto Rico since the 1950s. In 1950, approximately 50 percent of the labor force in manufacturing was female. By 1990, the female proportion of the manufacturing workforce in the island was still 46.7 percent. Of course, as manufacturing changed so did the employment profile of women. In 1950, women were concentrated in industries producing apparel and related products. More than 90 percent of the 15,176 persons employed in this industry in 1950 were women (Ríos 1995; Acevedo 1990; Baerga 1987, 1993; Rivera-Quintero 1980; Safa 1986). In 1990,

Figure 5.1   Growth of White-Collar Occupations in Puerto Rico, 1953–90

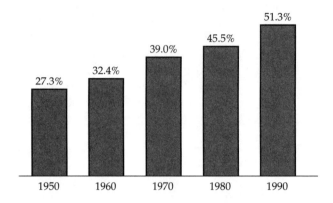

Sources: U.S. Census of Population and Housing, 1950–90; for 1950 and 1960, as cited in Friedlander (1965), table 4.4; for 1970 to 1990: 5% PUMS for Puerto Rico.

approximately 53 percent of the 35,000 workers employed in the electronic machinery and professional and scientific industries were female. The high concentration of women in Puerto Rico's manufacturing sector is a phenomenon shared with other economies that are host to foreign investments. Foreign-owned export-oriented assembly plants, whether in Puerto Rico, Mexico, the Dominican Republic, or other parts of the world, tend to have high proportions of women in their labor forces. Whatever the reason—lower costs, greater productivity, or the segregation of women into certain jobs—employers in such plants prefer to hire women as laborers (Fernández-Kelly and Sassen. 1995; Fernández-Kelly 1983).

The Growth in White-Collar Occupations

The period from 1950 to 1990 was remarkable not only for the industrial changes that occurred but also for the occupational transformation that took place. During this period, the proportion of the labor force in white-collar occupations grew sharply, reflecting a gradual upgrading of the skills of the Puerto Rican workforce. Workers in white-collar occupations made up less than 30 percent of the labor force in 1950 but more than half of the labor force by 1990 (figure 5.1). The considerable improvements in education discussed in chapter 4 greatly contributed to the improvement in occupational status. Since the 1950s, there has been considerable growth in the number of executives, professionals,

Table 5.2   Overrepresentation of Women in Low-Paying Occupations

	Proportion Female, 1990	Average Hourly Wage in the Occupation
Secretaries	97.0%	$5.48
Private household occupations	91.0	4.78
Registered nurses	88.0	7.42
Elementary school teachers	79.0	7.41
Physicians and dentists	30.0	14.64
Lawyers	27.0	15.78
Computer analysts and scientists	27.0	14.81
Engineers	10.0	15.46

Sources: 1980 and 1990 U.S. Census of Population and Housing: Puerto Rico, 5% PUMS.
Note: Data for employed women between 16 and 64 years of age.

and technical workers, primarily in the trade, service, and government sectors. The contraction of jobs in the blue-collar occupations was especially significant for farm laborers, household service workers, and machine operators. (See table 3.4 for the occupational distribution of employment in Puerto Rico in 1990.)

Traditionally, women have been overrepresented in white-collar occupations. Within the white-collar sector, however, the female labor force has also been clustered or segregated in lower-paying clerical and administrative-support occupations (Mulero 1990; Núñez 1990). This changed to some extent in the 1980s, when women became more visible in some of the high-paying occupations traditionally dominated by men. For instance, the proportion of women in executive, administrative, and managerial occupations grew from 27.9 percent in 1980, to 37.7 percent in 1990, a significant increase. On the other hand, the proportion of women in technical occupations declined in the 1980s.

The well-documented segregation of women in low-paying occupations continues.[2] Table 5.2 presents the proportion of the female labor force in a set of occupations and the average hourly wage prevailing in those occupations in 1990. As average hourly wages rise, the proportion of women in the corresponding occupations drops sharply. The average hourly wage for secretaries in Puerto Rico in 1990 was $5.48, and women made up 97 percent of the secretarial labor force in 1990. In comparison, the hourly wage rate for engineers in 1990 was $15.46, and women constituted 10 percent of the engineering workforce.

2. For analyses of this issue, see Rivera (1987), Azize Vargas (1987, 1992), and Valdivia (1992).

Figure 5.2   Labor Force Participation in Puerto Rico, 1970–90

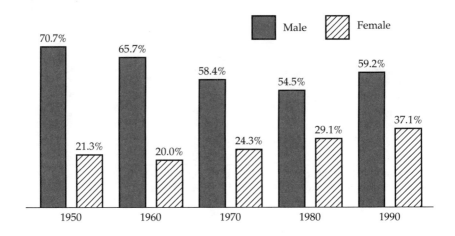

Sources: U.S. Census of Population and Housing, 1950–1990; for 1950 and 1960, as cited in Friedlander (1965), table 4.3; for 1970 to 1990: 5% PUMS for Puerto Rico. Authors' tabulations.
Note: Data for persons 16 years and older.

Changes in Labor Force Participation

The labor force participation rate measures the share of the population that is economically active—either employed or searching for employment (unemployed). It is one of the leading indicators of a society's economic well-being. Generally, the higher the labor force participation rate, the greater is the level of economic activity.

The male labor force participation rate declined sharply in Puerto Rico between 1950 and 1980, rising again between 1980 and 1990 (figure 5.2). Several factors contributed to the declining rate up to 1980. The first was the increased retention of the young population in educational institutions, with the rising enrollments of Puerto Ricans in elementary and secondary education beginning in the 1950s and an increased proportion of the population completing at least some college education. The labor force participation rate of men aged 16 to 19 years thus dropped from 54.2 percent in 1950, to 24 percent in 1980. A second factor was earlier retirement. As an economy's per capita income rises and older cohorts of the population are able to reach a certain level of savings at a younger age, the proportion of people retiring increases rapidly, drawing workers away from the labor force. In Puerto Rico, the labor force participation rate of men aged 65 or older dropped from

57.7 percent in 1950, to 15.1 percent in 1980. A third factor was the changing economic situation in the 1970s, when a sustained economic recession led to hard times and sharply higher unemployment rates. As a consequence, the island began to suffer from "discouraged-worker syndrome," with the lack of new job opportunities eventually leading unemployed workers to withdraw from the labor force altogether.

The labor force participation rate of women has trended upward since the early 1960s, increasing from 20 percent in 1960, to 29.1 percent in 1980. The same forces that reduced labor force participation rates among men were also at work among women during this period. Female labor force participation rates among the younger and older cohorts also declined. The labor force participation rate of women aged 16 to 19 fell from 32.9 percent in 1950, to 9.9 percent in 1980. For women over 65, the rate fell from 6.3 percent in 1950, to 2.4 percent in 1980. These changes, however, were minor compared with the sharply rising labor force participation rates of women in the 25–55 age group, which were associated with the increased demand for female labor in the manufacturing and service sectors, as well as shifting societal attitudes that made the idea of married women working outside the home more acceptable.

The Determinants of Labor Force Participation in the 1980s

The labor force participation rates of both men and women rose in the 1980s. The increase among women was much more substantial than for men. As figure 5.2 displays, the proportion of men in the labor force increased from 54.5 percent in 1980, to 59 percent in 1990; the proportion of women jumped from 29 percent in 1980, to 37 percent in 1990.

As a measure of the labor supplied by persons in the workforce, the labor force participation rate is affected by the unemployment rate in the labor market, general economic conditions, the demographic structure of the population, and public policies toward employment and wages, among other factors (Santiago 1981, 1983). Moreover, the labor force participation rate has cyclical as well as secular characteristics. In the short run, the labor force participation rate may vary substantially in response to the business cycle. An economic downturn may result in workers leaving the labor force because of general discouragement over the lower likelihood of obtaining a job (the "discouraged-worker" effect). At the same time, other family members may enter the labor force to supplement declining household income (the "added-worker effect"). These responses are not mutually exclusive and often vary by gender. Thus, what is important is the magnitude of the countervailing forces and their net impact.[3]

We carried out an exploratory econometric analysis to get an idea of the determinants of labor force participation in Puerto Rico. The dependent variable in our analysis is whether an individual is a labor force participant (either employed or searching for work) or a nonparticipant. Our statistical analysis sought to identify the impact of various individual characteristics on the probability or likelihood of participating in the labor market. Based on this analysis, table 5.3 presents a simple tabulation of how labor force participation rates vary among Puerto Ricans on the basis of age, educational attainment, and gender.[4]

It is apparent from the data presented in table 5.3 that labor force participation rates increased significantly between 1980 and 1990 in all age and educational categories considered for both men and women. This suggests that demographic factors do not account for the rise of labor force participation in the 1980s. Still, as in most other economies, labor force participation rates in Puerto Rico vary with age, rising up to the 40–49 age group and dropping after the age of 50. As table 5.3 shows, in 1990, the labor force participation rate was 61 percent for the 20–29 age group and 65 percent for the 30–39 age group. But it drops to 60 percent and below for older cohorts.

Schooling has a strong positive impact on the labor force participation of persons older than 19 years of age. As table 5.3 indicates, the participation rate of persons between the ages of 20 and 55 who had a high school diploma in 1990 was 18 percentage points higher than that of people who had not obtained a high school diploma. This is crucial since persons with less than a high school education constitute approximately 50 percent of the population in Puerto Rico in 1990. A college degree is associated with another quantum leap in labor force participation. Persons aged 20–55 with a college degree had labor force participation rates almost 15 percentage points higher than those of persons without a college degree.

Work disabilities are another factor accounting for differences in labor force participation in the population. Table 5.4 displays the proportion of people 16 years of age or older who were out of the labor force in 1990 and who were affected by disabilities that either limit work participation or that prevent any work at all. The proportion of men

3. Some economists contend that during the initial downswing in economic activity in a recession the discouraged-worker effect is dominant and reduces the labor force. But, if the probability of finding employment continues to decline or fails to improve, the added-worker effect predominates, and the size of the labor force increases (Santiago and Rossiter 1995).
4. The technical, econometric results of this analysis are available from the authors upon request.

**Table 5.3   Labor Force Participation by Gender, Age, and Education,
1980 and 1990**

	Labor Force Participation Rate	
	1980	1990
	All persons aged 20 to 55	
Age		
20–55	54.2%	60.9%
20–29	53.6	60.7
30–39	59.3	65.1
40–49	52.9	60.3
50–55	43.2	51.3
Educational attainment		
Less than high school	41.7	46.0
High school	62.0	64.3
Some college	⊤	63.8
Finished college	68.4	78.5
More than college	⊥	87.7
	All men aged 20 to 55	
Age		
20–55	71.4	74.3
20–29	66.7	71.7
30–39	78.5	79.1
40–49	72.6	74.3
50–55	63.0	69.2
Educational attainment		
Less than high school	63.0	64.0
High school	79.3	80.1
Some college	⊤	75.4
Finished college	68.4	86.2
More than college	⊥	90.6
	All women aged 20 to 55	
Age		
20–55	39.2	49.0
20–29	42.2	50.3
30–39	42.4	53.0
40–49	35.7	48.0
50–55	25.3	35.6
Educational attainment		
Less than high school	22.3	27.4
High school	46.7	49.1
Some college	⊤	54.4
Finished college	60.4	73.8
More than college	⊥	84.9

Sources: 1980 and 1990 U.S. Census of Population and Housing: Puerto Rico, 5% PUMS.
Note: The data for 1980 were not decomposed by college category.

Table 5.4   Disability and Handicap Rates among Persons Out of the
Labor Force in Puerto Rico, 1980 and 1990

	Proportion of Persons out of the Labor Force with Some Handicap or Disability		Proportion of Persons out of the Labor Force with Some Work-Limitation or Work-Prevented Status	
	1980	1990	1980	1990
Men	35.3%	37.9%	35.1%	36.2%
Women	18.8	25.7	18.5	23.8

Sources: 1980 and 1990 U.S. Census of Population and Housing: Puerto Rico, 5% PUMS.
Note: Data for persons 16 years of age and older.

out of the labor force because of some handicap or disability was over
a third in both 1980 and 1990. In 1990, 36 percent of men out of the
labor force fit in the work-limitation or work-prevented category. The
extent of disability or handicap among women out of the labor force
was lower. In 1990, 24 percent of women out of the labor force had
some disability. The proportion of those out of the labor force because
of handicaps or other limiting factors rose in the 1980s. Although improvements in working conditions and health care facilities may reduce this problem in the future, the aging of the Puerto Rican population suggests that the portion of the population out of the labor force
suffering from physical or health-related limitations is likely to go up.
Another group in the island with low labor force participation is disabled veterans. It is noteworthy that Puerto Ricans in the United States
are also subject to comparatively high rates of disabilities (Rivera-Batiz
and Santiago 1994). The ability to incorporate the disabled into the
workforce represents a major challenge to Puerto Rican policymakers
and society, especially in face of the prevailing high rates of joblessness
overall.

The Crisis in Unemployment

The unemployment rate in Puerto Rico began to skyrocket in the 1970s.
Among men, unemployment rose from under 5 percent in 1970, to 14
percent in 1980, and among women, it increased from under 7 percent
in 1970, to 16 percent in 1980 (figure 5.3). Unemployment continued
to rise in the 1980s, climbing to 19 percent among men in 1990, and to
22 percent among women. These numbers are even more striking when
it is recalled that Puerto Rico's economy experienced significant *positive*

Figure 5.3   Changes in the Unemployment Rate in Puerto Rico, 1970–90

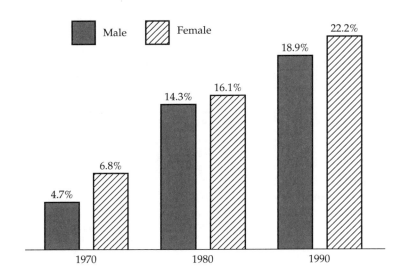

Source: 1970, 1980, and 1990 U.S. Census of Population and Housing for Puerto Rico, 5% PUMS.
Note: Data for persons 16 years of age and older.

economic growth and per capita household income rose sharply during the 1980s.

Explaining the Incidence of Unemployment

An array of variables influences the likelihood of employment of a person in a local labor market (DeFreitas 1991; Rivera-Batiz 1992b; Santiago 1986). Labor demand swings may result in a sudden expansion of employment opportunities or, alternatively, in a surge of layoffs and unemployment. Given labor demand conditions, the characteristics of individuals can have a significant impact on the likelihood of their employment. For instance, higher educational levels raise the probability of employment. Similarly, the older the person and the greater his or her labor market experience, the higher the likelihood of employment. Personal characteristics, such as gender and migration status, can influence the probability of getting a job.

Table 5.5 illustrates the influence of a set of key demographic and socioeconomic variables on the unemployment rate in Puerto Rico. First, it appears that the unemployment rate among teenagers in Puerto Rico is at crisis levels. In 1990, 54 percent of men between the ages of

Table 5.5   Unemployment Rates in Puerto Rico by Age, Education, and Migrant Status, 1980 and 1990

	Male		Female	
	1980	1990	1980	1990
Age				
Younger than 16	14.3%	18.9%	16.1%	22.2%
16–19	50.0	53.9	51.9	61.9
20–29	19.6	24.3	18.7	29.4
30–39	10.5	14.8	12.3	16.8
40–49	8.8	13.1	10.4	13.9
50–59	8.5	12.3	8.8	13.4
60 and older	10.4	15.3	15.5	18.9
Educational attainment				
All persons 25 or older	10.6	14.4	12.0	16.5
Less than high school	15.4	21.7	21.2	27.7
High school	8.9	13.1	11.8	19.4
Some college	5.4	9.9	7.4	15.6
Finished college	2.5	4.4	3.0	5.5
Migrant status				
Did not migrate to the United States between 1980 and 1990 (1970–80)	(12.9)	17.3	(14.5)	20.4
Migrated 1988–90 (1978–80)	(34.9)	40.5	(37.0)	46.3
Migrated 1985–87 (1975–77)	(19.2)	23.4	(24.2)	30.3
Migrated 1980–84 (1970–74)	(13.4)	20.6	(19.3)	29.6

Sources: 1980 and 1990 U.S. Census of Population and Housing, 5% PUMS.
Note: Data for persons aged 16 and older.

16 and 19 in the labor force were unemployed, as were 62 percent of the women of this age group in the labor force. Unemployment rates were generally lower for older cohorts. For example, the unemployment rate among men in the labor force aged 50 to 59 in 1990 was 12 percent, substantially below the 19 percent overall unemployment rate among men. Among women in the 50–59 age cohort, the unemployment rate was 13 percent, again below the 22 percent overall unemployment rate for women.

Educational attainment is another major determinant of the likelihood of employment. The unemployment rate in 1990 for men with less than a high school education was 22 percent. In contrast, the unemployment rate for men with a high school diploma was 13 percent. And men with a college degree had a dramatically lower unemployment rate of slightly over 4 percent. The same negative correlation between unemployment and educational attainment held true for women in 1990.

Given the high rate of mobility of Puerto Ricans between the island and the U.S. mainland, the recency of migration to Puerto Rico is another major factor affecting the likelihood of employment. Puerto Ricans who did not migrate to the United States between 1980 and 1990 had substantially lower unemployment rates than persons who lived in the United States for some period of time during the decade. Among persons who resided in Puerto Rico in the 1980s, 17 percent of the men and 20 percent of the women in the labor force were unemployed in 1990. Among men who moved to the island between 1988 and 1990, the unemployment rate was 40.5 percent in 1990, and among women who moved to the island during this period, it was 46 percent. The migration of people back and forth between Puerto Rico and the United States is disruptive economically and leads the high unemployment.

What stands out from table 5.5 is the fact that the unemployment rate went up for every group in the 1980s, despite the substantial growth of household income discussed in chapter 4. The implication is that demand factors associated with the overall economic activity on the island are behind most of the high unemployment rates. Although the characteristics of persons clearly affect the distribution of unemployment within the labor force, it is the absence of sustained employment growth across most sectors and groups in the economy that has characterized the Puerto Rican labor market since the 1970s.

As we have seen, household income grew briskly in Puerto Rico during the 1980s. This suggests that, in spite of higher unemployment rates, earnings rose during the decade. As a result, although the rate of employment creation lagged, those who were fortunate enough to have employment gained substantially in real wages. This increase of both real wages and unemployment is puzzling and leads us to look for an explanation in the effects of changes in the minimum wage.

The Employment Effects of Minimum Wage Changes

Economists have argued for decades that minimum wage setting, by raising the relative cost of labor, could raise unemployment, especially in the youth labor market, where the effects would bite the most. Given significant changes in minimum wage legislation applying to Puerto Rico in the 1970s, the question arises whether the increasing unemployment in the island is a result of these changes.

Puerto Rico has been covered by the Fair Labor Standards Act (FLSA) since its inception in 1938. However, historically, the minimum wage was applied differently to Puerto Rico than to the mainland

United States. For the first few years after the passage of the FLSA, the federal statutory minimum wage was fully applied to Puerto Rico. However, since average wages on the island were substantially below the U.S. standard, this led many firms into financial difficulties and resulted in layoffs and widespread noncompliance (Reynolds and Gregory 1965). To counteract these effects, the application of the FLSA to Puerto Rico was changed so that a local minimum-wage board could determine exemptions on an industry-by-industry basis to the minimum wage provisions of the FLSA for firms engaged in interstate commerce. Insular minimum wages were also set for firms engaging in commerce within the island.

A major change in the application of federal minimum wages to Puerto Rico occurred in 1974, when the federal minimum-wage boards were abolished. The objective of the legislation was to gradually eliminate the exemptions to the federal statutory minimum wage so that the standards would be automatically extended to Puerto Rico. By the end of the 1970s, the $3.35 federal minimum wage had been fully applied to all relevant industries (although most of manufacturing is covered by the FLSA, other industries are not). Furthermore, the minimum wages were binding to many firms. By the early 1980s, the ratio of the minimum wage to average manufacturing wages was very high. Thus, in contrast to the United States, a relatively large fraction of the Puerto Rican workforce is potentially under the influence of changes in the minimum wage. According to the labor economist Alan Krueger (1995, 4): "Once all industries became covered by the U.S. minimum wage, the U.S. minimum wage became the modal wage paid on the island. In 1983, one-quarter of Puerto Rican workers were paid within 5 cents of the U.S. minimum wage of $3.35. In 1988, 28% of workers were paid within 5 cents of $3.35 per hour, even though the average wage on the island rose in nominal dollars." The federal minimum wage was increased again in 1989, from $3.35 to $4.25 per hour. However, the application of the new standard to Puerto Rico was staggered for a number of industries so that the full effect of the new standard was not obtained until 1995.

Studies of the impact of minimum wage legislation have had a long history in Puerto Rico. The work of Reynolds and Gregory (1965) is still considered to be the definitive study on the effects of minimum wages in Puerto Rican economic development. Reynolds and Gregory found that the increase in real wages that occurred during the 1950s was due, in part, to changes in the minimum wage. They argued that minimum wages pushed real wages upward by generating improvements in productivity. On the other hand, Lastra (1964, 90–91) suggested that the productivity effects hypothesized by Reynolds and Gregory were dependent on the ability of specific industries to quickly generate technical changes in production. From the sample of firms he studied, he concluded that a number of establishments did not have such flexibility and were thus deeply affected financially by the higher minimum wages: "The effects of minimum wages . . . has [*sic*] been to eliminate the sectors of low wages, starting with the disappearance of domestic needlecraft, and continuing with other low wage sectors. . . . The case studies indicate that some sectors have decreased employment and that the imposition of minimum wages has been one factor accounting for this decrease. . . . It is significant that about 45 percent of the firms answered . . . that they would close their plant if the minimum wage rates were increased by 25 cents." The issue of the employment effects of minimum wages in Puerto Rico has been revisited by others over the years using a variety of data sources, including time-series and cross-sectional data. Castillo-Freeman and Freeman (1992) and Santiago (1986, 1989) found significant disemployment effects of revisions to the minimum wage on the island. However, Krueger (1995) and Card and Krueger (1995) found the evidence for significant disemployment effects to be weak.

The literature on the impact of minimum wages on Puerto Rico suffers from the fact that the available data are not perfectly suitable for studying the issue. First, there exists no establishment-based information for examining the particular impact of the minimum wage hikes on firms over time. Second, it is not possible, using the aggregate, economy-wide data on which most of the existing literature is based, to isolate the impact of minimum wages on the economy from the effects of other factors. For instance, minimum wages were increased— and applied more widely—in the 1970s and 1980s, a period when unemployment grew sharply. However, the minimum wage rate hike was not the only major shock that affected the economy during these years. There was also a lingering recession on the island. In addition, there was increased competition for labor-intensive foreign investment from developing and newly industrialized nations. These shocks to the economy all acted, in one way or another, to reduce the demand for labor in Puerto Rico, and it is difficult to disentangle the role played by these forces on unemployment from the particular impact of higher minimum wages.

The impact of the minimum wage, even when considered alone, is also highly complex. Some of its effects act to increase unemployment and others to ameliorating it. For instance, the value of the minimum wage declined sharply in the 1980s since it was not indexed to inflation. By the end of the decade, the average wage in Puerto Rico exceeded the minimum wage by a considerable amount. However, for the substantial number of industries relying on unskilled labor, such as the apparel industry, the minimum wage was still binding, effectively preventing these establishments from hiring additional workers at lower wages. At the same time, some of these firms were able to afford the minimum wage through increased productivity, an effect emphasized by Reynolds and Gregory, as well as Krueger. These firms could sustain their employment despite the higher minimum wages. For them, the minimum wage rate had a limited effect on employment.

The employment impact of minimum wages is also difficult to determine because minimum wage hikes affect the economy in a number of ways. For example, the higher minimum wages in the 1980s raised the earnings of employed workers. This was an incentive for persons to enter the labor force. The resulting increase in labor supply would have raised unemployment rates, although some of this rise in unemployment may not have been seen because of the emigration of unemployed workers to the mainland. Castillo-Freeman and Freeman (1992, 203) argue that "absent migration of the less skilled [to the United States], imposition of a U.S.-level minimum on the island would have raised unemployment so much as to call into question the viability of such a policy."

The evidence on the role that minimum wages play on unemployment is mixed. Overall, however, the weight of the evidence leads to the conclusion that the two variables are positively related in Puerto Rico, even though the magnitude of the relationship has not been precisely established.

The Rise of Real Earnings in the 1980s

Earnings growth in Puerto Rico during the 1980s was brisk. It also appears to have been somewhat stronger for women than for men. Among full-time male workers aged 24–64, earnings, when adjusted for inflation, rose by 18 percent between 1979 and 1989. Real earnings for full-time female workers in the same age group increased by 20 percent. Table 5.6, in which the data are disaggregated by age, reveals strong earnings growth in all the major age cohorts.

Is the Gender Gap in Earnings Declining?

Historically, there has been substantial inequality in the earnings of men and women in Puerto Rico (Picó 1980). In 1979, the average earnings of full-time female workers aged 25–64 were equal to 74 percent of the earnings of full-time male workers. In the 1980s, this gap narrowed by over three percentage points, and in 1989, women's annual earnings had risen to 78 percent of men's (table 5.7). The census data show that the gap in earnings between men and women varies by age group, with less of a gap among the younger cohorts. Nevertheless,

**Table 5.6   Annual Earnings of Men and Women Working Full-Time in
Puerto Rico, 1979 and 1989 (1989 dollars)**

	1979	1989	Percent Change, 1979–89
Age 25–64			
Male	$13,089	$15,480	18.3%
Female	9,698	11,407	20.1
Age 25–34			
Male	11,670	13,011	11.5
Female	9,497	11,407	20.1
Age 35–44			
Male	13,964	16,748	19.9
Female	9,857	12,698	28.8

Sources: 1980 and 1990 U.S. Census of Population and Housing, 5% PUMS.
Note: The 1979 figures have been adjusted upward for inflation using the consumer price index in Puerto Rico between 1979 and 1989.

**Table 5.7   Earnings Ratio between Men and Women Employed Full-
Time in Puerto Rico, 1979 and 1989**

	1979	1989
Age 25–64	74.1%	77.7%
Age 25–34	81.4	87.7
Age 35–44	70.5	75.8

Sources: 1980 and 1990 U.S. Census of Population and Housing, 5% PUMS.
Note: Ratio shows women's earnings as a percentage of men's.

the earnings gap narrowed among all age groups in the 1980s. In 1979, the annual earnings of women aged 25–34 were 81 percent of men's. By 1989, they were 88 percent. For women aged 35–44, the fraction of earnings relative to men in the same age group rose from 70.5 percent in 1979 to 76 percent in 1989. Part of the explanation for this narrowing of the male-female earnings gap is that the occupational distributions of men and women in Puerto Rico became more similar during the 1980s. This occupational convergence is related to substantial improvements in educational attainment among women and to the sharp increase in female participation in professional degree programs in such areas as law, medicine, and veterinary science.

One reason why women in general have had substantially lower personal incomes than men is their greater concentration, and segregation, into part-time employment. This reduces women's earnings compared to men's. In the 1980s, the proportion of both men and women working full-time in Puerto Rico increased substantially. The proportion of women employed full-time year-round rose from 14 percent in 1979, to 20 percent in 1989. The proportion of fully employed men also rose, from 34 percent in 1979, to 40 percent in 1989.

Despite the recent changes, women still earn substantially less than men. Women are still segregated into low-paying jobs in the labor market and, on average, continue to have substantially lower income than men (Rivera-Batiz 1994). This inequality is best seen by considering the economic status of women living in female-headed households. In 1990, 29.8 percent of all women 14 years of age or older were living in such households. The personal income of these women was approximately two-thirds that of the rest of the population, and close to 40 percent of them were receiving income from public assistance (which includes Aid to Families with Dependent Children, food stamps, and other federal and state transfers), compared to 21 percent among the general population in the same age group. Public assistance constituted a major source of personal income for women 14 years of age or older living in female-headed households. The average share of public assistance as a proportion of personal income for these women was 30.7 percent, compared to 15.7 percent among the overall population in the same age group. It is clear that there are still substantial inequities in pay and income between men and women.

The Economic Returns to Education in Puerto Rico

Increased educational levels are associated with the acquisition of skills, which makes people more competitive in the labor market. This generates greater labor force participation, lower unemployment, and increased pay. The importance of education as a factor in success in the labor market grew during the 1980s in Puerto Rico. This means that persons with high levels of education benefited relatively more from Puerto Rico's economic expansion during the second half of the decade.

This pattern is clearly seen in the changes in earnings over the past decade. For example, although the average earnings adjusted for inflation of all women aged 25–34 employed full-time increased during the 1980s, the wages of those with less than a college degree barely increased during the same time period (table 5.8). The inflation-adjusted earnings of female workers with no high school diploma rose by a mere 1.3 percent in the 1980s, while the inflation-adjusted earnings of women with only a high school diploma did not rise at all. Only among women with a college or post-college degree was there a significant increase in earnings in the 1980s. The earnings of women with a post-college education rose by nearly 9 percent. A similar pattern of change according to educational attainment holds for men.

Table 5.8   **Economic Returns to Education in Puerto Rico, 1979 and 1989 (1989 dollars)**

	Earnings		Percent Change, 1979–89
	1979	1989	
Less than high school			
Men	$8,271	$8,160	−1.3%
Women	7,384	7,459	1.0
High school graduate			
Men	11,662	11,371	−2.4
Women	9,489	9,510	0.2
College graduate			
Men	18,581	19,047	2.5
Women	12,471	13,072	4.8
Post-college education			
Men	23,210	25,965	11.9
Women	16,465	17,915	8.8

Sources: 1980 and 1990 U.S. Census of Population and Housing: Puerto Rico, 5% PUMS.
Note: Data show average annual earnings of full-time workers, 25–34 years old. The data for 1979 have been adjusted by the change in the consumer price index for Puerto Rico between 1979 and 1989, as published by the Puerto Rico Planning Board, *Economic Report to the Governor.*

Employed workers with college degrees benefited from an increased standard of living in the 1980s; those with less than a college degree did not progress and were likely to suffer a *reduction* of their economic standard of living. This suggests that there was an increase in the returns to education in Puerto Rico during the decade. In 1979, the earnings of women with a college degree were 31.4 percent higher than those of women with a high school diploma. By 1989, the earnings of women with a college degree were 37.8 percent higher than those of women with a high school diploma. The higher value of a college degree relative to a high school diploma in Puerto Rico also applies among men.

The causes of the rise in the returns to education in Puerto Rico are many. Economic restructuring, in the form of the flight of blue-collar manufacturing from the island and an increase in white-collar service sector employment, led to a relative drop in economic opportunities for unskilled, blue-collar workers. Research conducted by the economists Kevin Murphy and Finis Welch (1993) and Alan Krueger (1993) suggests that most of the drop in the wages of unskilled workers relative to educated labor in the United States during the 1980s was related to technological changes in the workplace, such as the use of computers. These changes reduced the demand for unskilled workers, shifting the

Table 5.9   Economic Returns to Education by Gender, 1979 and 1989

		1979	1989
Increased earnings of college grad-uates relative to those with just a high school diploma	Men	59.3%	67.5%
	Women	31.4	37.8
Increased earnings of persons with education greater than col-lege relative to those with a high school diploma	Men	99.0	128.0
	Women	73.5	88.4

Source: Table 5.8.
Note: Based on average annual earnings of full-time workers, 25–34 years old.

demand for highly educated labor upward. The result was an increase in the wage premium paid to education in the labor market. Similar changes may be occurring in Puerto Rico.

Although increased education is related to higher pay for both men and women, the linkage between these two variables is stronger for men than for women, that is, the economic returns to education are higher for men. In 1989, the economic gain from a college degree—relative to a high school diploma—for men in the 25–34 age group was 67.5 percent, meaning that the earnings of men with college degrees were 67.5 percent higher than the earnings of men with a high school diploma (table 5.9). For women in this age cohort, on the other hand, the economic returns of a college education—38 percent—were much lower. The gap in the returns to education between men and women is equally wide for post-college education. In 1989, the returns to education for men with post-college education were 128 percent compared to those with a high school diploma; for women they were 88 percent.

One explanation for the lower rates of return to education among women has been offered by Picó (1980, 224), who argues that "traditionally, female occupations such as nurses and teachers require more educational attainment than the average. Yet, they have lower pay than other, male-dominated, occupations requiring the same levels of educational attainment. Another explanation is that women are segregated into lower-paying occupations despite their educational accomplishments. They are also paid less than men for the same work."

The Informal Sector and Economic Dualism in the Puerto Rican Economy

It is important to keep in mind that Puerto Rico's economy is, in many ways, a developing economy. As such, it has features quite distinct from those of the economies of the states of the U.S. mainland. The notion of economic dualism, which is a useful concept in analyzing many developing economies, is therefore useful in examining Puerto Rico's economic development (Santiago and Thorbeque 1984, 1988; Santiago 1988). Dualism has many different meanings but it refers here to sectoral differences that tend to persist over time.[5]

Examined within a multisectoral dualistic framework, the long-term trends and changes in the Puerto Rican labor market are seen to be characterized by two basic dimensions, the first, regional and the second, technological. Regional dualism refers to differences between rural and urban areas, while technological dualism refers to differences between the formal and informal sectors. The informal sector consists primarily of self-employed, but non-incorporated, workers and unpaid family labor. The formal sector is made up of all wage and salary employees, workers employed within their own corporations, and all public sector workers. Urban areas are those defined by the census as metropolitan statistical areas (MSAs); rural areas are defined as all non-MSAs. Although the theoretical constructs of urban/rural and formal/informal may not always match the standard census classifications, the important point is that the operational definitions remain unchanged and appropriate comparisons can be made over time.

Whereas differences between rural and urban areas are easily understood, differences between formal and informal sectors are often not. The urban informal sector has received considerable attention among development economists since the mid-1970s. Some have looked at this sector as a repository of surplus labor. According to this approach, persons residing in rural areas are spurred to migrate to urban areas by the promise of high wages and unrealistic expectations of future employment, leading to an excess supply of labor in urban areas (Harris and Todaro 1970; Fields 1975; Rivera-Batiz 1986). The inability of the formal sector to employ the many migrants coming from rural areas resulted, according to some scholars, in a crisis of "overurbanization." Thus, to some, the urban informal sector represents a large, poverty-ridden population with few realistic prospects for escaping the squalor and inequities of marginal urban life. Others have argued that the urban informal sector represents pent up entrepreneurship that has been relegated to an economic realm outside of the mainstream due to bur-

---

5. In this respect, labor market segmentation and dualism need not refer to the same phenomenon. However, both segmentation and dualism incorporate barriers to mobility across sectors. Labor market segmentation refers to a situation where identical individuals (in terms of skills, education, age, and so forth) tend to have different labor market outcomes (earnings, employment) because of lack of mobility among labor market segments. Dualism, on the other hand, is more related to regional and technological differences in production sectors of the economy, and it may or may not be associated with lack of labor mobility across labor market segments.

Table 5.10 **Unemployment Rates in a Dualistic Framework by Region and Type of Activity**

	1980	1990
Formal sector	15.0%	20.9%
Informal sector	6.1	9.4
Urban	13.4	19.5
Rural	18.1	28.1
Rural non-farm	13.6	21.4
Rural farm	57.2	65.6
Urban formal	13.4	20.0
Urban informal	5.7	9.1
Rural non-farm formal	13.6	22.9
Rural non-farm informal	6.6	10.0
Rural farm formal	57.2	68.3
Rural farm informal	8.9	22.2

Sources: 1980 and 1990 U.S. Census of Population and Housing: Puerto Rico, 5% PUMS.

densome government interference and regulation (De Soto 1989). From this viewpoint, the informal sector is characterized by high rates of employment, with people thriving in an underground economy unrestricted by taxes and governmental regulation. However, the true characteristics of the urban informal sector lie somewhere between these extremes.

Table 5.10 presents rates of unemployment for Puerto Rico in 1980 and 1990 by major sectors within the dualistic framework. Although unemployment rates are high across the board, there are significant differences across sectors. Formal-sector unemployment rates, for example, are higher than those in the informal sector. This is to be expected if the informal sector is a thriving regulation-free, underground economy. However, formal-sector workers are covered by unemployment compensation and other programs that subsidize, in some measure, job search and retraining. This is not the case in the informal sector, where many of the institutional features of the labor market, such as unemployment benefits, minimum wage provisions, occupational health and safety provisions, and the like may not be available. It is also apparent from the data in table 5.10 that rural unemployment rates tend to be higher than those in urban areas, and unemployment rates in the rural farm sector surpass those in the rural non-farm sector.

An examination of real earnings growth across sectors also shows noteworthy patterns of change from 1979 to 1989. The data in table 5.11 demonstrate that, contrary to expectation, informal-sector earnings surpassed those prevailing in the formal sector in both 1979 and

Table 5.11   **Real Annual Earnings in a Dualistic Framework by Region and Type of Activity (in 1989 dollars)**

	1979	1989	Percent Change, 1979–89
Formal sector	$7,136	$8,206	15.0%
Informal sector	8,160	8,945	9.6
Urban	7,984	8,266	3.5
Rural	5,717	5,939	3.9
Rural non-farm	5,879	6,223	5.9
Rural farm	3,695	2,375	−35.7
Urban formal	7,871	8,400	6.7
Urban informal	9,351	9,336	− 0.2
Rural non-farm formal	5,846	6,521	11.5
Rural non-farm informal	6,328	5,776	− 8.7
Rural farm formal	3,775	2,437	−35.4
Rural farm informal	3,308	2,083	−37.0

Sources: 1980 and 1990 U.S. Census of Population and Housing: Puerto Rico, 5% PUMS.

1989, although the gap between the two has closed a bit. Again, this is hardly characteristic of a marginal sector of low-income activities. Rather, the picture of the informal sector obtained from these data is one that includes high-paying activities as well as low-paying ones. It is also noteworthy that while urban and rural non-farm formal earnings grew during the 1980s, this was not the case in the rural farm or rural informal sectors. By 1989 informal-sector earnings in rural areas had fallen below earnings in the rural formal sector. Thus, there was a noticeable bias in the 1980s against rural employment and rural earnings. The Puerto Rican economy continues to gravitate toward urban non-farm activities, leaving the rural sector marginalized from the rest of the economy.

Summary: The Labor Market and the Unemployment Crisis

1. The decline of employment in agriculture is one of the most important developments in the Puerto Rican economy over the last forty years. In 1950, 35 percent of the Puerto Rican labor force was employed in agriculture, compared to only 3.7 percent in 1990. This drastic transformation was associated with the decline of agriculture as an income-generating sector in the economy. As policymakers engaged in Operation Bootstrap, with its urban-based "industrialization-first" development strategy, the agricultural labor force was siphoned into rapidly expanding urban areas.
2. Trade, services, and public administration have all greatly increased as employment sectors. Manufacturing employment has been stable since 1950, accounting on average for about 19 percent of the labor force. Women have been heavily involved in manufacturing employment in Puerto Rico. In 1950, approximately 50 percent of the labor force employed in manufacturing was female. In 1990, the female proportion of the manufacturing workforce in the island was still 46.7 percent.
3. From 1950 to 1990, the proportion of the labor force in white-collar occupations grew sharply, reflecting an upgrading of the skills of the Puerto Rican workforce. Workers in white-collar occupations made up less than 30 percent of the labor force in 1950, but more than half by 1990. Improvements in education greatly contributed to the improvement in occupational status.
4. Historically, women have been overrepresented in white-collar occupations. Within the white-collar segment, however, the female labor force has been clustered or segregated into lower-paying clerical and administrative-support occupations.
5. Male labor force participation rates declined sharply between 1950 and 1980, and rose between 1980 and 1990. In 1950, the male labor force participation rate was 70.7 percent; by 1990, it was 59.2 percent. This drop is related to lower participation rates among persons below 20 years of age (due to greater educational attainment), and among those above 64 years (related to earlier retirement). The rising unemployment since the early 1970s has resulted in *discouraged* workers, who drop out of the labor force.
6. The labor force participation rate of women has trended upward since the early 1960s, rising from 20 percent in 1960, to 37.1 percent in 1990. The same forces operating to reduce labor force participation rates among younger and older men were also operating among women during this time period. These changes, however, were minor compared with the sharply rising labor force participation rates of women in the 25–55 age group. This was associated with an increased demand for female labor in manufacturing and service sectors, as well as with shifting attitudes toward women's work in Puerto Rican society.
7. Unemployment exploded in the 1970s and 1980s. Among men, unemployment rose from 4.7 percent in 1970, to 14.3 percent in 1980, to 18.9 percent in 1990. Among women, unemployment increased from 6.8 percent in 1970, to 16.1 percent in 1980, to 22.2 percent in 1990.
8. The incidence of unemployment varies among various demographic groups in the population. Age is crucial: the unemployment rate among teenagers in Puerto Rico is at crisis levels. In 1990, 53.9 percent of the

men between the ages of 16 and 19 in the labor force were unemployed. Among women in this age group, 61.9 percent of the labor force was unemployed. Educational attainment is another major determinant of unemployment. The unemployment rate is substantially lower among college-educated persons. Given the high rate of mobility of Puerto Ricans between the island and the mainland, recency of migration to the island is a third major factor affecting unemployment. A fourth factor affecting unemployment is location: rural areas in the island tend to have substantially higher unemployment rates.

9. The massive increase in unemployment in Puerto Rico in the 1970s and 1980s affected almost every demographic group in the island. The crisis was to a large extent associated with a sustained drop in the aggregate demand for labor caused by a severe recession that lasted until the late 1980s. In addition, increased competition from other developing and newly industrialized nations for foreign investment resulted in a reduction of labor-intensive U.S. investments in Puerto Rico.

10. Federal minimum wage legislation applies to Puerto Rico. The evidence of the role that federal minimum wages play on unemployment on the island is mixed. However, the weight of the evidence leads to the conclusion that the two variables are positively related, even though the magnitude of the relationship has not been precisely established.

11. Earnings growth in Puerto Rico during the 1980s was brisk. It also appears to have been somewhat stronger for women than for men. As a result, the gender gap in earnings declined in the 1980s. In 1979, the average earnings of women working full-time in Puerto Rico were 74.1 percent of the earnings of full-time male workers. In the 1980s, this gap narrowed by more than three percentage points. Part of the explanation for the narrowing of the male-female earnings gap is that the occupational distributions of men and women in Puerto Rico became more similar during the 1980s.

12. The returns to education increased in Puerto Rico just as they did in the United States. Although higher education is related to higher pay for both men and women, the economic returns to education are higher among men.

13. One of the things that differentiates Puerto Rico's economy from the economy of the mainland, is that it is, in many ways, a developing economy. The notion of dualism, between formal and informal sectors, and between rural and urban areas, an important concept in analyzing developing economies, applies to Puerto Rico. The urban informal sector in Puerto Rico appears to be thriving and dynamic, with comparatively low unemployment rates and high earnings. In contrast, both the formal and informal sectors in rural areas are stagnant.

CHAPTER 6

Immigration and the Population Born outside Puerto Rico

T HE MIGRATION of persons born outside Puerto Rico to the island has boomed over the last thirty years. In 1960, there were 59,316 persons born elsewhere living in Puerto Rico. By 1990, the number had risen to 320,234, or 9.1 percent of the total population. This is a high figure by international standards, reflecting Puerto Rico's history of attracting persons born outside its borders. The foreign-born population of the United States—often referred to as the land of immigrants—was also around 9 percent in 1990.

More than two-thirds of the persons residing in Puerto Rico in 1990 who were born outside the island originated in the United States. Of these 229,304 individuals, the great majority had Puerto Rican parentage, that is, at least one of their parents was born in Puerto Rico. These are the children of the hundreds of thousands of Puerto Ricans who emigrated to the United States in the past. The immigration of persons to Puerto Rico born outside the United States (the so-called foreign-born) has also increased substantially over the last thirty years. Between 1960 and 1990, the number of foreign-born persons residing on the island increased almost ninefold, from 10,414 in 1960, to 90,930 in 1990. Cuban-born and Dominican-born immigrants constitute a substantial part of this flow.

In recent years, the undocumented immigration population in the island also appears to have grown significantly. As the number of these immigrants has increased, their role in the island's economy has become a controversial topic among the public and in the press. Questions about the impact of the immigrants on the labor market dominate this discussion, and opinions vary, from those who feel that the immi-

Table 6.1   The Population of Puerto Rico by Nativity, 1980–90

	1980	1990	Growth, 1980–90
Puerto Rico, total	3,197,000	3,522,027	10.2%
Born in Puerto Rico	2,934,084	3,201,793	9.1
Born outside Puerto Rico	262,916	320,234	21.8
Born in the mainland United States	199,524	229,304	14.9
Puerto Ricans born in the continental United States	176,198	207,787	17.9
Persons born in the continental United States not of Puerto Rican parentage	23,326	21,517	−7.7
Born outside the United States (the foreign-born)	63,392	90,930	43.4

Sources: 1980 and 1990 U.S. Census of Population and Housing: Puerto Rico, 5% PUMS.

grants contribute positively to the economy, to those who believe that they take jobs away from Puerto Ricans and raise unemployment.

The Population Born outside Puerto Rico

In 1990, Puerto Rico had a population of about three and a half million. Of this population, 91 percent were native-born.

The population of Puerto Rico born outside the island is growing quickly. While the native-born population of Puerto Rico grew by 9 percent over the 1980s, the population born outside the island grew by 22 percent (table 6.1). The foreign-born population grew faster still, rising by 43 percent. This influx of persons born outside Puerto Rico was the continuation of a trend that began in the 1960s. Of those born outside Puerto Rico living on the island in 1990, close to half had moved there during the 1980s (table 6.2). Over 28 percent had migrated to Puerto Rico between 1970 and 1979. Only about 5 percent had moved to the island before 1960.

The Foreign-Born Population

The foreign-born population of Puerto Rico—persons born outside Puerto Rico and the United States—has expanded exponentially during the last three decades (figure 6.1). The number of foreign-born immigrants residing in the island remained below 15,000 from the turn of the century until 1960. Between 1960 and 1990, however, this

**Table 6.2   Population Born outside Puerto Rico by Years of
In-Migration, 1990**

In-Migration Cohort	Number	Percentage of Total
All persons born outside Puerto Rico	320,234	100.0%
1985–90	104,905	32.7
1980–84	52,277	16.3
1970–79	90,569	28.3
1960–69	58,044	18.1
Before 1960	14,439	4.6

Sources: 1980 and 1990 U.S. Census of Population and Housing: Puerto Rico, 5% PUMS.

Figure 6.1   Foreign-Born Population of Puerto Rico, 1900–90

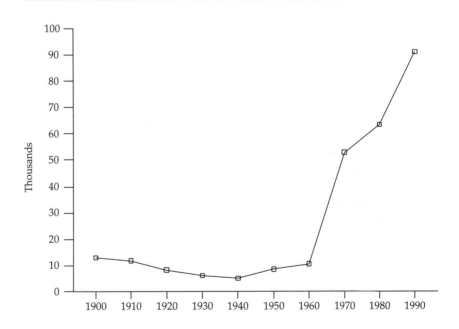

Sources: 1900 to 1960: Vázquez Calzada (1988); after 1960: 1970, 1980, and 1990 U.S. Census of Population: Puerto Rico, table for selected social and economic characteristics.

Table 6.3   Foreign-Born in Puerto Rico by Country of Origin

	1980	1990	Growth, 1980–90
Foreign-born, total	63,351	90,930	43.5%
Dominican Republic	20,558	41,193	100.4
Cuba	22,811	19,755	−13.4
Europe	7,449	9,108	22.3
South America	5,424	7,140	31.6
Central America	1,702	6,651	290.8
Other	5,407	2,917	−46.0

Sources: 1980 and 1990 U.S. Census of Population and Housing: Puerto Rico, 5% PUMS.

population increased almost ninefold, from 10,414 in 1960, to 90,930 in 1990. Most of these migrants came to Puerto Rico from other Latin countries in the Caribbean, and from Central and South America. Puerto Rico's Hispanic culture, its comparatively higher per capita income, and its proximity make it attractive to the Spanish-speaking migrants from these areas.

In 1990, the largest immigrant group in Puerto Rico was made up of those born in the Dominican Republic (table 6.3). The Dominican-born residing in Puerto Rico doubled during the 1980s, increasing from 20,558 in 1980, to 41,193 in 1990. Dominican migration to Puerto Rico first became significant in the 1960s.[1] From 1930 to 1961, the restrictive out-migration policies of the Dominican Republic under the rule of the Trujillo regime were linked to a comparatively small flow out of the island. In the 1960s, however, emigration of Dominicans to Puerto Rico was stimulated by various forces, with the number of Dominicans in Puerto Rico increasing from 1,070 in 1960, to 10,843 in 1970.

The admission of immigrants to Puerto Rico is determined by federal immigration policy as administered by the U.S. Immigration and Naturalization Service (INS). Major changes in U.S. immigration policy in the 1960s, such as those related to the U.S. Immigration Family Reunification Act, stimulated Dominican migration to Puerto Rico as well as to the United States (Hernández, Rivera-Batiz, and Agodini 1995). The turmoil caused by political strife in the Dominican Republic (such as the overthrow of President Juan Bosch in 1963) also promoted emigration. Since the 1970s, however, economic motives have driven Dominican emigration.

1.   For analyses of the Dominican population in Puerto Rico, see Duany (1994), and Vázquez Calzada and Morales del Valle (1979).

The explosion of Dominican migration to Puerto Rico in the 1980s and 1990s was directly linked to the sharply deteriorating economic situation in the Dominican Republic during this period. The Dominican Republic's GNP declined almost every year between 1982 and 1992, and per capita consumption dropped by 22 percent. A ballooning external debt and the deterioration in commodity prices and export markets led to a severe crisis. With the per capita GNP in Puerto Rico nearly three times as high as in the Dominican Republic, the recession of the 1980s proved a powerful stimulus to migration. A 1987 survey of Dominican migrants in San Juan conducted by the University of the Sacred Heart in Puerto Rico found that close to 60 percent of the persons in the sample had migrated to Puerto Rico "to find employment." Other reasons for migration included "to study" (6.4 percent), "family reunion" (13 percent), and "the political situation in the Dominican Republic" (3.7 percent) (Hernández Angueira 1990, 75).

The second-largest immigrant group in Puerto Rico in 1990 was the Cuban-born population of 19,755 persons. In contrast to Puerto Rico's Dominican population, its Cuban-born population *declined* in the 1980s, a continuation of a trend that began in the 1970s. The height of the Cuban migration to Puerto Rico occurred in the 1960s and early 1970s, as refugees fled from the socialist policies of Fidel Castro.[2] In 1960, there were approximately 500 Cubans residing in Puerto Rico. By 1970, there were 26,000. This number continued to increase until 1973, when the "freedom flights" moving Cuban exiles to the United States ended. After 1973, there were no major inflows of Cubans to Puerto Rico, and a significant number of Cubans left Puerto Rico for the United States.

As table 6.3 illustrates, the fastest-growing population in Puerto Rico in the 1980s was not the Dominican-born. Although the number of Central Americans living in Puerto Rico is still small compared to the number of Dominicans and Cubans, Central American immigration to the island has surged in recent years. While in 1980 there were only 1,702 immigrants from Central America living in Puerto Rico, by 1990 there were 6,651, an increase of almost 300 percent.

Undocumented Immigrants

The numbers of foreign-born residents of Puerto Rico cited here derive from the decennial U.S. census. Insofar as undocumented immigrants avoid being counted by the census, these figures represent a lower-bound estimate of the total immigrant population residing in Puerto Rico. This is of particular significance with respect to the Dominican

2. For detailed analyses of Cuban immigrants in Puerto Rico, see Rivera-Batiz (1995), Duany (1989), Esteve (1984), Vázquez Calzada and Morales del Valle (1979), and Montaner (1971).

population estimate, since Dominicans constitute the great majority of the undocumented immigrant population. Between April 1987 and May 1994, INS statistics indicate that 21,186 undocumented immigrants were apprehended in Puerto Rico. Of these, 19,893, or nearly 94 percent, were born in the Dominican Republic.

Estimates of the undocumented population of the island range from 100,000 to 300,000, according to INS officials. However, these estimates are questionable. Just as for the U.S. mainland, there is a tendency to exaggerate the undocumented presence in Puerto Rico. In 1986, the Immigration Reform and Control Act allowed undocumented immigrants who had resided in the United States before 1982 to apply for legalization. Close to two million people did so, but only 4,521 persons applied from Puerto Rico. No doubt some undocumented immigrants were afraid to apply for legalization, and undocumented migration to Puerto Rico appears to have accelerated since the mid-1980s. Even so, it is highly unlikely that the undocumented population in Puerto Rico is as high as 300,000. If anything, it is probably closer to, but less than, 100,000.

One of the difficulties in estimating the number of undocumented immigrants in Puerto Rico is the large flow of these immigrants who move in and out of the island every day. In recent years, Puerto Rico has been a stepping-stone for undocumented immigrants seeking entry to the mainland United States. Travel between Puerto Rico and the mainland does not normally require any immigration documentation. INS officers sometimes make visual checks of passengers at airports and may ask some individuals for identification and documents. This is a cursory process, however, and few undocumented persons are discovered. This means that any undocumented immigrant who successfully makes it to Puerto Rico without being intercepted by the INS can almost be ensured entry into the United States.

Tens of thousands of undocumented immigrants enter Puerto Rico undetected every year by sea. Aided by smugglers, hundreds set out daily from the Dominican Republic toward Puerto Rico in frail and crowded boats, crossing the treacherous waters of the Mona Passage that separates Puerto Rico from the Dominican Republic. Many die in the attempt. Every year, hundreds of undocumented migrants are reported drowned. Many are never located.

Some of the undocumented immigrants come from Cuba, Jamaica, and even from as far away as China and India. Of the Dominicans, who form the great majority of these immigrants, a small fraction stays in Puerto Rico, working illegally in a variety of businesses. Most of them, though, soon continue their travel to the United States, usually to New York City. As one Dominican construction worker in San Juan said to *New York Times* reporter Larry Rohter in 1992, "I don't think

Table 6.4   Household Income of the Population of Puerto Rico by Nativity, 1989

	Household Income	Persons in Household	Per Capita Household Income
Puerto Rico, average	$14,843	4.15	$4,099
Puerto Rican–born	14,523	4.15	3,983
Foreign-born	23,394	3.71	7,386
Cuban-born	31,300	3.26	10,627
Dominican-born	16,968	4.01	4,712
Puerto Ricans born in the mainland United States	14,686	4.34	3,916
Persons born in the mainland United States, not of Puerto Rican parentage	26,943	3.81	9,160

Source: 1990 U.S. Census of Population and Housing: Puerto Rico, 5% PUMS.

there is a single town in my country that doesn't have somebody who made it to New York by going through Puerto Rico." This flow of undocumented immigrants through Puerto Rico makes it difficult to estimate the portion of those immigrants who stay in the island.

The Socioeconomic Status of the Population Born outside Puerto Rico

Stereotypes about immigrants abound in the recipient countries. In Puerto Rico, for example, the Dominican immigrants as a group are perceived to be people with very low levels of educational attainment on the lowest rungs of the income ladder. Stereotypes, however, are often groundless, and this is certainly the case of immigrants in Puerto Rico.

A comparison of average annual household income in Puerto Rico in 1989, decomposed by nativity, reveals significant diversity in the dispersion of income among the various groups considered (table 6.4). On average, persons born in the mainland United States without any Puerto Rican parentage had the highest household income. They were followed by the foreign-born, whose income was more than 60 percent higher than the native-born. Among immigrants, the Cuban population had the highest household income. This is not surprising since many of the Cuban refugees who arrived in Puerto Rico in the 1960s and 1970s were professional and technical workers. And, in contrast to popular perceptions, the average annual household income of the Dominican population of Puerto Rico was also higher than that of the native-born population. In fact, the $16,989 average household income of the Dominicans exceeded the $14,523 income of the native-born by 17 percent.

These household income differentials on the basis of nativity persist even in a comparison of per capita income. Indeed, in some cases, the differences are magnified because the population groups with the lowest household incomes also tend to have the largest households. As table 6.4 shows, the native-born and Puerto Ricans born in the mainland United States—the two groups with the lowest household income in 1989—also had the largest households, with 4.15 and 4.34 persons per household, respectively. On the other hand, for the Cuban-born and Dominican-born populations, whose average household incomes in 1989 were greater than the native-born population's, the average number of persons per household was 3.26 and 4.01, respectively. As a result, the per capita income of Cubans was more than two and a half times that of the native-born.

The higher income of the foreign-born compared to the native-born in Puerto Rico is unusual relative to the mainland United States, where the income of the foreign-born population on average is lower than that of the native-born population. In 1989, for instance, the average household income of the native-born population in the United States was $41,485. In comparison, for the foreign-born population of the United States it was $40,969. Of course, some immigrant groups in the United States—such as the Russian and the Japanese populations— have higher incomes than the native-born population. This raises the question of what forces determine differentials in household income across groups in the population.

Income differentials can be explained by differences in key labor market outcomes that vary by nativity. The average household income of a particular group is closely related to: (1) the labor force participation of persons in that group, (2) the employment or unemployment rates of those in the labor force, (3) the proportion of employed persons who are working full-time, and (4) the earnings of those who are employed. Of course, labor force participation, earnings, and the like are in turn determined by other fundamental socioeconomic variables, such as educational attainment (higher educational attainment is usually linked to greater labor force participation rate as well as increased earnings), age and labor market experience (the older the person, the more experienced he or she is likely to be and, therefore, the higher his or her earnings).

Labor Force Participation and Unemployment

The labor force participation rate in Puerto Rico is much higher for persons born outside the island than among those born in Puerto Rico

Table 6.5   Labor Force Participation Rates in Puerto Rico by Nativity, 1990

	Male	Female
Puerto Rico, average	59.2%	37.1%
Persons born in Puerto Rico	58.0	35.9
Foreign-born	75.3	46.4
Persons born in Cuba	77.5	46.2
Persons born in the Dominican Republic	77.8	51.1
Puerto Ricans born in the mainland United States	67.2	49.8
Persons born in the mainland United States, not of Puerto Rican parentage	70.7	47.1

Source: 1990 U.S. Census of Population and Housing: Puerto Rico, 5% PUMS.
Note: Data for persons 16 years and older.

Table 6.6   Unemployment Rates in Puerto Rico by Nativity, 1990

	Male	Female
Puerto Rico, average	18.8%	22.1%
Persons born in Puerto Rico	19.1	22.0
Foreign-born	7.3	8.3
Persons born in Cuba	3.0	6.9
Persons born in the Dominican Republic	12.4	24.4
Puerto Ricans born in the mainland United States	22.3	25.4
Persons born in the mainland United States, not of Puerto Rican parentage	7.5	17.0

Source: 1990 U.S. Census of Population and Housing: Puerto Rico, 5% PUMS.
Note: Data for persons 16 years and older.

(table 6.5). Among men, the labor force participation of the Puerto Rican–born population 16 years of age or older in 1990 was 58 percent; it ranged between 78 percent and 67 percent for the groups born outside the island. The labor force participation rate for native-born Puerto Rican women in 1990 was 36 percent, while for all other groups of women it was at least 10 percentage points higher.

The data on the proportion of the labor force that was unemployed in 1990, decomposed by nativity, reveal wide unemployment differentials among the various groups examined (table 6.6). The highest unem-

Table 6.7   Proportion of Persons Working Full-Time Year-Round in
            Puerto Rico by Nativity, 1989

	Male	Female
Puerto Rico, average	39.6%	20.0%
Persons born in Puerto Rico	38.2	19.3
Foreign-born	59.8	28.2
Persons born in Cuba	68.3	33.7
Persons born in the Dominican Republic	51.3	21.9
Puerto Ricans born in the mainland United States	47.9	30.7
Persons born in the mainland United States, not of Puerto Rican parentage	68.0	26.5

Source: 1990 U.S. Census of Population and Housing: Puerto Rico, 5% PUMS.
Note: Data for all persons aged 25–64 living in households.

ployment rates occur among Puerto Ricans born in the mainland
United States, 22 percent for males and 25 percent for females. The
unemployment rates for native-born Puerto Ricans—19 percent for
men and 22 percent for women—did not lag far behind. In contrast,
the unemployment rate in 1990 for foreign-born men was 7 percent,
and for women it was 8 percent. The unemployment rates of the Cuban-born population were particularly low: 3 percent for men and 7
percent for women. There was a substantial unemployment gap between Dominican-born men and women. Dominican-born men had an
unemployment rate of 12 percent in 1990, while Dominican-born
women had an unemployment rate of 24 percent. This gap in the unemployment rates of Dominican-born men and Dominican-born women
residing in Puerto Rico is partly related to the significantly higher educational attainment of the former.

Full-Time versus Part-Time Employment

Individuals who are either employed or actively seeking employment
are considered to be labor force participants. However, some persons
want and obtain full-time employment, while others seek part-time
work. Part-time employment, of course, reduces earnings compared to
full-time employment. A significant part of the income shortfall of the
native-born population of Puerto Rico relative to the population born
outside the island results from substantial differences in full-time employment (table 6.7).

Among Puerto Rican–born men aged 25–64, only 38 percent were
working full-time year-round in 1989. For all the groups born outside

the island the proportion of men working full-time year-round in 1989 was much higher. Among Cuban-born men, it was 68 percent, the highest of any group on the island, and among men born in the Dominican Republic, it was 51 percent. These figures correlate with the household incomes for these groups: the Cuban-born population of Puerto Rico also had the highest level of household income in 1989, and the Dominican-born population also had a higher average household income than the native-born population.

There is also a gap between the native-born female population working full-time year-round and the female population born outside the island. However, in all groups, the proportion of women working full-time was significantly lower than among men in 1989. Only 19 percent of all women born in Puerto Rico aged 25–64 were working full-time, compared to 34 percent of Cuban-born women, and 22 percent of Dominican-born women. The lower participation of women in full-time work is a phenomenon that applies in the United States as well. The traditional division of labor by gender is associated with greater participation of married women in household production compared to men. As a result, a higher proportion of married women than men have participated in the labor market on a part-time basis. Economic pressures associated with stagnating household income and rising unemployment, as well as changing societal roles by gender, have resulted in a greater proportion of women working full-time, yet a substantial gap remains between male and female full-time employment.

Earnings and Personal Income

In addition to the roles played by gaps in labor force participation, unemployment rates, and full-time labor market commitment in determining income, differences in earnings also play a part in creating the gaps in income between the various groups in Puerto Rico divided according to nativity.

In 1989, the average annual earnings of full-time workers aged 25–64 born in Puerto Rico were $13,562 for men and $11,557 for women (table 6.8). The comparable figures for the foreign-born population were $22,558 and $13,072. On the other hand, the earnings of persons born in the Dominican Republic were *lower* than those of the native-born population: $12,216 for men and just $8,728 for women.

Most of the personal income of immigrants is obtained from their earnings in the labor market. Among immigrants aged 16 or older, earnings accounted for 83.8 percent and 68.6 percent of the personal incomes of men and women, respectively. In comparison, the proportion of personal income generated by earnings among the Puerto Rican–born population was 63.3 percent for men and 46.4 percent for women.

One of the most controversial issues relating to immigration is the

Table 6.8   **Annual Earnings of Men and Women Working Full-Time in Puerto Rico by Nativity, 1979 and 1989**

	Male	Female
Puerto Rico, average	$14,233	$11,693
Persons born in Puerto Rico	13,562	11,557
Foreign-born	22,558	13,072
Cuban-born	25,829	15,139
Dominican-born	12,216	8,728
Puerto Ricans born in the mainland United States	16,772	12,895
Persons born in the mainland United States, not of Puerto Rican parentage	28,699	16,318

Source: Table 6.5.
Note: Data for employed persons aged 25–64.

extent to which immigrants participate in public assistance programs. In the United States, recent policy initiatives have sought to eliminate the access of immigrants to a number of public assistance programs. These initiatives are mostly politically motivated, and the question of what use immigrants actually make of public assistance remains. The census data provide some information on this issue with respect to Puerto Rico. The census questionnaire asks individuals to identify the income they receive from various sources, including supplemental security income payments made by federal, Commonwealth, or local welfare agencies to low-income persons who are 65 or over, blind, or disabled; Aid to Families with Dependent Children; food stamps or nutritional assistance grants; and general public assistance. This measure of public assistance does not include Social Security income, permanent disability insurance payments, Medicare and Medicaid payments, or unemployment insurance benefits.

The proportion of immigrants aged 16 years or over in 1989 receiving public assistance was 4.3 percent for men and 14.4 percent for women. The average assistance received by immigrants in 1989 was $91 for men and $253 for women. These figures are considerably smaller than those for the native-born population, among which 16.9 percent of the men and 27.7 percent of the women received public assistance in 1989. The amount of assistance received on average by the native-born in 1989 was $303 for men and $513 for women. Women in general received a greater amount of public assistance. This is explained by the lower earnings of women in the labor market as well as by the number of female-headed households, which have the highest poverty rates.

The greater participation of the native-born population of Puerto Rico in public assistance programs, compared to immigrants, is related to the lower household income of the Puerto Rican–born population. Still, the proportion of Puerto Ricans receiving public assistance is substantially lower than has been suggested by some observers. Chavez (1991, 151), for example, claims that "Puerto Ricans are well versed in public assistance. . . . About 70 percent of all persons living in Puerto Rico receive some form of government assistance." The census data, which include a substantial share of public assistance payments for the purpose of determining income, do not support this observation.

Explaining the Differences in Labor Market Outcomes According to Nativity

The variation in the labor market outcomes between persons born inside and outside Puerto Rico is substantial. Economic studies of the determinants of labor force participation, employment rates, and earnings have identified some key variables that explain variations in labor market outcomes. The two most significant factors are educational attainment and the average age of the population. Higher educational attainment typically raises worker productivity and labor market attachment, and is thus related to increased labor force participation, improved employment rates, and higher earnings. And the older the population is, the greater its labor market and on-the-job experience is likely to be, which in turn raises annual earnings, lowers unemployment rates, and raises labor force participation.

Among the native-born population of Puerto Rico, 13 percent of those 25 years of age or older had received a college degree in 1990 (table 6.9). This proportion is lower than that observed among persons born outside Puerto Rico: 38 percent of the Cuban-born population and 15 percent of the Dominican population had a college degree in 1990.

At the other end of the educational spectrum, 52 percent of the native-born population 25 years of age or older was without a high school diploma in 1990, a greater percentage than for all other groups except Dominicans, 56.5 percent of whom were without a high school diploma. This suggests that the Dominican-born population in Puerto Rico has a bi-modal distribution, with a comparatively higher proportion of people at the top and the bottom of the educational ladder relative to the native-born population. A significant portion of the Dominican population in Puerto Rico with low levels of education consists of undocumented immigrants. According to a recent study, the average

Table 6.9   **Educational Status of the Population of Puerto Rico by Nativity, 1990**

	Percentage of the Population Completing			
	Less than High School	High School	Some College	College or More
Puerto Rico, average	50.4%	21.0%	14.3%	14.3%
Puerto Rican–born	52.4	21.1	13.4	13.1
Foreign-born	39.3	16.5	16.7	27.3
Cuban-born	27.4	16.0	18.8	37.8
Dominican-born	56.5	15.6	13.1	14.8
Puerto Ricans born in the mainland United States	18.0	24.1	31.9	26.0
Persons born in the mainland United States, not of Puerto Rican parentage	13.2	21.4	26.8	38.5

Source: 1990 U.S. Census of Population and Housing: Puerto Rico, 5% PUMS.
Note: Data for persons 25 years and older.

number of years of education among undocumented Dominican immigrants in Puerto Rico was eight (Duany, Hernández Angueira, and Rey 1995).

The overall greater educational attainment of the population born outside the island explains to a large extent the higher income of these groups relative to native-born Puerto Ricans since the labor market compensates those with greater education with higher earnings, lower unemployment, and higher labor force participation. Educational outcomes can also explain the lower earnings of the Dominican-born population in the island relative to other groups: the relatively high proportion of Dominican-born persons without a high school diploma tends to push down the earnings of that population. The situation is more critical among women: the proportion of Dominican-born women 25 years of age or older without a high school education was 60.9 percent in 1990, compared to 50.7 percent among Dominican-born men. Similarly, the proportion of Dominican-born women 25 years of age or older with a college degree or more was 13 percent in 1990, compared to 17.1 percent among Dominican-born men.

There are significant variations in the average age among the various groups considered (table 6.10). In 1990, the average age of persons born in Puerto Rico was 32. Among the foreign-born population, both the average age of the Cuban-born population—49.9—and the Dominican-born population—35.7—were significantly higher. The average age of the population born in the mainland United States is less than that of the native-born population: 26.5 for Puerto Ricans born in the United

Table 6.10   Age of the Population of Puerto Rico by Nativity, 1990

	Mean Age
Puerto Rico, average	31.5
Persons born in Puerto Rico	32.0
Foreign-born	39.1
Persons born in Cuba	49.9
Persons born in the Dominican Republic	35.7
Puerto Ricans born in the mainland United States	20.6
Persons born in the mainland United States, not of Puerto Rican parentage	26.5

Source: 1990 U.S. Census of Population and Housing: Puerto Rico, 5% PUMS.

States and 20.6 for those born in the United States not of Puerto Rican parents.

In general, persons residing in Puerto Rico who were born outside the island have done well economically. However, there is considerable diversity of experience among the various immigrant groups in the population.

Summary: Immigration and the Population Born outside Puerto Rico

1. The migration of persons born outside Puerto Rico to the island has boomed over the last thirty years, rising from 59,316 in 1960, to 320,234 in 1990. Persons born outside Puerto Rico in 1990 can be decomposed into these groups: Puerto Ricans born in the mainland United States (229,304); the foreign-born, that is, persons born outside the United States (90,930); and persons born in the mainland United States not of a Puerto Rican parent (21,517).
2. Dominicans constituted the largest immigrant group in Puerto Rico in 1990. The Dominican-born population of Puerto Rico almost doubled in the 1980s, from 20,558 in 1980, to 41,193 in 1990. The second-largest immigrant group in Puerto Rico in 1990 was the Cuban-born population, although this population shrank in the 1980s.
3. Overall, immigrants have done very well in Puerto Rico compared to the native-born population. In terms of household income, for example, the major groups born outside the island residing in Puerto Rico had average annual household income exceeding that of the native-born population in 1989. Among the foreign-born, the Cuban-born population had the highest household income, equal to over twice the household income of the native-born population. The Dominican-born population had household income close to 17 percent higher than the native-born population.

4.   The average gaps in income exhibited by the groups born outside the island compared to the native-born population can largely be explained by the following:
     (a)   all the major groups born outside the island—including both men and women—had higher rates of labor force participation in 1990 than persons born in Puerto Rico
     (b)   the proportion of persons born outside Puerto Rico employed full-time year-round is generally higher than the equivalent for the Puerto Rican–born population
     (c)   for most, though not all, of the groups born outside Puerto Rico, unemployment rates in 1990 were below those for the native-born
     (d)   with the exception of the Dominican-born population, workers born outside Puerto Rico receive higher annual earnings than the native-born

5.   These gaps in labor market outcomes between the populations born in Puerto Rico and those born outside the island are explained by two key factors:
     (a)   average educational attainment: the overall educational attainment of the persons born outside Puerto Rico tends to surpass that of the native-born population. For instance, only 13.1 percent of the native-born population had a college degree or more in 1990, compared with 37.8 percent of the Cuban-born and 14.8 percent of Dominican-born populations. For the latter population, however, the proportion of persons with educational attainment below a high school diploma was also significantly higher than for other groups, generating a bi-modal educational distribution, with a higher proportion of people at the top and the bottom of the educational ladder relative to the native-born. Furthermore, among the Dominican-born population, women had substantially lower educational attainment than men. This partly explains the higher unemployment and lower earnings of Dominican-born women compared to native-born women.
     (b)   The foreign-born population is comparatively older than the native-born population, and its on-the-job experience is thus significantly greater. The average age among the native-born in 1990 was 31.5, compared to 49.9 for the Cuban-born population and 35.7 for the Dominican-born population.

6.   Higher educational attainment and greater on-the-job experience improve economic opportunities in the labor market, resulting in higher labor force participation rates, lower unemployment, and increased earnings, all of which are associated with the higher income received by those born outside the island compared to people born in Puerto Rico.

7.   The participation of immigrants in public assistance programs is comparatively small in Puerto Rico. The proportion of immigrants aged 16 years or over in 1989 receiving a positive amount of public assistance was 4.3 percent for men and 14.4 percent for women. In comparison, among the native-born population, 16.9 percent of men and 27.7 percent of women 16 years of age or older received a positive amount of public assistance payments in 1989.

CHAPTER 7

The Puerto Rican Population in the United States

IT IS a widely accepted belief that Puerto Ricans, in contrast to other Hispanic groups, have failed to achieve significant economic progress in the United States, especially in recent years, and that they are at risk of becoming an "underclass." This suggestion was first made early in the 1960s by Nathan Glazer and Daniel Moynihan in *Beyond the Melting Pot.* Later studies suggested that the economic situation of Puerto Ricans was deteriorating over time. Tienda (1989, 106) noted that "among Hispanics, between 1970 and 1985 Puerto Ricans experienced a sharp deterioration in economic well-being while Mexicans experienced modest, and Cubans substantial, improvement in economic status." Lemann (1991, 96) asserts that "Puerto Ricans are the worst-off ethnic group in the United States." Chavez (1991, 140), one of the most vocal exponents of this viewpoint, depicts Puerto Ricans as occupying "the lowest rung of the social and economic ladder among Hispanics."

Our study shows, however, that Puerto Ricans in 1990 *were not* at the bottom of the socioeconomic ladder among Hispanics, being about average within this group, and that—as the first part of this chapter demonstrates—they exhibited substantial economic progress during the 1980s, narrowing the economic gap between themselves and white Americans. Even so, there are grounds for concern about the current socioeconomic status of Puerto Ricans in the United States because the economic gap in relation to whites remains substantial and income inequality within the Puerto Rican population is sharp, being associated with one of the highest poverty levels in the nation.

The second part of this chapter focuses on the mobility of the Puerto Rican population within the United States and on a comparison be-

Table 7.1   Puerto Ricans in the United States

	Population	Percent Change (annual average)
1940	69,967	2.8%
1950	301,375	14.6
1960	892,513	10.8
1970	1,391,463	4.4
1980	2,014,000	3.7
1990	2,728,000	3.0

Sources: 1960 U.S. Census of Population and Housing, *Puerto Ricans in the United States,* subject report PC(2)-1D, table A, p. viii; 1970 U.S. Census of Population and Housing, *Puerto Ricans in the United States,* PC(2)-1E, June 1973, table 1, p. xi; and 1980 and 1990 U.S. Census of Population and Housing.

tween movers and non-movers. The Puerto Rican population is becoming increasingly dispersed throughout the United States and traditional areas of settlement have lost some of their drawing power. Puerto Ricans are moving out of the major urban centers, particularly New York City, toward such mid-sized northeastern cities as Hartford, Connecticut, and Springfield, Massachusetts. At the same time, there is also a regional shift underway toward the Southeast and the West. These changes reflect the movements of Puerto Ricans already living within the United States as well as the movements of new migrants arriving from Puerto Rico.

How many Puerto Ricans are there in the United States? To answer this question, it is necessary to first address the more basic question of who is considered to be Puerto Rican. This study relies on U.S. census data. Both the 1980 and 1990 censuses classified residents of the mainland United States as Puerto Rican on the basis of self-identification. The census questionnaires asked individuals to identify themselves by choosing from a list of ethnic identifications, of which Puerto Rican was one.

In the 1980s, the number of Puerto Ricans in the United States increased by 35 percent, from close to two million in 1980, to over 2.7 million in 1990 (table 7.1). In comparison, the overall population of the United States increased by close to 10 percent between 1980 and 1990. Net emigration of more than 100,000 persons from the island to the mainland accounted for part of the growth of the Puerto Rican population during the decade. Natural population growth of Puerto Ricans residing in the mainland accounted for the rest. According to the 1990 census, over 50 percent of all Puerto Ricans in the United States were born on the mainland, and this population is growing rapidly.

Table 7.2   **Changes in Mean Household Income of Puerto Ricans in the United States, 1979 and 1989 (in 1989 dollars)**

	Mean Household Income	Persons in Household	Mean Per Capita Household Income
1979	$23,463	4.13	$6,490
1989	29,264	3.95	8,370
Proportional change, 1979–89	24.7%	−4.4%	29.0%

Source: 1990 U.S. Census of Population and Housing: Puerto Rico, 5% PUMS.
Note: The income data for 1979 have been converted into 1989 dollars, using the consumer price index between 1979 and 1989.

Changes in the Socioeconomic Status of Puerto Ricans in the 1980s

Puerto Ricans in the United States made substantial economic advances during the 1980s. The mean household income adjusted for inflation of Puerto Ricans rose by 25 percent between 1979 and 1989, from an average of $23,463, to $29,264 (table 7.2). This economic gain is magnified in terms of per capita income because the size of the average Puerto Rican household declined in the 1980s. In 1979, there were 4.13 persons per household among Puerto Ricans in the United States, compared to 3.95 in 1989. As table 7.2 shows, mean per capita income rose from $6,490 in 1979, to $8,370 in 1989, a 29 percent increase.

The Puerto Rican income gains compare favorably to those made by other ethnic and racial groups in the United States in the 1980s. In the period 1979–89, the non-Hispanic white population had the highest per capita income and the Hispanic population the lowest (table 7.3). Within the Hispanic population groups considered, Cubans had the highest per capita income in both 1979 and 1989, and Dominicans the lowest.

The rate of income growth among Puerto Ricans in the 1980s was one of the highest in the country overall. As a consequence, although in 1979 the per capita income of Puerto Ricans was significantly below that of the average Hispanic and lower than that of Mexicans, the largest Hispanic group, by 1989 Puerto Rican income was about the same as that of the average Hispanic and exceeded the income of Mexicans by a significant amount. Indeed, the surprising statistic from table 7.3 is the slow growth of income among the Mexican population compared to other groups. The 5 percent increase in Mexican income between 1979 and 1989 was nearly six times slower than the 29 percent rate of growth among Puerto Ricans. Of all the groups considered in

Table 7.3   Mean Per Capita Household Income of Puerto Ricans and Other Ethnic/Racial Groups in the United States, 1979 and 1989 (in 1989 dollars)

	1979	1989	Proportional Change, 1979–89
United States, average	$11,928	$14,052	17.8%
Non-Hispanic white	12,954	15,593	20.4
Asian	11,692	13,519	15.6
Non-Hispanic black	7,489	8,779	17.2
Hispanic	7,771	8,397	8.1
Cuban	10,851	12,634	16.4
South American	8,990	11,793	31.2
Puerto Rican	6,490	8,370	29.0
Central American	7,190	7,935	11.2
Mexican	7,196	7,561	5.0
Dominican	5,523	6,871	24.4

Source: 1990 U.S. Census of Population and Housing: Puerto Rico, 5% PUMS.
Note: The income data for 1979 have been converted into 1989 dollars, using the consumer price index between 1979 and 1989.

table 7.3, only the South Americans exhibited higher mean per capita income growth than Puerto Ricans.

The economic gains made by Puerto Ricans in the United States in the 1980s varied depending on their place of birth. Figure 7.1 illustrates the changes in household income of Puerto Ricans residing in the United States, decomposed according to whether they were born in the mainland United States or in Puerto Rico. Although both groups experienced significant income gains, Puerto Ricans born in the mainland United States exhibited a larger increase in mean per capita household income during the decade (32 percent, compared to 29 percent for Puerto Ricans born on the island). In 1989, the mean per capita household income of the island-born population slightly exceeded the average income of the U.S.-born group. This did not hold for other Hispanic groups in the United States. For example, among Mexicans, immigrants had an average per capita income of $6,415 in 1989, compared to $8,163 for the U.S.-born.

There are a number of reasons for the sharp rise in average income among Puerto Ricans in the United States relative to other ethnic and racial groups. Labor force participation among Puerto Rican women rose significantly (by close to 10 percentage points between 1980 and 1990). Educational attainment improved sharply. The proportion of Puerto Ricans 25 years of age or older with less than a high school

Figure 7.1   Changes in the Mean Per Capita Income of Island-Born and U.S.-Born Puerto Ricans in the United States, 1979 and 1989

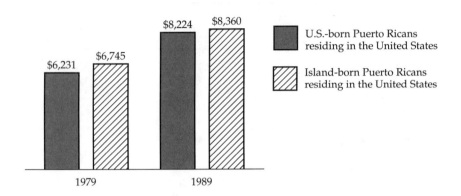

Source: U.S. Bureau of the Census, 1990 Census of Population and Housing 5% PUMS for Puerto Rico.
Note: The income measure is per capita household income. The data for 1979 have been converted into 1989 dollars, using the consumer price index between 1979 and 1989.

education dropped from 57.7 percent to 46.5 percent. Although the proportion of Puerto Ricans completing college only increased from 6.1 percent in 1980, to 9.5 percent in 1990, the proportion completing at least some college education rose by a greater amount. Associated with this increase in schooling was an upgrading of the occupational status of the population. The proportion of Puerto Ricans in managerial, professional, technical, sales, and administrative positions rose from 39.9 percent in 1980, to 47.4 percent in 1990. This led to a substantial rise in the average earnings of Puerto Ricans in the United States (Rivera-Batiz and Santiago 1994; Enchautegui 1992 and 1993).

The Great Divide: The Income Shortfall of Puerto Ricans in the United States

Despite substantial income gains made by Puerto Ricans in the United States in the 1980s, there remain serious grounds for concern about their overall economic well-being. Their per capita household income is still lower than that of non-Hispanic whites, non-Hispanic blacks, and Asians. For example, the per capita household income of Puerto Ricans in 1989 was only 53 percent of that of non-Hispanic whites. Although this represents an increase from 1979 (when the corresponding figure was 50 percent), the absolute shortfall of Puerto Rican income relative to the white population is huge. However, Puerto Ricans have almost closed the gap with non-Hispanic blacks. In 1989, their per capita household income was 95.3 percent of that for blacks.

Another reason for not overemphasizing the average income gains Puerto Ricans made in the 1980s is that this growth was not shared equally among all Puerto Ricans. Indeed, there is sharp inequality of income among Puerto Ricans in the United States, with a significant portion of the Puerto Rican population stuck at the lowest rungs of the income ladder.[1] The poverty rate among Puerto Ricans in the United States declined from 36 percent to 30 percent during the 1980s, but this remained among the highest levels among the various ethnic groups in the nation. Associated with this high poverty rate was a persistently high unemployment rate. In 1990, the unemployment rate of Puerto Ricans in the United States was approximately 12 percent, about twice that in the country overall. This high jobless rate was the product of the massive exodus of manufacturing from the Northeast over the last twenty years (Falcón and Hirschman 1992; Pérez 1993; Torres and Bonilla 1993). In 1980, Puerto Ricans had the highest proportion of workers employed in manufacturing of all groups. During the 1980s, however, the proportion of the Puerto Rican workforce in manufacturing fell from 32.7 percent to 20.3 percent.

Moreover, these changes occurred during a period of strong U.S. economic growth. The 1980s were a decade of sharply rising income and employment in the mainland United States. The recession of the early 1990s reversed some of these gains, and data from the U.S. Department of Commerce's Current Population Survey suggest that the Puerto Rican population and Latinos in general were severely affected by the economic slowdown. By 1994, the poverty rate among Puerto Ricans in the United States may have risen by three percentage points, compared to 1989. It is still too early to say whether the economic recovery of the mid-1990s will lead the Puerto Rican population in the United States to regain the income it lost in the early 1990s, or whether the step back was a permanent one.

The Dispersion of the Puerto Rican Population in the United States

According to the 1990 census, close to 50 percent of the Puerto Rican population residing in the United States in March 1990 had moved since March 1985. This is a remarkably high percentage, reflecting in

1. Growing income inequality was not an exclusively Puerto Rican phenomenon. It was one of the main economic trends observed in the United States in the 1980s. See Levy (1995), and Blackburn, Bloom, and Freeman (1990).

part the significant migration of Puerto Ricans from the island to the mainland in the 1980s. This high rate of mobility among Puerto Ricans compared to other ethnic and racial groups in the United States is typical of populations in which immigrants or the foreign-born are an important component, such as other Latinos and Asians. The rate of residential mobility among Puerto Ricans born in the United States is similar to, although still somewhat higher than, that of other U.S.-born groups in the population. Figure 7.2 illustrates the rate of residential mobility between 1985 and 1990 of persons born in the mainland United States and residing in New York City in 1990 by race and ethnicity. A third of Puerto Ricans born in the United States moved between 1985 and 1990, a rate of residential mobility not much higher than for other racial and ethnic groups.

Of all Puerto Ricans who moved their residence between 1985 and 1990, nearly a quarter moved to California, Florida, and Texas. These movers were older than other Puerto Rican migrants. Of those Puerto Ricans moving to the South, a significant fraction are emigrants from Puerto Rico, many of whom are highly educated workers with college degrees in professional, technical, and managerial occupations. We estimate that approximately 12,000 professionals moved to the United States from Puerto Rico during the 1985–90 period. About a third located in Florida and Texas.

The Increasing Dispersion by State

In 1980, nearly three-quarters of the Puerto Rican population of the United States resided in the northeastern states of New York, New Jersey, Massachusetts, Pennsylvania, and Connecticut. By 1990, the Puerto Rican population was more widely dispersed, with only 68.3 percent living in these states (table 7.4). Despite its increased geographical dispersion, over the course of the decade, the Puerto Rican population continued to grow in those states in which it had previously made inroads. Approximately 90 percent of the Puerto Rican population still resides in ten states. But the growth rate of the Puerto Rican population in the Northeast is now exceeded by the rate in the southern states of Florida and Texas.

New York, New Jersey, and Illinois had the largest concentration of Puerto Ricans in 1980. These were the states with the slowest rates of population growth among Puerto Ricans between 1980 and 1990. By 1990, Florida, Massachusetts, Pennsylvania, and Connecticut all were home to more Puerto Ricans than Illinois, although the bulk of the Puerto Rican population continues to reside in New York and New Jersey.

The states with the most rapid increase in the Puerto Rican popula-

**Figure 7.2   Mobility of Puerto Ricans and Other Groups in the
United States**

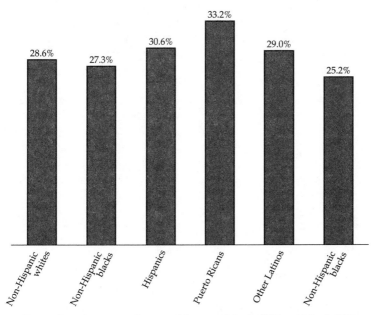

Proportion of persons who moved between March 1985 and March 1990

Sources: 1980 and 1990 U.S. Census of Population and Housing.
Note: Data for persons born in the continental United States, New York City residents,
March 1990.

tion between 1980 and 1990—on an average annual basis—were Florida (9.6 percent), Massachusetts (7.7 percent), Texas (6.7 percent), and
Connecticut (5.1 percent). At a national level, the 1980s were characterized by a significant shift in population away from the Midwest and
Northeast. This represented a continuation, at a slower pace, of the
Snowbelt-to-Sunbelt migration observed during the 1970s (Frey 1995).
The expansion of the Puerto Rican population in the slow-growing
states of the Midwest and Northeast during the 1980s runs counter to
the trend among the overall population.

The Dispersion by City

In 1980, 52 percent of the total Puerto Rican population in the United
States resided in four large cities: New York City, Chicago, Philadelphia, and Newark. By 1990, only 41 percent of the Puerto Rican popula-

Table 7.4　Geographic Distribution of Puerto Ricans in the United States by State

	1980 Population	1990 Population	Percent of Total Puerto Rican Population Residing in State, 1990	Percent of Total State Population That Is Puerto Rican, 1990
New York	978,616	1,086,580	39.8%	6.0%
New Jersey	243,540	320,133	11.7	4.1
Florida	94,775	247,010	9.1	1.9
Massachusetts	76,450	151,193	5.5	2.5
Pennsylvania	91,802	148,988	5.5	1.3
Connecticut	88,361	146,842	5.4	4.5
Illinois	129,165	146,059	5.4	1.3
California	93,038	126,417	4.6	0.4
Ohio	32,442	45,853	1.7	0.4
Texas	22,938	42,981	1.6	0.3

Sources: 1980 U.S. Census of Population and Housing, Persons of Spanish Origin by State, supplementary report PC80-S1-7, table 1, p. 6; 1990 U.S. Census of Population and Housing, Summary Tape File 1C.

tion resided in these cities and only in Philadelphia did the total Puerto Rican population increase significantly (table 7.5). One of the more significant findings of the 1990 census is that Puerto Ricans are increasingly residing in relatively smaller cities. Springfield, Massachusetts, and Hartford and Bridgeport, Connecticut, emerged as centers of Puerto Rican concentration in the 1980s (table 7.6).

In 1980, 65 percent of the total Puerto Rican population lived in the cities listed in tables 7.5 and 7.6; by 1990 that figure had fallen to approximately 55 percent. A couple of additional findings emerged from the 1990 census data. First, Puerto Ricans continue to be concentrated in a few cities. If "population presence" is defined as the fraction of a state's (or city's) population that is made up of any particular group, for the cities listed, the "Puerto Rican presence" within the state in which a city is located is generally less than that of the city itself. For example, Puerto Ricans make up only 4.5 percent of Connecticut's population, even though they make up 27 percent of Hartford's, 21 percent of Bridgeport's, and 11 percent of Waterbury's total populations. Buffalo, New York, as well as Tampa and Miami in Florida, are exceptions. However, Puerto Ricans living in the Sunbelt are not as concentrated in cities as Puerto Ricans elsewhere. It is in the Northeast where Puerto Ricans cluster in cities. For instance, in 1990, the Puerto Rican populations of New York City, Yonkers, Rochester, and Buffalo accounted for more than 86 percent of the total Puerto Rican population of New York state. In contrast, the cities of Miami and Tampa accounted for only 7 percent of Florida's total Puerto Rican population.

Therefore, there appears to be a movement of Puerto Ricans away from traditional areas of settlement and large urban centers and a continuous process of concentration in mid-size cities within traditional areas of settlement, particularly in the northeastern United States.

A second finding is that the cities that showed the most rapid Puerto Rican population growth between 1980 and 1990 were not the largest urban centers. That is, among the top cities of Puerto Rican residence, growth was most pronounced in the smaller cities and in cities where the Puerto Rican presence initially was not large, such as Springfield and Lawrence in Massachusetts, Hartford, Connecticut, Lancaster, Pennsylvania, and Bridgeport and Waterbury in Connecticut, whose metropolitan areas range in size from approximately 130,000 to 800,000 in total population.

Differences among Puerto Rican Communities in the United States

As table 7.7 demonstrates, mean household income and mean per capita household income in the metropolitan statistical areas (MSAs) with

Table 7.5 Cities with the Largest Concentration of Puerto Ricans in the United States

	1980 Population	1990 Population	1980–90 Growth (average annual)	Share of Total Puerto Rican Population (1990)
New York City, New York	860,552	896,763	0.4%	32.87%
Chicago, Illinois	112,074	119,866	0.7	4.39
Philadelphia, Pennsylvania	46,587	67,857	3.8	2.49
Newark, New Jersey	39,732	41,545	0.4	1.52
Hartford, Connecticut	24,615	38,176	4.4	1.40
Jersey City, New Jersey	26,830	30,950	1.4	1.13
Bridgeport, Connecticut	22,146	30,250	3.1	1.11
Paterson, New Jersey	24,326	27,580	1.2	1.01
Boston, Massachusetts	18,899	25,767	3.1	0.94
Springfield, Massachusetts	12,298	23,729	6.6	0.87
Camden, New Jersey	...	22,984	—	0.84
Cleveland, Ohio	12,267	17,829	3.7	0.65
Rochester, New York	10,545	16,383	4.4	0.60
Lawrence, Massachusetts	5,726	14,661	9.4	0.54
Yonkers, New York	...	14,420	—	0.53
Los Angeles, California	13,835	14,367	0.4	0.53
Buffalo, New York	6,865	12,798	6.2	0.47
Worcester, Massachusetts	5,433	12,165	8.1	0.45
Waterbury, Connecticut	5,819	12,080	7.3	0.44
Elizabeth, New Jersey	...	12,062	—	0.44
Miami, Florida	12,320	12,004	−0.2	0.44
Passaic, New Jersey	10,529	11,626	1.0	0.43
Reading, Pennsylvania	6,957	11,612	5.1	0.43
New Britain, Connecticut	5,358	10,325	6.5	0.38
Lancaster, Pennsylvania	5,967	10,305	5.5	0.38
Tampa, Florida	4,038	9,863	8.9	0.36
Allentown, Pennsylvania	4,279	9,670	8.1	0.35
Lorain, Ohio	8,033	9,382	1.5	0.34
Trenton, New Jersey	6,148	9,350	4.2	0.34

Sources: 1980 U.S. Census of Population and Housing, Census Tracts; 1990 U.S. Census of Population and Housing, Summary Tape File 1C.

Table 7.6   Puerto Rican Presence in Cities with Greater Concentrations of Puerto Ricans

U.S. City	Percent of Total City Population That Is Puerto Rican	
	1980	1990
Hartford, Connecticut	18.08%	27.31%
Camden, New Jersey	. . .	26.27
Bridgeport, Connecticut	15.54	21.35
Lawrence, Massachusetts	9.06	20.88
Passaic, New Jersey	20.06	20.00
Paterson, New Jersey	17.63	19.58
Lancaster, Pennsylvania	10.90	18.55
Springfield, Massachusetts	8.07	15.12
Newark, New Jersey	12.07	15.10
Reading, Pennsylvania	8.84	14.82
New Britain, Connecticut	. . .	13.68
Jersey City, New Jersey	12.00	13.54
Lorain, Ohio	10.65	13.17
New York City, New York	12.17	12.25
Waterbury, Connecticut	5.63	11.09
Elizabeth, New Jersey	. . .	10.96
Trenton, New Jersey	6.67	10.54
Allentown, Pennsylvania	4.12	9.20
Yonkers, New York	. . .	7.67
Worcester, Massachusetts	3.36	7.17
Rochester, New York	4.36	7.07
Boston, Massachusetts	3.35	4.49
Chicago, Illinois	3.73	4.31
Philadelphia, Pennsylvania	2.78	4.28
Buffalo, New York	1.92	3.90
Cleveland, Ohio	2.14	3.53
Tampa, Florida	1.49	3.52
Miami, Florida	3.55	3.34
Los Angeles, California	0.47	0.41

Sources: 1980 U.S. Census of Population and Housing, census tract data; 1990 U.S. Census of Population and Housing, Summary Tape File 1C.

the largest Puerto Rican concentrations vary widely.[2] Puerto Ricans in Los Angeles, California, have a mean per capita income nearly three times that of Puerto Ricans living in Lawrence, Massachusetts. Furthermore, of the top ten cities in terms of income listed in table 7.7, six are located in three states—California, Florida, and New Jersey—

2.   The figures in table 7.7 are in nominal terms and have not been adjusted for differences in the cost of living across cities. This should be kept in mind when comparing cities of different size as well as cities that are distant from each other.

while, of the bottom ten cities in income, seven are located in Massachusetts and Pennsylvania. This geographical pattern of income inequality gives rise to concerns about growing inequality among Puerto Ricans in the United States.

The diverse economic status of Puerto Ricans in different metropolitan areas could be due to different overall economic outcomes across cities. In all of the MSAs listed in table 7.7, mean per capita household income of Puerto Ricans is less than mean per capita household income of the overall population. However, there is a great deal of variance between cities. In some metropolitan areas, such as Los Angeles–Long Beach, Tampa, and Miami, Puerto Ricans have per capita mean household incomes that approximate those of the total community. On the other hand, Puerto Rican residents in such MSAs as Lawrence-Haverhill and Worcester in Massachusetts have per capita mean household incomes that are about a third of the mean for all residents. In the five largest urban centers of the Northeast and Midwest where there is a significant Puerto Rican presence (New York City, Chicago, Philadelphia, Newark, and Boston), mean per capita household income of Puerto Ricans is comparatively low—less than 50 percent of that of all residents. To put this in perspective, the ratio of mean per capita household income of *all* Puerto Ricans residing in the United States in 1990 to the mean per capita household income of the overall American population was approximately 60 percent.

The data in table 7.7 suggest that the overall relative prosperity of a metropolitan area and the relative economic status of Puerto Ricans within that area are closely related. For instance, Puerto Ricans in the Los Angeles–Long Beach metropolitan area had the highest mean per capita income in our sample of cities. At the same time, Puerto Rican per capita household income was closest to that of the overall population in this metropolitan area. In contrast, Puerto Ricans in the Lawrence-Haverhill metropolitan area had the lowest mean per capita household income in the sample *and* one of the lowest ratios of per capita income relative to that of the overall population.

There appears to be little correspondence between the relative economic position of Puerto Ricans across MSAs and the growth rate of the Puerto Rican population in these communities between 1980 and 1990, or the increased presence of Puerto Ricans in these MSAs between 1980 and 1990.[3] Thus, the relative lack of affluence or poverty of Puerto

3. This result is based on a statistical analysis wherein the ratio of Puerto Rican to total per capita household income in an MSA is regressed on the growth of the Puerto Rican population between 1980 and 1990, the change in Puerto Rican presence between 1980 and 1990, and the level of per capita income in 1990. The results are available from the authors.

Table 7.7   Distribution of Mean Per Capita Household Income among Puerto Ricans in Metropolitan Areas, 1989

	Mean Per Capita Household Income	Mean Per Capita Household Income of Puerto Ricans Relative to That of the Overall Population
Los Angeles–Long Beach, California	12,032	79.5%
Tampa–St. Petersburg– Clearwater, Florida	9,267	67.3
Jersey City, New Jersey	9,214	65.3
Trenton, New Jersey	8,979	50.3
Miami, Florida	8,903	68.9
Newark, New Jersey	8,562	45.0
New York City, New York	7,989	49.2
Chicago, Illinois	7,685	48.9
Lorain-Elyria, Ohio	7,660	61.0
Bridgeport, Connecticut	7,549	46.5
Cleveland, Ohio	7,276	50.5
Boston, Massachusetts	7,186	38.8
Waterbury, Connecticut	6,932	50.1
Rochester, New York	6,780	44.8
Allentown-Bethlehem- Easton, Pennsylvania	6,193	42.8
Hartford, Connecticut	6,095	32.6
Philadelphia, Pennsylvania	6,078	38.8
Lancaster, Pennsylvania	5,409	39.5
Reading, Pennsylvania	5,234	37.5
Buffalo, New York	5,194	38.9
Worcester, Massachusetts	5,142	34.2
Springfield, Massachusetts	4,658	37.3
Lawrence-Haverhill, Massachusetts	4,228	35.2

Source: 1990 U.S. Census of Population and Housing: Puerto Rico, 5% PUMS.

Ricans within their MSAs in 1990 was not largely associated with the growth of the Puerto Rican population in these areas between 1980 and 1990. This can be interpreted to mean that the Puerto Rican population has not been growing faster in areas of relatively high income than in the lower-income cities. There does not appear to be a pattern of Puerto Ricans exiting low-income communities on the basis of income. The Puerto Rican populations in both low-income and high-income communities appear to be expanding equally.

The Relative Economic Influence of Puerto Ricans in Metropolitan Areas of the United States

In analyzing the relative economic influence of Puerto Ricans within particular MSAs in the United States, we have used an index of relative economic influence in which 1.0 would mean Puerto Ricans were the only group accounting for income in that MSA and zero if the income of Puerto Ricans in that MSA were zero. The actual value of the index varies across MSAs and the closer it is to 1.0, the stronger the economic influence of the Puerto Rican community in the MSA.[4] The index of economic influence of Puerto Ricans in a metropolitan area is determined by two ratios: (1) mean per capita household income of Puerto Ricans relative to that of the overall MSA (the larger this ratio, the greater the economic influence of Puerto Ricans in the MSA, all other things being constant), and (2) the number of Puerto Ricans within an MSA relative to the overall population (the larger the Puerto Rican population in the city, the greater the economic influence, income being held constant).

Table 7.8 shows the value of the index of economic influence of Puerto Ricans in the twenty-five MSAs with the largest Puerto Rican populations. The index is the highest in Bridgeport, Connecticut, Hartford, Connecticut, Jersey City, New Jersey, Lorain, Ohio, and Lawrence, Massachusetts. At the other extreme, the impact of Puerto Ricans is smallest in such large MSAs as Los Angeles, Buffalo, Boston, and Philadelphia.

The general portrait of economic change among Puerto Rican communities in the United States obtained from the data presented in table 7.8, and elsewhere, is mixed and many questions remain. In some expanding communities Puerto Ricans have faced a relatively good labor market and their performance was quite satisfactory, but in other communities where there was also substantial growth in the Puerto Rican population in the 1980s, the economic status of Puerto Ricans worsened. Thus, a paradox emerges: Puerto Ricans seem to be agglomerating in areas of both economic prosperity and economic distress.

For example, the Puerto Rican populations of both Tampa, Florida, and Allentown, Pennsylvania, grew substantially during the 1980s (9 percent in Tampa and 8 percent in Allentown, on an average annual basis). Both metropolitan areas had approximately 10,000 residents who identified themselves as Puerto Rican, and their economic impact was

---

4. Other factors, such as community cohesiveness and quality of leadership, play fundamental roles in the economic impact of a particular group on the population at large in a city. These and other factors are not accounted for in our comparisons.

Table 7.8   **Relative Economic Influence of Puerto Rican Communities in Various Metropolitan Areas of the United States**

	Index of Relative Economic Impact
Bridgeport, Connecticut	0.0993
Hartford, Connecticut	0.0890
Jersey City, New Jersey	0.0884
Lorain, Ohio	0.0803
Lawrence, Massachusetts	0.0735
Lancaster, Pennsylvania	0.0733
Newark, New Jersey	0.0679
New York City, New York	0.0603
Springfield, Massachusetts	0.0563
Reading, Pennsylvania	0.0556
Waterbury, Connecticut	0.0556
Trenton, New Jersey	0.0531
Allentown, Pennsylvania	0.0393
Rochester, New York	0.0316
Worcester, Massachusetts	0.0245
Tampa, Florida	0.0237
Miami, Florida	0.0230
Chicago, Illinois	0.0211
Cleveland, Ohio	0.0178
Boston, Massachusetts	0.0174
Philadelphia, Pennsylvania	0.0166
Buffalo, New York	0.0152
Los Angeles, California	0.0032

Sources: 1980 and 1990 U.S. Census of Population and Housing.
Note: The index of relative economic impact is equal to the ratio of mean per capita household income of Puerto Ricans in the MSA to the overall MSA mean per capita household income in 1990, multiplied by the fraction of the total MSA population that was Puerto Rican.

nearly the same (0.0237 for Tampa and 0.0393 for Allentown). However, the mean per capita household income of the Puerto Rican residents of Tampa was high relative to that of the total population of Tampa (67 percent), while for the Puerto Rican residents of Allentown, it was less than half (43 percent) that of the total population. These differences may be explained by relative levels of educational attainment, occupation, or migration history, but the fact remains that in both metropolitan areas the Puerto Rican population expanded at high rates during the 1980s. It is easy to understand why the Puerto Rican population expanded in Tampa but more difficult to understand the increased Puerto Rican presence in Allentown. This leads to a discussion of why Puerto Rican population growth was high in communities that were economically depressed (at least for Puerto Ricans) during the 1980s.

Table 7.9   Characteristics of Puerto Rican Movers and Non-Movers Residing in the United States by Gender, Age, and Marital and Headship Status

	Non-Movers	Movers from Puerto Rico	All Other Movers
Gender			
Male	47.2%	46.8%	49.5%
Female	52.8	53.2	50.4
Age			
20–29	15.8	33.1	28.6
30–39	16.8	18.8	22.2
40–49	16.3	10.2	11.2
50–55	7.6	3.2	3.7
Over 55	16.3	7.7	6.7
Marital and headship status			
Never married	50.5	52.6	52.6
Married	33.8	34.6	32.9
Widowed	3.9	2.5	2.0
Divorced	6.9	5.8	7.4
Separated	4.9	4.5	5.1
Female-headed household	34.1	35.3	32.1

Source: 1990 U.S. Census of Population and Housing, 5% PUMS.
Note: Data for movers/non-movers during 1985–90.

The Characteristics of Puerto Rican Movers and Non-Movers in the United States

The 1990 census identifies as recent migrants those who answered yes to the question: "Did you live in this residence on April 1, 1985?" People who responded affirmatively to this question are referred to as "non-movers," and those who answered negatively as "movers" (recent migrants).

In order to determine the characteristics of Puerto Rican non-movers and movers (migrants), we differentiated between (1) those movers to the United States who resided in Puerto Rico in 1985 (the recent emigrants from Puerto Rico), and (2) other Puerto Rican movers, who relocated within the United States during the period 1985–90. Comparisons of demographic and socioeconomic characteristics between non-movers, movers from Puerto Rico, and all other movers follow.

Gender, Age, Marital Status, and Female-Headed Households

As table 7.9 reveals, the majority of movers identified by the 1990 census were female, but gender did not significantly differentiate movers

Table 7.10   Characteristics of Puerto Rican Movers and Non-Movers Residing in the United States by Education, Earnings, Poverty Rates, and Labor Force Status

	Non-Movers	Movers from Puerto Rico	All Other Movers
Education			·
Less than high school	64.4%	59.5%	58.6%
High school	20.0	18.6	20.7
Some college	10.7	14.1	14.6
College	3.1	5.0	4.0
More than college	1.9	2.9	2.1
Mean annual earnings	$18,231	$12,808	$17,402
Poverty rates	27.0	41.6	27.0
Labor market status			
Participation rate	57.3	57.9	64.0
Unemployment rate	11.4	17.4	12.1

Source: 1990 U.S. Census of Population and Housing, 5% PUMS.
Note: Data for movers / non-movers during 1985–90.

from non-movers. On the other hand, movers are generally younger than non-movers. Among the population 20 years of age and older, over 50 percent of movers fall between the ages of 20 and 39 years. Only 32 percent of non-movers fall into this age group. Movers from Puerto Rico are even younger, on average, than other Puerto Rican movers. This has significant implications because the propensity to participate in the labor force, the likelihood of being unemployed, and the level of earnings also vary by age. In general, labor force participation rates rise with age, peaking between 35 and 55 years of age, and then decline. Unemployment rates are higher for the young and earnings rise with age and then decline after retirement.

Marital status and the fraction of households headed by females do not vary significantly among movers and non-movers. There is a slightly higher percentage of female-headed households among movers from Puerto Rico (35 percent), compared to all other movers (32 percent), but the difference is not significant.

Educational Attainment, Earnings, Poverty, and Labor Market Status

There are substantial differences between movers and non-movers in terms of educational attainment and labor market outcomes, as shown in table 7.10. Recent movers from Puerto Rico have higher levels of education than the population of non-movers in the United States: 84 percent of all non-movers have a high school education or less; this is true of only 78 percent of movers from Puerto Rico and 79 percent of all other movers. Similarly, while 16 percent of all non-movers have at least some college education, 22 percent of movers from Puerto Rico and 21 percent of all other movers fall into this category.

However, these differences in educational attainment do not translate into higher earnings and lower poverty rates. The mean annual earnings of non-movers in 1989 were 42 percent higher than earnings of movers from Puerto Rico, while all movers earned 36 percent more than movers from Puerto Rico. This difference is also reflected in poverty rates, where 42 percent of all movers from Puerto Rico in 1990 had incomes at or below the poverty level, compared to 27 percent of non-movers and all other movers alike. Unemployment rates among movers and non-movers also reflect these differences. Movers from Puerto Rico had unemployment rates of 17 percent, compared to unemployment rates of 11 percent and 12 percent for non-movers and other movers, respectively. On the other hand, movers from Puerto Rico participated in the labor market in similar proportions to non-movers and all other movers.

Other recent immigrant groups in the United States have faced similar shortfalls in income and labor market status relative to U.S.-born persons with comparable education (Borjas 1990, 97). Those who move to the United States, whether from Europe, Asia, or Puerto Rico, find it harder to adjust to a new and different labor market, compared to non-movers and other movers who are already in the country. Many recent migrants do not have the comprehensive networks and contacts necessary to identify available jobs, which take time to develop. As a consequence, the recent migrant may face a longer spell of unemployment prior to getting initial job offers.

These difficulties may be aggravated by linguistic or cultural factors. English-language proficiency, in particular, may vary between non-migrants and migrants, deeply influencing economic outcomes (Bloom and Grenier 1993; McManus, Gould, and Welsh 1983; Rivera-Batiz 1991). The ability to speak English is highly valued in the U.S. labor market, and many recent arrivals from Puerto Rico are disadvantaged in this respect. According to the 1990 census, a third of recent movers from Puerto Rico indicated that they did not speak English at all or did not speak it well. This compares with 18 percent of Puerto Rican non-movers and 14 percent of all other Puerto Rican movers.

The fact that recent movers from Puerto Rico have relatively high levels of educational attainment and are still at a considerable disadvantage in the U.S. labor market may also signal discrimination against recent immigrants and/or the belief on the part of employers that education received in Puerto Rico is inferior to that received on the mainland.

A clear pattern emerges in table 7.11, which illustrates the composi-

Table 7.11   Percentage of Non-Movers, Movers from Puerto Rico, and
All Other Movers in Various Metropolitan Areas, 1990

	Non-Movers	Movers from Puerto Rico	All Other Movers
Lawrence-Haverhill, MA	24.2%	26.5%	49.3%
Worcester, Massachusetts	27.3	20.3	52.4
Waterbury, Connecticut	29.3	16.1	54.6
Rochester, New York	29.3	11.1	59.6
Lancaster, Pennsylvania	29.6	12.9	57.6
Tampa–St. Petersburg–			
Clearwater, FL	31.0	15.4	53.6
Reading, Pennsylvania	31.6	14.9	53.5
Springfield, MA	32.0	17.7	50.3
Miami, Florida	33.7	12.4	53.9
Buffalo, New York	33.7	15.3	51.0
Boston, Massachusetts	35.8	11.5	52.6
Hartford, Connecticut	35.9	14.5	49.6
Bridgeport, Connecticut	38.0	9.6	52.4
Cleveland-Lorain-Elyria, Ohio	38.5	12.1	49.4
Allentown-Bethlehem-			
Easton, PA	39.9	11.7	48.4
Trenton, New Jersey	41.0	10.9	48.1
Chicago, Illinois	42.4	5.1	52.5
Los Angeles–Long Beach, CA	43.6	4.8	51.6
Newark, New Jersey	44.7	9.1	46.2
Philadelphia, PA	44.9	7.5	47.6
Lorain-Elyria, Ohio	47.4	5.3	47.2
Jersey City, New Jersey	50.6	5.7	43.7
New York City, NY	63.0	3.5	33.5

Source: 1990 U.S. Census of Population and Housing, 5% PUMS.

tion of the MSAs of greater Puerto Rican residence by mobility status. The larger, more established urban areas, such as New York City, Newark, Chicago, and Philadelphia, are receiving fewer recent migrants directly from Puerto Rico compared to the smaller, more rapidly growing cities of the Northeast and Southeast. The figures also attest to the considerable mobility of Puerto Ricans in the United States, either within or across state boundaries.

Traditional migration routes may be changing, although the existence of sequential migration (or circular migration for that matter) with New York City as the hub cannot be ruled out. Puerto Rican communities in Massachusetts, Florida, and western New York appear to be major recipients of movers from Puerto Rico and other localities. These areas also showed considerable growth in their Puerto Rican populations during the 1980s.

The comparison of three MSAs, presented in table 7.12, provides a more detailed look at the issue of mobility and economic status among Puerto Ricans. The MSAs selected—Lawrence-Haverhill, Massachusetts, Tampa–St. Petersburg–Clearwater, Florida, and New York City—illustrate important features of the Puerto Rican population in the United States. The Puerto Rican population increased dramatically in the first two during the 1980s, compared to the third. Puerto Ricans in Lawrence are in a relatively disadvantaged economic position compared to those in Tampa who are better off than the overall population of that metropolitan area. New York City is included as a basis of comparison since it continues to be home to the largest concentration of Puerto Ricans in the United States.

Educational attainment varies considerably both across and within these three MSAs. Of the three, the Tampa area has the Puerto Rican population with highest educational attainment, followed by New York City and Lawrence. Recent movers from Puerto Rico exhibit greater educational attainment than non-movers and other movers in all three metropolitan areas, with greater differences in Lawrence and smaller differences in New York City. As noted earlier, these differences in educational attainment do not translate into a better relative economic position for movers from Puerto Rico. Movers from Puerto Rico earn, on average, 35 percent, 58 percent, and 20 percent less than Puerto Rican non-movers in Lawrence, Tampa, and New York City, respectively. This pattern of differences holds for poverty and unemployment rates. In all respects, recent movers from Puerto Rico are in a disadvantaged economic position compared to non-movers and other movers.

Certain patterns are also evident for the category of recent movers who did not reside in Puerto Rico in 1985—the group referred to as "other movers." In Lawrence, these individuals earn considerably less than non-movers although they have similar levels of educational attainment. They also have higher poverty rates. This contrasts sharply with "other movers" in Tampa and New York City, where "other movers" have higher average annual earnings than non-movers. It is possible that the "other movers" in Lawrence are those who have fled the economic distress of large urban centers. This does not appear to be the case in either Tampa or New York City, however. The "other movers" in Tampa may be individuals with retirement income or those with skills in search of better jobs in the growing Southeast. Those in New York City may be the upwardly mobile who are moving to the suburbs and outlying areas.

Puerto Ricans in New York City

New York City used to dominate discussions of the Puerto Rican population in the United States. The early waves of Puerto Ricans migrating

Table 7.12   **Non-Movers, Movers from Puerto Rico, and All Other Movers in the MSAs of Lawrence, Tampa, and New York City**

	Non-Movers	Movers from Puerto Rico	All Other Movers
Lawrence-Haverhill, MA			
Education			
Less than high school	76.0%	65.6%	78.5%
High school	17.1	17.2	14.5
Some college	4.4	12.9	5.5
College	1.9	3.7	1.2
More than college	0.6	0.6	0.3
Mean annual earnings	$16,557	$12,266	$13,716
Poverty rates	48.8	66.1	58.5
Labor market status			
Participation rate	55.8	46.3	45.0
Unemployment rate	28.3	29.8	36.2
Tampa, St. Petersburg, Clearwater, FL			
Education			
Less than high school	52.4	50.7	51.1
High school	24.8	19.6	22.2
Some college	14.2	18.2	17.5
College	5.0	8.4	6.1
More than college	3.7	3.1	3.1
Mean annual earnings	$16,965	$10,716	$18,186
Poverty rates	13.6	27.7	18.6
Labor market status			
Participation rate	66.6	67.5	70.6
Unemployment rate	7.3	15.5	7.9
New York City			
Education			
Less than high school	66.7	59.9	61.3
High school	19.2	21.3	20.5
Some college	10.3	11.8	13.2
College	2.6	3.5	3.5
More than college	1.2	3.5	1.6
Mean annual earnings	$18,109	$15,136	$18,905
Poverty rates	35.5	48.6	36.4
Labor market status			
Participation rate	50.5	48.1	58.3
Unemployment rate	13.8	18.5	13.4

Source: 1990 U.S. Census of Population and Housing, 5% PUMS.

to the mainland flocked to the city, and by 1960 close to two-thirds of all Puerto Ricans residing in the United States lived there. However, this pattern has been reversed during the last three decades. By 1980, only 43 percent of all Puerto Ricans in the United States lived in the city, and by 1990 the proportion had dropped to 33 percent.

The drop in the significance of New York City as the destination for emigrants from Puerto Rico is reflected in the fact that only 26,000 of all the emigrants who moved from the island to the United States during the 1985–90 period were residing in New York City in 1990 (City of New York 1993, table 9-1). Many more Puerto Ricans *left* New York City to move to the island between 1985 and 1990 than moved from the island to the city.[5] On a net basis, the migration of Puerto Ricans between New York and the island was −28.457.

New York City continues to be the metropolitan area with the largest number of Puerto Rican residents. But the rate of growth of the Puerto Rican population in New York City was only 0.8 percent between 1980 and 1990. There were only 13,821 more Puerto Ricans residing in New York City in 1990 than in 1980. Furthermore, the expansion of Puerto Rican population in the city in recent years has been totally due to natural increase. Between 1985 and 1990, the number of Puerto Ricans who moved out of New York City exceeded the number who moved in by 86,687. Most moved to Puerto Rico (39 percent), elsewhere in New York state (17 percent), Florida (14 percent), and New Jersey (9 percent) (City of New York 1993, table 9-1). As Carmen Carrasquillo, a former resident of the Chelsea section of New York City who moved to Osceola County in Central Florida, recently said, "We wanted to raise our son in a different environment, out of the city, but we wanted to own our home and New York was too expensive. . . . For a lot of people, it's a dream to be able to own your house. . . ."[6]

The socioeconomic status of Puerto Ricans in New York City was lower than that of the overall Puerto Rican population in the United States in 1990. The mean per capita household income of Puerto Rican New Yorkers in 1989 was $7,989, compared to $8,370 for the overall Puerto Rican population (table 7.13). Associated with this lower per capita income was a higher poverty rate of 36.5 percent, compared to 30 percent for the Puerto Rican population as a whole.

Despite the lower average socioeconomic status exhibited by Puerto

5. The number of Puerto Ricans who left New York City between 1985 and 1990 to locate in Puerto Rico was 54,405, and 25,948 people moved from the island to New York City, for a net emigration of Puerto Ricans out of New York City to the island of 28,457.

6. Larry Rohter, "A Puerto Rican Boom for Florida," *New York Times*, January 31, 1994.

Table 7.13   Mean Per Capita Household Income of Puerto Ricans in New York City, and in the United States, 1979–89 (in 1989 dollars)

	New York City	United States
1979	$6,203	$6,490
1989	7,989	8,370
Proportional change, 1979–89	28.8%	29.0%

Source: 1990 U.S. Census of Population and Housing: Puerto Rico, 5% PUMS.
Note: The income data for 1979 have been converted into 1989 dollars, using the consumer price index for the New York City metropolitan area between 1979 and 1989.

Table 7.14   Mean Per Capita Household Income of Puerto Ricans and Other Ethnic/Racial Groups in New York City, 1979 and 1989 (in 1989 dollars)

	1979	1989	Proportional Change 1979–89
New York City average	$12,765	$16,226	27.1%
Non-Hispanic white	16,336	22,892	40.1
Asian	11,471	13,421	17.0
Non-Hispanic black	8,600	10,753	25.0
Hispanic	7,085	8,496	19.9
Cuban	11,697	14,462	23.6
South American	8,673	10,480	20.8
Puerto Rican	6,203	7,989	28.8
Central American	6,900	9,260	34.2
Mexican	8,315	8,933	7.4
Dominican	5,920	6,389	7.9

Source: 1990 U.S. Census of Population and Housing: Puerto Rico, 5% PUMS.
Note: The income data for 1979 have been converted into 1989 dollars, using the consumer price index for the New York City metropolitan area between 1979 and 1989.

Ricans in New York City, the economic progress of this population during the 1980s was similar to that of the overall Puerto Rican population. The increase in their per capita mean household income during the past decade was just about the same as that of Puerto Ricans overall. While remarkable by national standards, the 28.8 percent gain shown by Puerto Rican New Yorkers was not unusual by New York City standards. The second half of the 1980s were years of solid economic growth for New York City, and this was reflected in the income gains of many ethnic and racial groups in the population (table 7.14). The growth in per capita household income among Puerto Ricans was close to the average gain for the city as a whole, although it pales in comparison to the 40 percent increase in mean per capita household income of non-Hispanic whites in the city. The greater income gains of whites relative to Puerto Ricans meant that the gap between the two groups in New York City widened during the 1980s, while the opposite occurred at the national level.[7]

7. For more details on the Puerto Rican population of New York City, see Rivera-Batiz (1994).

Summary: The Puerto Rican Population in the United States

1. The number of Puerto Ricans in the United States increased from close to two million in 1980, to over 2.7 million in 1990. This rate of growth of 35 percent was more than three times the rate of growth of the overall population in the United States during the decade.
2. The 1980s saw Puerto Ricans dispersing across America at rates unprecedented in previous decades. Substantial Puerto Rican populations now exist in Texas, Florida, and California, where a significant part of the new emigrants from Puerto Rico are locating. By 1990, Florida had the third-largest population of Puerto Ricans in the United States, with approximately 10 percent of the total. Most Puerto Ricans, however, still reside in the Northeast and Midwest. New York had the largest Puerto Rican population in 1990 (39.8 percent of the total), followed by New Jersey (11.7 percent). Massachusetts, Pennsylvania, Connecticut, Ohio, and Illinois also have significant portions of Puerto Rican populations.
3. The growth of Puerto Rican communities declined in large, urban centers in the Northeast and Midwest and accelerated in smaller cities within the Northeast and in the southern and western United States. While the Puerto Rican population doubled or more in such cities as Tampa (Florida), Springfield (Massachusetts), and Lawrence (Massachusetts), during the 1980s, it increased by only 4 percent in New York City, 6.9 percent in Chicago, and 4.5 percent in Newark.
4. The traditional association of Puerto Ricans with New York City is now a matter of the past. While in 1960 close to two-thirds of all Puerto Ricans in the United States lived in New York City, by 1990 only a third did. The attractiveness of New York City for Puerto Rican migrants declined sharply in the 1980s. More Puerto Ricans *moved out* of New York City between 1985 and 1990 than moved in during that period. Those moving out migrated mostly to other areas of New York state, Florida, New Jersey, and Puerto Rico itself.
5. Puerto Ricans exhibited substantial income growth in the United States in the 1980s. Their mean per capita household income adjusted for inflation increased by close to 30 percent during the 1980s. This increase was the highest among all the major racial and ethnic groups in the United States. It was significantly higher than the growth in mean per capita household income of the overall American population, which was 17.8 percent.
6. Associated with the income gains of the 1980s was a sharp increase in labor force participation among Puerto Rican women, higher educational attainment, and a significant upgrading of the occupational distribution of Puerto Ricans in the United States.

7. Despite the economic gains exhibited by the Puerto Rican population as a whole, the socioeconomic advancement of the 1980s was not shared by all Puerto Ricans, and some groups among them actually suffered a deterioration in economic status. Puerto Ricans who had not completed high school suffered significant losses in earnings, employment, and income. A substantial portion of first-generation migrants from Puerto Rico also lagged behind in socioeconomic development. The situation is desperate among unskilled migrants who moved to cities such as Lawrence, Springfield, or Worcester where they face unemployment rates of 20–30 percent.

8. The Puerto Rican community appears to be becoming polarized with respect to economic opportunity and outcomes. This polarization, however, is not necessarily based on the traditional urban-suburban patterns observed among other groups in the population. Rather, there are a number of Puerto Rican communities plagued with poverty and joblessness in mid-sized urban areas of the Northeast and, at the same time, many affluent, booming communities in the southern and western United States. The mean per capita household income of Puerto Ricans in the Los Angeles metropolitan area in 1989 was $12,032, and $9,267 in Tampa, Florida. In contrast, for Puerto Ricans in Lawrence, Springfield, and Worcester, Massachusetts, it was $4,228, $4,658, and $5,142, respectively.

CHAPTER 8

Between Two Worlds:
Puerto Rico Looks toward
the Twenty-First Century

IN FEBRUARY 1949, Luis Muñoz Marín took office as the first freely
elected governor of Puerto Rico. In his inaugural address, Muñoz
Marín, who was the main architect of Puerto Rico's subsequent
economic development strategy, likened the task faced by his
government to planting seed: "This is the moment when, depending on
our actions, the seed can either become a bumper crop or a wasteland of
weeds" (Muñoz Marín 1980, 4). What resulted from the seed planted by
Muñoz Marín and his government? Did it blossom into a bumper crop
or into a field of weeds?

The 1990 census paints a rather paradoxical picture of Puerto Rico's
current socioeconomic status. At times over the last fifty years Puerto
Rico has exhibited rapid, occasionally extraordinary gains in per capita
income and in its standard of living. These changes were associated with
substantial improvements in health, nutrition, and education. Yet, since
the early 1970s, the economy has suffered from a devastating upward
trend in unemployment. And inequality of economic outcomes has
sharply increased: persons residing in female-headed households, rural
households, the unskilled, the uneducated, and the young, all suffer from
high levels of poverty. In recent years, such social ills as growing crime
rates and substance abuse, and the lethal virus-related AIDS have become rampant among some segments of the population.

The industrialization of Puerto Rico shows conflicting faces. On the
one hand, Puerto Rico was the pioneer of policies later adopted worldwide. Its outward-oriented approach to trade and investment, based
on tax exemptions and other incentives to attract foreign investment
and export-oriented industries, is now commonplace. Even before eco-

152

nomic integration became a fashionable word in academic circles, Puerto Rico's common market and common currency union with the United States had a long history. And the island's experiences with health, housing, education, and population policies also have been at the forefront of the developing world. On the other hand, the speed at which industrialization proceeded in Puerto Rico made the process of adjustment extremely difficult for many. Accompanying the industrialization was a rapid migration of people from rural to urban areas and a massive emigration of Puerto Ricans to the mainland United States. In 1990, there were 2.7 million Puerto Ricans in the United States and 3.5 million persons residing on the island. It is not clear whether the sharp increase in per capita income in Puerto Rico since 1940 would have occurred without this migratory movement since the economic expansion that would have been required to absorb the labor force that left the island would have been enormous.

The waves of emigration to the United States have been painful to many. Esmeralda Santiago's book, *When I Was Puerto Rican*, is an autobiographical narrative of the trials and tribulations of a young girl growing up, first in Puerto Rico, and later in New York City. When it appeared in 1993, it struck a cord among Puerto Ricans. Yet its portrayal of the difficulties of navigating between many different worlds and contexts has universal appeal. The author's story begins in the rural barrio of Macún, where "our house stood in the center, its shiny zinc roof splotched with rust at the corners. Next to the house was a kitchen shed, from which a thin curl of smoke wove into the air. . . . The chicken coop squatted between the pigsty and the mango tree, a branch of which held one end of Mami's laundry line, the other end stretched to the trunk of an acerola bush." From this rural setting, the author's family moves first to La Parada 26 in urban Santurce (San Juan) and then to Brooklyn. The story of Esmeralda is the story of many Puerto Ricans and their families over the last half century. What stands out is the magnitude and extent of the change occurring over a single generation. The shift from agriculture to industry, the rural-to-urban migration process, the emigration to the United States, all transpired at tremendous speed.

The social and cultural impact of the changes undergone by Puerto Rico over the last fifty years has been deep. But rather than succumbing to the vicissitudes of rapid economic growth and industrialization, the Puerto Rican population has exhibited remarkable resiliency. Despite the influence of its intimate ties with the United States, the glue that binds the Puerto Rican nation remains strong. This is true not only on the island but also throughout the diaspora in the mainland United States. That over 2.7 million individuals living in the United States, whether born in Puerto Rico or not, identify themselves as Puerto Rican is a significant statement of cultural affirmation. This is reinforced by the close contact and frequent visits of Puerto Ricans in the United States to the island.

The story of Puerto Rico and Puerto Ricans over the last half century is eloquently told in literature, both fiction and nonfiction. In this volume, we have attempted a similar understanding—illustrating the dramatic changes, displacement, struggle, and settlement of the island and its people—but within the context of social science and relying on the empirical foundation provided by the decennial census. It is important to bear in mind, however, that behind the numbers lie families, institutions, and people of real flesh and blood. As the Puerto Rican author Luis Rafael Sánchez (1985, 29–30) sums up, in a short story of the Puerto Rican migrant,

> It is the story that history books do not tell. It is the underside of rhetoric that politics does not see. . . . It is the belated justice that compensates for the shipwreck of those who from aboard the Borinquen steamboat and the Coamo saw their dear island evaporate forever; it is the vindication of those dumb-founded pioneers who went up into the fourteen hours of confinement inside the uncomfortable, narrow and trembling flying-machines of Pan American Airlines; it is the devastating course of reality and its hallucinatory proposal of a new and furiously conquered space: that of a floating nation going back and forth, smuggling hopes between two ports.

Key Socioeconomic Trends in Puerto Rico

It is easier to depict and examine past events than it is to chart future paths. Nonetheless, we think it necessary to present issues that will have a bearing on the future policy agenda respecting Puerto Rico, realizing full well that competing paradigms, philosophies, and objectives play a role in the direction and scope of public policy. In presenting the findings of our study and providing a broad interpretation of the reasons for the socioeconomic contrasts occurring in Puerto Rico since the 1940s, we stress not only what we see as critical trends but also delineate a number of myths about Puerto Rico that we find to be inconsistent with the facts. We remain hopeful that *informed* discussion and debate will provide the indispensable foundation for effective policymaking.

The Economy: Growth, Stagnation, and Inequality

After decades of accelerated economic growth, the Puerto Rican economy came to a standstill in the mid-1970s and stayed that way until the mid-1980s. Brisk economic growth began again only in the second half of the 1980s when per capita income surged. Mean per capita household income rose 22 percent in the 1980s, and by the end of the decade income levels had recovered to the levels of the early 1970s.

However, the average income gains made by Puerto Rico over the last fifty years were not equally distributed. The degree of income inequality in Puerto Rico is very high. The poorest 40 percent of all families on the island received only 7.5 percent of all family income in 1989. In contrast, in the United States, the poorest 40 percent of all families received 15 percent of the nation's family income. The extent of inequality in Puerto Rico approximates that of other developing countries, such as Brazil and Panama.

The incidence of poverty in Puerto Rico is tempered by rising levels of federal transfer payments to the poor. However, the participation of Puerto Ricans in welfare programs has been widely exaggerated. There is a belief among some that most of Puerto Rico's population receives some form of public assistance payments from the government. However, our findings, based on census data, indicate that, among the native-born population in Puerto Rico, 17 percent of men and 28 percent of women 16 years of age or older received a positive amount of public assistance payments in 1989.

Industrialization and Growing Urbanization

The decline of employment in agriculture is one of the most remarkable developments in the Puerto Rican economy of the last forty years. In 1950, 35 percent of the Puerto Rican labor force was employed in agriculture; by 1990, it was under 4 percent. This drastic transformation was associated with the decline of agriculture as an income-generating sector in the economy. As policymakers engaged in Operation Bootstrap, with its urban-biased, "industrialization-first" development strategy, the agricultural labor force was rapidly siphoned into expanding urban areas. The numbers of Puerto Ricans employed in trade, services, and public administration greatly increased. Manufacturing, on the other hand, has accounted for about 19 percent of the labor force on average since 1950. Women have been heavily involved in manufacturing, constituting about 50 percent of the manufacturing labor force since 1950.

The shift in economic activity from agriculture to other sectors was associated with massive rural-to-urban migration. Urban areas began to expand, and metropolitanization has boomed in recent years. The metropolitan population of Puerto Rico rose from 62 percent of the population in 1980, to 89.5 percent in 1990.

Education and the Labor Force

Educational attainment has greatly increased in Puerto Rico over the last forty years. In 1950, 93 percent of the population 25 years of age or older did not have a high school diploma. The proportion had dropped to 50 percent by 1990. Similarly, the proportion of the population 25 years of age or older with a college degree or more rose from 2 percent in 1950, to 14 percent in 1990. Women have exhibited particularly substantial growth in educational attainment. By 1990, women in Puerto Rico were more likely to complete college than men. The proportion of men in Puerto Rico with a college degree or more in 1990 was 13 percent. Among women, the corresponding proportion was 15 percent.

Associated with this greater educational attainment has been an increase in the proportion of the labor force in white-collar occupations. Workers in white-collar occupations made up less than 30 percent of the labor force in 1950 but more than half of the labor force by 1990.

Male labor force participation rates declined sharply between 1950 and 1980, and then rose between 1980 and 1990. In 1950, the male labor force participation rate was 71 percent; by 1990 it was 59 percent. This drop is related to lower participation rates among persons below 20 years of age (due to greater educational attainment) and those above 64 years (related to lower retirement age). In addition, the rising unemployment since the early 1970s has produced *discouraged* workers who drop out of the labor force.

The labor force participation rate of women has trended upward since the early 1960s, rising from 20 percent in 1960, to 37 percent in 1990. The same forces operating to reduce labor force participation rates among younger and older men were also operating among women during this time period. These changes, however, were minor compared with the sharply rising labor force participation rates of women in the 25–55 age group. The latter is, in turn, associated with an increased demand for female labor in manufacturing and service sectors, as well as shifting attitudes toward women's work in Puerto Rican society.

Earnings growth in Puerto Rico during the 1980s was substantial, particularly among the most-educated. Consequently, the returns to education in Puerto Rico increased in the 1980s, just as they did in the United States. Although increased education is related to higher pay for both men and women, the economic returns to education are higher among men. Large numbers of women with college education are clustered or segregated into lower-paying clerical and administrative-support occupations, receiving wages below those received by men with comparable education and skills.

The Unemployment Crisis

Unemployment climbed dramatically in the 1970s and 1980s. Among men, unemployment rose from 5 percent in 1970, to 19 percent in 1990.

Among women, unemployment increased from 7 percent in 1970, to 22 percent in 1990. The incidence of unemployment varies among demographic groups in the population. The unemployment rate among teenagers in Puerto Rico is at crisis levels. The unemployment rate is also substantially higher among persons who do not have a high school diploma. And migrants who have recently returned to the island suffer from subtantially higher unemployment rates, as does the labor force residing in rural areas.

The massive increase in unemployment in Puerto Rico in the 1970s and 1980s affected almost every demographic group. The crisis was to a large extent associated with a sustained drop of the aggregate demand for labor, caused by a severe recession that lasted until the late 1980s. Increased competition from other developing and newly industrialized nations for foreign investment resulted in a reduction of labor-intensive U.S. investments in Puerto Rico. Another factor in the rise of unemployment was the full application of federal minimum wage legislation to Puerto Rico in the 1970s. The evidence of the role that federal minimum wages play on unemployment is mixed. Overall, however, the weight of the data leads one to conclude that the two variables are positively related, even if the magnitude of the relationship has not been precisely established.

Puerto Rico's economy is a developing economy. Indeed, the dual-economy concept used to characterize many developing economies applies well to Puerto Rico, where there is persistent segmentation between formal and informal sectors. The urban informal sector in Puerto Rico is thriving and dynamic, with comparatively low unemployment rates and high earnings. In contrast, in rural areas, both the formal and informal sectors are stagnant.

Population

The 1980s were one of the slowest periods of population growth of this century. This was mostly due to a reduction in the natural growth of the population resulting from a drop in the birth rate and an increase in the death rate during the decade. The drop in the birth rate was closely associated with increased educational attainment and labor force participation among women, as well as with a significant increase in the age at which women are marrying.

Death rates declined between 1950 and 1980, but turned around sharply in the 1990s. The increased mortality rate was partly related to the aging of the population and the consequent increased proportion of people 65 or older. There was an unusual increase in the mortality among the 25–44 age group in the 1980s due to the rise in AIDS-related deaths, and the growing incidence of accidents and homicides.

The Family

The role of the family as a unit of organization is on average stronger in Puerto Rico than in the mainland United States. In 1990, the proportion of all households in the United States that were also families was 71 percent, compared to 84 percent in Puerto Rico. However, as in many other countries, including the United States, the incidence of married-couple families is declining in Puerto Rico. Divorce rates have been climbing since the 1960s, and Puerto Rico now has one of the highest divorce rates in the world.

Families consisting of a female head with no spouse present have been a growing presence in Puerto Rican society in recent years. The population living in such households is in the worse economic condition of any group in Puerto Rico. The fact that 30 percent of all women 15 years of age or older live in female-headed households suggests that gender constitutes a significant force in the island's income distribution. Indeed, poverty rates in 1990 were substantially higher for women than among men.

In many industrialized economies, teenage pregnancy is an issue of growing concern for policymakers, but it does not appear to be on the rise in Puerto Rico. Single parenthood, on the other hand, has been increasing rapidly. The proportion of all women aged 18–55 who were single parents was 19 percent in 1990, up from 16 percent in 1980.

Migration between the United States and Puerto Rico

Puerto Rico has witnessed one of the most massive emigration flows of this century. Net migration from Puerto Rico to the United States peaked in the 1950s, when 470,000 persons left the island. Emigration slowed thereafter, especially in the 1970s, but surged again in the 1980s. The net outflow from Puerto Rico was almost 117,000 during the 1980s. Nonconverging wage and unemployment differentials between the island and the United States explain the continuation of mass Puerto Rican migration to the United States in the 1980s.

Worries about the emigration of Puerto Rican professional and technical workers and the possibility of a "brain drain" appear to be unfounded. The census data do not support the view that the recent emigration outflow from the island is composed mostly of highly skilled workers.

Return migrants to Puerto Rico have been a significant aspect of the demographic picture of the island since the 1950s. Return migration peaked in the 1970s and declined somewhat in the 1980s, when 150,000 return migrants moved to Puerto Rico. Recent return migrants to Puerto Rico have substantially lower educational attainment status compared to the island's overall population.

Policymakers worry about the potentially deleterious effects of back-and-forth migration between Puerto Rico and the United States on the income and social stability of the families involved. Census-based measurements suggest that circular migration is a significant phenomenon among Puerto Ricans, with as many as 130,000 circular migrants in the 1980s. Circular migration accounts for the fact that a large fraction of Puerto Rican migrants to the United States in the 1980s resided for a relatively short period of time in the United States.

Puerto Ricans in the United States

The 1980s saw Puerto Ricans dispersing across the mainland United States at rates unprecedented in previous decades. Substantial Puerto Rican populations now exist in Texas, Florida, and California, where a significant portion of the new emigrants from Puerto Rico are locating. By 1990, Florida had the third-largest population of Puerto Ricans in the United States, and approximately 10 percent of the total. Most Puerto Ricans, however, still reside in the Northeast and the Midwest. The growth of Puerto Rican communities declined in large, urban centers and accelerated in smaller cities. While the Puerto Rican population doubled or more in such cities as Tampa, Florida, and Springfield and Lawrence, Massachusetts, it increased by only 4 percent in New York City, 7 percent in Chicago, and 4.5 percent in Newark.

Puerto Ricans in the United States exhibited substantial income growth in the 1980s. Their mean per capita household income increased by close to 30 percent adjusted for inflation. This was the highest of all the major racial and ethnic groups in the United States. Associated with these income gains was a sharp increase in labor force participation among Puerto Rican women, higher educational attainment overall, and a significant upgrading of the occupational distribution.

Despite the economic gains exhibited by the U.S. Puerto Rican population as a whole in the 1980s, several very disturbing trends exist. Some groups actually exhibited a deterioration in economic status in the 1980s. Puerto Ricans who had not completed high school suffered significant losses in earnings, employment, and income, and a substantial portion of first-generation migrants from Puerto Rico also lagged behind in these areas. Unskilled migrants moving to smaller cities in the Northeast face unemployment rates of between 20 and 30 percent.

Immigrants in Puerto Rico

The migration of persons born outside Puerto Rico to the island has boomed over the last thirty years, rising from nearly 60,000 in 1960, to 320,000 in 1990. The groups of persons born outside Puerto Rico in

1990 include Puerto Ricans born in the mainland United States (229,000), persons born outside the United States, the so-called foreign-born (91,000), and persons born in the mainland United States with no Puerto Rican parentage (21,500).

Dominicans constituted the largest immigrant group in Puerto Rico in 1990. The Dominican-born population in Puerto Rico almost doubled in the 1980s, to nearly 42,000 in 1990. The second-largest immigrant group was the Cuban-born population, although this population declined in the 1980s.

Overall, immigrants have done very well in Puerto Rico, compared to the native-born population. For example, the major groups born outside the island residing in Puerto Rico had average annual household incomes exceeding that of the native-born population in 1989. The public perception that the Dominican-born population has a substantially lower income and lower educational attainment than the population as a whole is unfounded. In 1989, the average household income of the Dominican-born population was 17 percent higher than that of the native-born population. As for educational attainment, 15 percent of the Dominican-born population had a college degree in 1990, compared to 13 percent of the native-born population. However, the proportion of Dominicans with educational attainment below a high school diploma was also significantly higher than for the population as a whole, resulting in a higher proportion of Dominicans at the top and bottom of the educational ladder relative to the native-born. Dominican-born women had substantially lower educational attainment than Dominican-born men.

The participation of immigrants to Puerto Rico in public assistance programs is comparatively small. The proportions of immigrants aged 16 years or over in 1989 receiving a positive amount of public assistance were only 4 percent of men and 14 percent of women.

Puerto Rico's Experience with Economic Integration

Throughout the world, countries of all sizes and income levels are forging closer economic ties with each other. In some cases, as with the North American Free Trade Agreement, these ties involve freer trade and investment flows among the participants. In other cases, as with the East and West German economic union and the European Economic Community, the movement is toward full integration of the economies involved, including common currency and common social and labor legislation. Puerto Rico's relationship to the United States falls in the latter category. Puerto Rico has common currency and customs arrangements with the United States, and there is free labor and capital mobility between the island and the mainland. Puerto Ricans are covered by U.S. minimum wage legislation and are eligible for federal transfer payments. Puerto Rico's immigration policy is dictated by the United States. Because of the wide differences in income between Puerto Rico and the United States, however, the island's close economic, social, and political ties with the mainland constitute a social experiment on a grand scale.

The economic union with the United States meant that the island had free access to the internal U.S. market. Without tariffs, quotas, or other barriers to the free flow of goods and services, government authorities in Puerto Rico understood that the island had an advantage over other developing countries in producing for export to the huge U.S. market. They proceeded, and have continued to the present, to develop tax-incentive schemes to attract U.S. capital to further such export production. This strategy was associated with sustained economic growth until the early 1970s. Since that time, Puerto Rico's economic record has been disappointing.

The recent failure of Puerto Rico's economic development has several roots. First, Puerto Rico's advantages as an export site have diminished over the years. As the United States and many other countries worldwide liberalized their external trade, Puerto Rico lost its pioneer status in externally oriented economic development. At present, the island enjoys no *major* advantages over other developing nations in trading with the United States. Mexico's admittance into the North American free trade area and the long list of would-be entrants headed by Chile, Colombia, and Argentina mean that Puerto Rico's advantageous position with respect to the American internal market is seriously in question.

A second problem relates to Puerto Rico's heavy reliance on U.S. capital. The tax incentives that Puerto Rico has used to attract this capital are under attack by federal authorities intent on reducing the federal budget deficit. Even if the subsidies were to continue, it is unlikely that they will serve the long-run growth needs of the Puerto Rican economy. Recently, in order to attract U.S. firms, Puerto Rico has had to offer heavy subsidies. This has become increasingly costly, not only in terms of tax revenues, but also because the subsidies, in encouraging capital-intensive firms to settle in the island, have produced relatively little gain in employment (Tobin 1976).

A third set of difficulties encountered by the economic integration strategy of Puerto Rico concerns the application of federal social legislation and, more specifically, minimum wages to the island. Given the differences in per capita income between Puerto Rico and the mainland, the adoption of federal minimum wages in Puerto Rico constituted a binding, biting restriction on the wages paid by industries that use low-wage, unskilled labor. With neighboring countries, such as the Dominican Republic and Mexico, offering an unskilled labor force with wages substantially below those in Puerto Rico, labor-intensive production on the island is simply not competitive. The potential for job-creation for those workers who need it the most—young persons with low educational attainment—is therefore bleak.

A fourth issue associated with the development crisis in Puerto Rico is connected to the migratory flow between the island and the mainland. The economic union with the United States effectively makes Puerto Rico an American region. Puerto Rico cannot utilize the major policy instruments available to sovereign countries, with respect to monetary or exchange rate issues. This means that the local government has no macroeconomic tools with which to deal with sudden economic shocks and disturbances.[1] In these circumstances, one of the key mechanisms through which an economy adjusts over time is labor migration (Eichengreen 1989). Wide wage differentials with other regions trigger emigration, while a booming local economy results in in-migration. In Puerto Rico, this basic concept of economic adjustment in integrated regions has operated with a vengeance.

Overall, Puerto Rico's experience with an externally oriented development strategy based on integration with the U.S. economy reflects the costs and the benefits of such a strategy, with the benefits very clearly seen in the period up to the early 1970s and the costs emerging more clearly since that time. Other countries and regions seeking the same sort of economic union that Puerto Rico has had with the United States will find a lesson in Puerto Rico's experience.

Toward the Year 2000: What Next for Puerto Rico in the Current Policymaking Environment?

Puerto Rico's policymakers are limited in their ability to promote economic growth and development given the many constraints they

---

1. This loss of macroeconomic policy control is not a totally bad thing. The ability of governments to initiate monetary and exchange rate policies also gives them the ability to misuse these policies. As a consequence, although in theory monetary independence gives policymakers the power to react to sudden economic disturbances, it also gives the government the ability to distort the economy, whether for political purposes or due to ignorance or ineptitude. Thus, many developing countries often forego devaluations of their currency for long periods of time, leading to eventual devaluations that create havoc in the financial markets. Mexico went through one of these episodes recently, in December 1994, with disastrous consequences. (See Sachs, Tornell, and Velasco 1995.)

face—some global in origin, others involving the federal government, and yet others involving the integration of Puerto Rico into the United States.

One of the key policymaking issues is the extent to which the public sector is able to effectively promote economic development in the global economy. Puerto Rico's development strategy has always had an active public sector component. Under Operation Bootstrap, the creation of infrastructure (social overhead capital), the regulation of labor, incentives to business, and the like were considered the responsibility of government. Today, however, there is considerable disagreement on the effectiveness of the public sector in fostering long-term economic growth and development. Calls for government downsizing, deregulation, and privatization are increasingly heard from those who believe that these reforms will lead to economic efficiency and increased competitiveness.

There is little question that the Puerto Rican government was an effective agent of economic change in Puerto Rico during the early years of Operation Bootstrap. The political concensus and social contract that allowed Operation Bootstrap to proceed were not without their costs and are unlikely to be repeated. And it might be argued that it was the massive emigration of Puerto Ricans to the United States during the 1950s, more than any governmental policy, that allowed the increased standard of living on the island.

As we have seen, Mexico's admittance to the North American free trade area and the potential expansion of NAFTA threaten Puerto Rico's competitive position in the Western Hemisphere. Puerto Rico is not immune to developments beyond its borders. The declining standards of living in the Dominican Republic during the 1980s that resulted in an inflow of Dominicans to Puerto Rico and the United States are a case in point. Puerto Rico's economic future is inextricably intertwined with that of its neighbors. It is conceivable that Puerto Rico can work out complementary and mutually beneficial trading arrangements in the present global alignment, but it is less likely that the Puerto Rican government can engage in policies to simultaneously promote economic development and insulate the island's economy from countervailing external forces.

A second issue that must be addressed in formulating public policy in Puerto Rico is the sometimes contradictory nature of U.S.–Puerto Rico relations. The objectives of the federal government and those of Puerto Rico do not always coincide and at times may even work at cross-purposes.

The federal minimum wage provisions, in particular, tend to exacerbate unemployment in the island. Another example is the attempt by Washington to curtail or eliminate the 936 provisions of the IRS code as they apply to Puerto Rico in order to help balance the federal budget. In an era in which public policy must be especially flexible and responsive to the needs of society at large, the federal-insular relationship puts strains on the ability of local policymakers to meet their objectives.

A third issue that impinges upon Puerto Rico's public policy is the existence of significant Puerto Rican communities in the United States, each with its own interests. These communities are not only increasingly dispersed geographically, but also display varied socioeconomic characteristics and priorities. Given the diversity among Puerto Ricans in the United States, the possibility arises of conflicts between the objectives of policymakers on the island and representatives of the various Puerto Rican communities in the United States. Moreover, Puerto Ricans residing in the United States maintain close ties with the island and participate in island political affairs in many ways—a clear example being the political status plebiscite of 1994.

One of the basic economic questions that confronts Puerto Rico is what alternative route of economic development can be devised to replace the failing Operation Bootstrap model (which is still followed to a large extent) in light of the many constraints facing policymakers on the island?

The most significant social and economic ill Puerto Rico faces is unemployment. The unemployment problem is most severe among young people with low levels of education. This suggests that the government must focus on raising educational attainment.[2] Educational growth stagnated in the 1980s, with government expenditures dedicated to education dropping sharply. Teachers' salaries declined to levels prevailing in the late 1960s. Educational quality appears to have deteriorated, as reflected in declining average scores in college entrance exams, and the increase in the proportion of the population graduating from college slowed down.

If the Puerto Rican economy is to deal seriously with high unemployment rates, the education of its workforce must be sharply increased. It is very difficult to raise the employment levels of unskilled labor in a developing country where federal minimum wage rates apply. A focus on education at all levels as a public policy objective is more likely to be successful in reducing unemployment. This accumu-

2.   An increase in the supply of highly skilled workers does not in general imply that unemployment levels will decrease. If there is a limited demand for skills in the economy, unemployment of educated workers may arise as the supply of new workers increases. In the case of Puerto Rico, as well as in many other newly industrialized economies in recent years, the demand for skills generally outstrips supply. This is reflected in rising rates of return to education (especially college education) and soaring salaries for some professionals and technical workers.

lation of human capital would also generate positive spillover effects: individual entrepreneurship, technological change, and innovation are all spurred by greater supplies of workers with a college degree or more. Economic growth is intimately related to human captial accumulation (Barro and Sala-i-Martin 1995). And skilled labor has also been shown to be complementary with unskilled labor, suggesting that increased supplies of highly educated workers may push the demand for unskilled labor upward (Rivera-Batiz and Sechzer 1991).

The next comprehensive census to be conducted in Puerto Rico is scheduled for the year 2000. At that time, it will be possible to determine whether the trends that we have identified on the basis of the 1990 census data have continued or been reversed. In any event, this study will have served its purpose if it promotes deeper understanding of present-day Puerto Rico, its people, and its society.

Appendix 1

Census Data

I N WRITING this report we relied primarily on data from the 1970, 1980, and 1990 censuses of population and housing of Puerto Rico and the public-use microdata samples (PUMS) derived from them. In addition, in examining the situation of Puerto Ricans and other groups in the U.S. mainland, we relied on data from the 1980 and 1990 censuses of population and housing of the United States and the associated PUMS.

The U.S. government has carried out censuses of the population of Puerto Rico ever since the island became a territory of the United States in 1898. The first census was conducted in November 1899, when a population of 953,243 persons was recorded. The next census was in 1910, and one has been conducted every ten years ever since. The Census Bureau of the U.S. Department of Commerce is in charge of the data collection activities. Each person whose usual residence is in Puerto Rico is targeted to be included in the census enumeration, without regard to that person's legal immigration status or citizenship.

The data collected by the census are obtained through questionnaires that are distributed to every household in Puerto Rico. The questionnaire asks basic demographic and socioeconomic questions in Spanish, although it is also available in English. Census enumerators pick up the questionnaires and make follow-up telephone calls and visits to ensure the fullest count of the population. In addition to seeking a count of—and basic information about—the population, the census also collects more detailed information from a sample of housing units. In 1990, for example, 17 percent of all persons enumerated by the census of Puerto Rico were provided with a longer questionnaire that included detailed questions on demographics, household composition, housing characteristics, and socioeconomic status.

The census questionnaire distributed to the population of Puerto Rico is slightly different from the one distributed to the population in the mainland United States. There are some questions that appear on the U.S. census questionnaire that are not asked in the census of Puerto Rico. Racial background, for example, has not been included in the Puerto Rico census for many decades. On the other hand, there are questions asked in the Puerto Rico census that do not appear on the census questionnaire for the mainland United States. The Puerto Rico census, for instance, asks whether the respondent is literate, that is, whether he or she can read or write. In addition, the census questionnaire for Puerto Rico includes several questions relating to migration and length of stay in the mainland United States, questions which allow a detailed study of patterns of return and circular migration to the island.

The public-use microdata samples (PUMS) are computer accessible files that contain records for a sample of housing units, with information on the detailed characteristics of each unit and the people in it. Information that would identify a household or an individual is excluded to protect the confidentiality of respondents. Within the limits of the sample size and geographic detail, these files allow users to prepare virtually any census-based tabulations about the population. PUMS files for Puerto Rico exist reaching back to 1970. For 1990, two separate public-use microdata samples are available, one representing 5 percent of the housing units in Puerto Rico and another representing 1 percent of the housing units. We used the 5 percent sample for this study.

Each microdata file is a stratified sample of the population that received census long-form questionnaires. Sampling was done by housing units in order to allow the study of family relationships and housing-unit characteristics. Sampling of persons in institutions and other group quarters was conducted on a person-by-person basis. Vacant units were also sampled. For Puerto Rico, the 5 percent PUMS for 1990 provides records for over 176,000 persons and over 59,000 housing units. For the United States mainland, the 5 percent PUMS for 1990 gives the user records for over 12 million persons and over 5 million housing units.

The census data provide the richest and most accurate information available on the population of Puerto Rico (a study of the coverage of the 1980 census of Puerto Rico indicates that the coverage patterns of that census are similar to that for blacks in the United States in 1980 [Robinson and Passel 1987]). Various agencies of the Commonwealth government in Puerto Rico collect data on national income accounts, labor market outcomes, and the like. These data sources provide information with substantially higher measurement errors compared to the census. Their samples, for one, are much smaller than those upon which the census is based. They also suffer from a number of data-collection and sampling difficulties. Indeed, prominent Puerto Rican researchers have for a long time complained about the inaccuracy of government socioeconomic data sources. For instance, it is generally recognized that the government estimates of migration flows between Puerto Rico and the United States are widely off the mark. In addition, estimates of employment and unemployment are widely considered to be unreliable. As Elias Gutiérrez (Montano and Gomez 1990, 1D), one of the most prominent Puerto Rican economists, has observed: "The statistical data that is supplied here (in Puerto Rico) contains exorbitant noise. The Labor Department has its own statistics, just as the Health, Education, and Commerce Departments also do, but these data consist of isolated numbers collected through various methodologies that do not have much practical value" (see also Sagardía 1992; Hernández-Soto 1988; Gomez 1988). The census-based analysis presented in this monograph provides results that often diverge drastically from Puerto Rican government figures. The unemployment rate, for example, is much higher when calculated from census data. However, the household survey upon which the Department of Labor in Puerto Rico estimates unemployment is based on a much smaller sample than the census. Furthermore, the sampling, methodology, and questionnaire used in the survey administered by the government in Puerto Rico have been repeatedly criticized by the island's economists (see Rodríguez 1995 and Hernández Soto 1988). Great care must be exercised by researchers in assessing published data based on Puerto Rican government sources.

Appendix 2

Measuring Migration to the United States

T HE DATA used in this monograph, as presented in table 3.1, are estimates of net emigration based on data recorded by the U.S. census of population and housing. There is an alternative, and very popular, source of information on the net balance of people moving in and out of Puerto Rico. The Planning Board of the Commonwealth of Puerto Rico collects annual data on the number of air travel passengers flowing into and out of the island. The net balance of these passenger flows represents the net amount of people moving in or out of Puerto Rico during a certain period of time. Computations of this balance usually arrived at negative numbers during the 1980s, indicating that more people were exiting than entering Puerto Rico. This is, of course, the same conclusion arrived at using census data. However, the passenger data suggest that the net movement of people out of Puerto Rico is substantially larger than census data do (table A2.1).

In the 1970–80 period, the net passenger outflow was 129,619 but the census-based net migration outflow was only 65,813, leaving an unexplained outflow of 63,806 persons. In the 1980–90 period, the gap between the net passenger outflow and the net migration outflow as recorded by the census is even greater, with an unexplained outflow of 170,947 persons.

Since the estimate of net migration provided by the census data is highly reliable, the gaps between the census-based and planning board estimates could be due to measurement errors in the planning board data. The latter is based on counts of thousands of air and sea travel connections involving over seven million travelers annually. Given the massive numbers to be counted, small errors could lead to major distortions in the estimate of net migration (Gomez 1988, 40).

169

Table A2.1   Measuring Net Migration from Puerto Rico

	1970–80	1980–90
Census-based net emigration	65,813	116,571
Planning board–based net emigration (net passenger outflow)	129,619	287,518
Difference between planning board and census-based net emigration	63,806	170,947

Source: Figures for the census-based net migration outflow are those in table 3.1. The data for net passenger outflow are as determined by Planning Board of Puerto Rico, Bureau of Economic and Social Planning.

There is an additional problem in using planning board net passenger flow measurements as an estimate of net migration of Puerto Ricans to the United States. To understand the issue, it must be remembered that Puerto Rico plays a crucial role as a stepping-stone for undocumented immigrants seeking entry to the mainland United States. Travel between Puerto Rico and the U.S. mainland does not normally require any immigration documentation. Immigration and Naturalization Service (INS) officers sometimes make visual checks of passengers at airports and may ask specific persons for identification. The process, however, is a cursory one and few, if any, undocumented persons are detected traveling from the island to the mainland. This means that any undocumented immigrant who successfully makes it to Puerto Rico without being intercepted by the INS can almost be ensured entry to the mainland. Undocumented immigrants who move illegally to Puerto Rico in order to move to the mainland appear as passengers exiting the island when they make their trip to the United States. Yet, they are not recorded by the Census of Population as out-migrants since they are never residents of Puerto Rico. The differences between the net outflow of passengers from the island and the net emigration from the island (as recorded by census data) may thus partly represent undocumented emigration. (Of course, measurement errors in the census data may explain part of the gap between the two figures. The Puerto Rico census is not without its own problems in terms of coverage and reporting errors. However, the available evidence confirms that the quality of the census data for Puerto Rico is relatively high, comparable to that for the black population in the mainland United States [Robinson and Passel 1988].)

Appendix 3

Population of Puerto Rico by *Municipio*

	1990	1980	Percent Change
Puerto Rico	3,522,037	3,196,520	10.18%
Adjuntas	19,451	18,786	3.54
Aguada	35,911	31,567	13.76
Aguadilla	59,335	54,606	8.66
Aguas Buenas	25,424	22,429	13.35
Aibonito	24,971	22,167	12.65
Añasco	25,234	23,274	8.42
Arecibo	93,385	86,766	7.63
Arroyo	18,910	17,014	11.14
Barceloneta	20,947	18,942	10.58
Barranquitas	25,605	21,639	18.33
Bayamón	220,262	196,206	12.26
Cabo Rojo	38,521	34,045	13.15
Caguas	133,447	117,959	13.13
Camuy	28,917	24,884	16.21
Canovanas	36,816	31,880	15.48
Carolina	177,806	165,954	7.14
Cataño	34,587	26,243	31.80
Cayey	46,553	41,099	13.27
Ceiba	17,145	14,944	14.73
Ciales	18,084	16,211	11.55
Cidra	35,601	28,365	25.51
Coamo	33,837	30,822	9.78
Comerío	20,265	18,212	11.27
Corozal	33,095	28,221	17.27
Culebra	1,542	1,265	21.90
Dorado	30,759	25,511	20.57

171

Appendix 3   (*continued*)

	1990	1980	Percent Change
Fajardo	36,882	32,087	14.94
Florida	8,689	7,232	20.15
Guanica	19,984	18,799	6.30
Guayama	41,588	40,183	3.50
Guayanilla	21,581	21,050	2.52
Guaynabo	92,886	80,742	15.04
Gurabo	28,737	23,574	21.90
Hatillo	32,703	28,958	12.93
Hormigueros	15,212	14,030	8.42
Humacao	55,203	46,134	19.66
Isabela	39,147	37,435	4.57
Jayuya	15,527	14,722	5.47
Juana Diaz	45,198	43,505	3.89
Juncos	30,612	25,397	20.53
Lajas	23,271	21,236	9.58
Lares	29,015	26,743	8.50
Las Marias	9,306	8,747	6.39
Las Piedras	27,896	22,412	24.47
Loiza	29,307	20,867	40.45
Luquillo	18,100	14,895	21.52
Manati	38,692	36,562	5.83
Maricao	6,206	6,737	−7.88
Maunabo	12,347	11,813	4.52
Mayagüez	100,371	96,193	4.34
Moca	32,926	29,185	12.82
Morovis	25,288	21,142	19.61
Naguabo	22,620	20,617	9.72
Naranjito	27,914	23,633	18.11
Orocovis	21,158	19,332	9.45
Patillas	19,633	17,774	10.46
Peñuelas	22,515	19,116	17.78
Ponce	187,749	189,046	−0.69
Quebradillas	21,425	19,728	8.60
Rincon	12,213	11,788	3.61
Rio Grande	45,648	34,283	33.15
Sabana Grande	22,843	20,207	13.04
Salinas	28,335	26,438	7.18
San German	34,962	32,922	6.20
San Juan	437,745	434,849	0.67
San Lorenzo	35,163	32,428	8.43
San Sebastian	38,799	35,690	8.71
Santa Isabel	19,318	19,854	−2.70
Toa Alta	44,101	31,910	38.20

Appendix 3   *(continued)*

	1990	1980	Percent Change
Toa Baja	89,454	78,246	14.32
Trujillo Alto	61,120	51,389	18.94
Utuado	34,980	34,505	1.38
Vega Alta	34,559	28,696	20.43
Vega Baja	55,997	47,115	18.85
Vieques	8,602	7,662	12.27
Villalba	23,559	20,734	13.62
Yabucoa	36,483	31,425	16.10
Yauco	42,058	37,742	11.44

Sources: 1980 and 1990 U.S. Census of Population and Housing: Puerto Rico.

Appendix 4

Multivariate Regression Analysis of the Growth and Presence of Puerto Ricans in 25 U.S. SMSAs, 1980–90

	Dependent Variables	
Independent Variables	Growth of the Puerto Rican Population, 1980–90	Changes in the Presence of Puerto Ricans, 1980–90
Constant	11.00413[a]	1.71730[a]
	(1.95)	(0.29)
Size of MSA in 1980	−0.0000015	−0.0000003[a]
	(0.00)	(0.00)
Share of MSA population that was Puerto Rican in 1980	−0.196327[a]	−0.0460290[a]
	(0.11)	(0.02)
Per capita household income	−0.000668[a]	−0.000104[a]
	(0.00)	(0.00)
Share of total Puerto Rican population	0.3914	0.1015[a]
	(0.36)	(0.05)
R^2	0.45	0.57
N	25	25

[a]Coefficient is statistically different from zero at the 10 percent level of significance.

References

Acevedo, Luz del Alba, "Industrialization and Employment: Changes in the Patterns of Women's Work in Puerto Rico," *World Development*, Vol. 18, March 1990, 231–55.

Acosta-Belén, Edna, "Puerto Rican Women in Culture, History, and Society," in Edna Acosta Belén, ed., *The Puerto Rican Woman: Perspectives on Culture, History and Society*, Praeger Publishers, New York, 1986, 1–29.

Alameda, José I., "Impacto de los ciclos económicos de los Estados Unidos en la economía de Puerto Rico," in R. J. Duncan, ed., *El Desarrollo Socioeconómico de Puerto Rico*, Universidad Interamericana de Puerto Rico, San Germán, 1979, 60–76.

Alameda, José I., and Wilfredo Ruíz Oliveras, "La fuga de capital humano en la economía de Puerto Rico: Reto para la actual década," *Revista de Ciencias Sociales*, Vol. 29, January–July 1985, 3–36.

Andic, Fuat M., *The Distribution of Family Incomes in Puerto Rico*, Institute of Caribbean Studies, Río Piedras, Puerto Rico, 1964.

———. "Un comentario en torno a la distribución del ingreso en Puerto Rico: Un estudio en base a los Años 1953–63," *Revista de Ciencias Sociales*, Vol. 9, December 1965, 363–71.

Aura, N. Alfara, "Many Puerto Rican Graduates of MIT Stay on Mainland," *Caribbean Business*, August 4, 1988.

Azize Vargas, Yamila, ed., *La Mujer en Puerto Rico: Ensayos en Investigación*, Ediciones Huracán, Río Piedras, Puerto Rico, 1987.

———, "Los sistemas estadísticos y la participación de las mujeres en la sociedad," in *Mujer y Estadísticas: Memorias del Primer Seminario*, Consejo de Educación Superior, Río Piedras, Puerto Rico, 1992.

Baer, Werner, *The Puerto Rican Economy and United States Fluctuations*, Ediciones Rumbos, Barcelona, 1960.

Baerga, María del Carmen, "La articulación del trabajo asalariado y no asalariado: Hacia una reevaluación de la contribución femenina a la sociedad Puertorriqueña (el caso de la industria de la aguja)," in Yamila Azize Vargas, ed., *La Mujer en Puerto Rico: Ensayos de Investigación*, Ediciones Huracán, Río Piedras, Puerto Rico, 1987, 89–112.

————, ed., *Género y Trabajo: La Industria de la Aguja en Puerto Rico y el Caribe*, University of Puerto Rico Press, Río Piedras, 1993.

Barro, Robert, and Xavier Sala-i-Martin, *Economic Growth*, McGraw-Hill, New York, 1995.

Bartlett, Frederic, and Brandon Howell, *Population Trends and Policies in Puerto Rico*, Planning Board of Puerto Rico, San Juan, April 1944.

Beardsley, Clarence, "Experto opina sangría de capital humano de la economía puertorriqueña," *El Mundo*, February 23, 1980.

Birdsall, Nancy, "Economic Approaches to Population Growth," in H. Chenery and T. N. Srinivasan, eds., *Handbook of Labor Economics*, North Holland Publishing, Amsterdam, 1988, 477–542.

Blackburn, McKinley L., David E. Bloom, and Richard Freeman, "The Declining Economic Position of Less Skilled American Men," in Gary Burtless, ed., *A Future of Lousy Jobs? The Changing Structure of U.S. Wages*, The Brookings Institution, Washington, D.C., 1990, 31–67.

Blasor, Lorraine, "Puerto Rico's Brain Drain: Curse or Blessing?" *Caribbean Business*, September 13, 1990.

Bloom, David E., and Giles Grenier, "Language, Employment and Earnings in the United States: Spanish-English Differentials from 1970 to 1990," National Bureau of Economic Research working paper 4584, December 1993.

Bofil, Jaime, *The Puerto Rican Development Model within an Interindustry Dynamic Framework*, Unpublished Ph.D. Dissertation, University College of Wales, 1987.

Borjas, George J., *Friends or Strangers: The Impact of Immigrants on the U.S. Economy*, Basic Books, New York, 1990.

Buitrago Ortiz, Carlos, "Estructura social y orientaciones valorativas en Esperanza, Puerto Rico y el Mediterráneo," in R. Duncan, ed., *La Investigación Social en Puerto Rico*, Interamerican University Press, San Juan, Puerto Rico, 1980, 153–182.

Card, David, and Alan Krueger, *Myth and Measurement: The New Economics of the Minimum Wage*, Princeton University Press, Princeton, N.J., 1995.

Castañeda, Rolando, and José A. Herrero, "La distribución del ingreso en Puerto Rico," *Revista de Ciencias Sociales*, Vol. 9, December 1965, 345–62.

Castillo-Freeman, Alida, and Richard Freeman, "When the Minimum Wage Really Bites: The Effect of the U.S.-Level Minimum on Puerto Rico," in George Borjas and Richard Freeman, eds., *Immigration and the Workforce*, University of Chicago Press, 1992, 177–211.

Chavez, Linda, *Out of the Barrio: Toward a New Politics of Hispanic Assimilation*, Basic Books, New York, 1991.

Choudhury, Parimal, *The Food Stamp Program in Puerto Rico*, Office of Research and Statistics, Department of Social Services, Commonwealth of Puerto Rico, 1978.

Choudhury, Parimal, and Fuat Andic, *The Impact of the Food Stamp Program in Puerto Rico*, Office of Research and Statistics, Department of Social Services, Commonwealth of Puerto Rico, 1977.

City of New York, *Puerto Rican New Yorkers in 1990*, Department of City Planning, New York, 1993.

Coale, Ansley, "The Demographic Transition," in John Eatwell, Murray Milgate, and Peter Newman, eds., *The New Palgrave: A Dictionary of Economics,* Macmillan Publishing, London, 1987.

Cobas, José A., and Jorge Duany, *Los Cubanos en Puerto Rico: Economía Étnica e Identidad Cultural,* Editorial de la Universidad de Puerto Rico, Río Piedras, 1995.

Colón, Leandro A. "Industrial Policy and Technological Capability in Puerto Rico," *Ceteris Paribus: Revista de Investigaciones Socioeconómicas,* Vol. 4, April 1994, 27–54.

Cunningham, Ineke, Carlos Ramos Bellido, and Reinaldo Ortiz Colón, *El SIDA en Puerto Rico: Acercamientos Multidisciplinarios,* Editorial Universidad de Puerto Rico, Río Piedras, 1991.

Curet, Eliezer, *Puerto Rico: Development by Integration to the U.S.,* Editorial Cultural, Río Piedras, Puerto Rico, 1986.

Danziger, Sheldon, and Peter Gottschalk, "Introduction," in Sheldon Danziger and Peter Gottschalk, eds., *Uneven Tides: Rising Inequality in America,* Russell Sage Foundation, New York, 1993.

Daubón, Ramón, "Section 936 as a Development Resource in the Caribbean: Suggestions for a More Effective Policy," Working Paper 13, Commission for the Study of International Migration and Cooperative Economic Development, December 1989.

DeFreitas, Gregory, *Inequality at Work: Hispanics in the U.S. Labor Force,* Oxford University Press, New York, 1991.

DeJesús Toro, Rafael, *Historia Económica de Puerto Rico,* Southwestern Publishing Company, Cincinnati, 1982.

De Soto, Hernando, *The Other Path: The Invisible Revolution in the Third World,* Harper and Row, New York, 1989.

del Valle-Caballero, Jaime L. "Technical Progress and Productivity in Puerto Rico: 1962–1977," *Ceteris Paribus: Revista de Investigaciones Socioeconómicas,* Vol. 4, October 1994, 31–46.

Dietz, James L., *Economic History of Puerto Rico,* Princeton University Press, Princeton, N.J., 1986.

Dietz, James L., and Emilio Pentojas-García, "Puerto Rico's Role in the Caribbean: The High Finance—Maquiladora Strategy," in Edwin Meléndez and Edgardo Meléndez, eds., *Colonial Dilemmas: Critical Perspectives on Contemporary Puerto Rico,* South End Press, Boston, 1993, 103–18.

Duany, Jorge, "The Cuban Community in Puerto Rico: A Comparative Caribbean Perspective," *Ethnic and Racial Studies,* Vol. 12, January 1989, 36–46.

———, "El impacto de la inmigración extranjera en el mercado laboral de Puerto Rico," *Homines,* Vol. 17, June 1994.

Duany, Jorge, Luisa Hernández Angueira, and César A. Rey, *El Barrio Gandul: Economía Subterránea y Migración Indocumentada en Puerto Rico,* Universidad del Sagrado Corazón, Santurce, Puerto Rico, 1995.

Duncan, Ronald J., "El análisis social de las poblaciones Puertorriqueñas de 1950 a 1980," in R. J. Duncan, ed., *Investigación Social en Puerto Rico,* Interamerican University Press, San Juan, Puerto Rico, 1980.

Earnhardt, Kent C., *Development Planning and Population Policy in Puerto Rico,* University of Puerto Rico Press, Río Piedras, 1982.

Easterlin, Richard, *Population, Labor Force and Long Swings in Economic Growth: The American Experience*, Columbia University Press, New York, 1968.

Ehrenberg, Ronald G., and Robert S. Smith, *Modern Labor Economics: Theory and Public Policy*, HarperCollins, New York, 1994.

Eichengreen, Barry, "One Money for Europe? Lessons from the U.S. Currency Union," *Economic Policy*, Vol. 4, April 1989, 118–87.

Enchautegui, María E., "Geographical Differentials in the Socioeconomic Status of Puerto Ricans: Human Capital Variations and Labor Market Characteristics," *International Migration Review*, Vol. 26, December 1992, 1267–90.

———, "Education, Location, and Labor Market Outcomes of Puerto Rican Men During·the 1980s," *Eastern Economic Journal*, Vol. 19, March 1993, 295–308.

Escobar, Manuel, *The 936 Market: An Introduction*, Borinquén Lithographers, San Juan, Puerto Rico, 1982.

Estado Libre Asociado de Puerto Rico, Departamento del Trabajo y Recursos Humanos, *Serie Estadística sobre Empleo y Desempleo, 1970 al 1985*, February 1986.

———, Junta de Planificación, *Caracteristicas de la Población Migrante de Puerto Rico*, 1984.

———, *Informe Económico al Gobernador, 1984*, San Juan, Puerto Rico, 1985.

———, *Serie Histórica del Empleo, Desempleo y Grupo Trabajador en Puerto Rico, 1984*, San Juan, Puerto Rico, October 1985.

———, *Indicadores Socioeconómicos de la Mujer en Puerto Rico*, March 1987.

———, *Informe Económico al Gobernador, 1988*, San Juan, Puerto Rico, 1987.

———, *Informe Económico al Gobernador, 1990*, San Juan, Puerto Rico, 1991.

———, *Serie Histórica del Empleo, Desempleo y Grupo Trabajador en Puerto Rico, 1990*, San Juan, Puerto Rico, October 1991.

———, *Informe Económico al Gobernador, 1991*, San Juan, Puerto Rico, 1992.

———, *Informe Económico al Gobernador, 1992*, San Juan, Puerto Rico, 1993.

Esteve, Himilce, *El Exilio Cubano en Puerto Rico: Su Impacto Político Social*, Editorial Raíces, San Juan, Puerto Rico, 1984.

Falcón, Luis M., and Charles Hirschman, "Trends in Labor Market Position for Puerto Ricans in the Mainland, 1970–1987," *Hispanic Journal of Behavioral Sciences*, Vol. 14, February 1992, 16–51.

Fernández-Kelly, María, *For We Are Sold: I and My People, Women and Industry in Mexico's Frontier*, State University of New York Press, Albany, 1983.

Fernández-Kelly, María, and Saskia Sassen, eds., "Recasting Women in the Global Economy: Internationalization and Changing Definitions of Gender," in Christine Bose and Edna Acosta-Belén, eds., *Women in the Latin American Development Process*, Temple University Press, Philadelphia, 1995, 99–124.

Fernández Méndez, Eugenio, *Portrait of a Society*, University of Puerto Rico Press, Río Piedras, 1972.

Fields, Gary S., "Rural-Urban Migration, Urban Unemployment and Underemployment, and Job Search Activity in LDCs," *Journal of Development Economics*, Vol. 2, June 1975, 165–87.

Fleisher, Belton, "Some Economic Aspects of Puerto Rican Migration to the United States," *Review of Economics and Statistics*, August 1963.

Frey, William, "The New Geography of Population Shifts," in Reynolds Farley, ed., *State of the Union: America in the 1990s*, Vol. 2, Social Trends, Russell Sage Foundation, New York, 1995, 271–336.

Freyre, Jorge, *El Modelo Económico de Puerto Rico*, Interamerican University Press, San Juan, Puerto Rico, 1979.

Friedlander, Stanley, *Labor Migration and Economic Growth*, MIT Press, Cambridge, 1965.

Gomez, A. R., "Inciertas las cifras de migración," *El Nuevo Día*, July 26, 1988.

González, José Luis, *El País de Cuatro Pisos y Otros Ensayos*, Edición Huracán, Río Piedras, Puerto Rico, 1980.

González, R. L., "Alegan dominicanos en Puerto Rico hacen trabajos 'forzosos'," *El Reportero*, September 4, 1987.

Gutiérrez, Elías R., *Factor Proportions, Technology Transmission and Unemployment in Puerto Rico*, Editorial Universitaria, Universidad de Puerto Rico, Río Piedras, Puerto Rico, 1977a.

———, "The Transfer Economy of Puerto Rico: Towards an Urban Ghetto," in J. Heine, ed., *Time for Decision: The United States and Puerto Rico*, North-South Publishing, Lanham, MD, 1983, 117–34.

Gutiérrez, Elías R., et al., "Riqueza nacional e inversión externa: Una visión desde la planificación Puertorriqueña," *Revista Interamericana de Planificación*, September 1977b.

Harris, John, and Michael P. Todaro, "Migration, Unemployment and Development: A Two-Sector Analysis," *American Economic Review*, Vol. 60, March 1970, 126–42.

Heine, Jorge, and Juan M. García Passalacqua, "An Economy in Transition," *Foreign Policy Association Headline Series*, No. 266, November–December 1983.

Hernández, Ramona, Francisco L. Rivera-Batiz, and Roberto Agodini, *Dominican New Yorkers: A Socioeconomic Profile*, The CUNY Dominican Studies Institute, Dominican Research Monographs, New York, 1995.

Hernández Alvarez, José, *Return Migration to Puerto Rico*, University of California Press, Berkeley, 1967.

Hernández Angueira, Luisa, "La migración de mujeres dominicanas hacia Puerto Rico," in Jorge Duany, ed., *Los Dominicanos en Puerto Rico: Migración en la Semi-periferia*, Ediciones Huracán, Río Piedras, Puerto Rico, 1990, 73–88.

Hernández Cruz, Juan, "Migración de retorno o circulación de obreros Boricuas?" *Revista de Ciencias Sociales*, Vol. 29, January–June 1985, 81–112.

Hernandez-Soto, Héctor, "Las cifras del desempleo," *El Mundo*, October 28, 1988.

Hirschman, Albert, *The Strategy of Economic Development*, Yale University Press, New Haven, Conn., 1958.

Krueger, Alan B., "How Computers Changed the Wage Structure: Evidence and Implications," *Brookings Papers on Economic Activity*, 1993, 209–35.

———, "The Effects of the Minimum Wage When It Really Bites: A Reexamination of the Evidence for Puerto Rico," in Solomon Polachek, ed., *Research in Labor Economics*, JAI Press, Greenwich, Conn., 1995, 1–22.

Lastra, Carlos J., "The Impact of Minimum Wages on a Labor-Oriented Industry," Technical Paper 1, Government Development Bank for Puerto Rico, San Juan, 1964.

Lemann, Nicholas, "The Other Underclass," *The Atlantic Monthly*, December 1991.

Levy, Frank, "Incomes and Income Inequality," in Reynolds Farley, ed., *State of the Union: America in the 1990s*, Russell Sage Foundation, New York, 1995, Vol. 1, 1–52.

Lewis, Gordon K., *Puerto Rico: Libertad y Poder en el Caribe*, Editorial Edil, Río Piedras, Puerto Rico, 1969.

Long, Frank, "The Puerto Rican Model of Industrialization: New Dimensions in the 1980s," *Development Policy Review*, 1988.

Maldonado, Rita, "Why Puerto Ricans Migrated to the United States, 1947–1973?" *Monthly Labor Review*, September 1976.

Maldonado Denis, Manuel, *Puerto Rico: Una Interpretación Histórico-social*, Siglo XXI, México, 1969.

———, *The Emigration Dialectic: Puerto Rico and the U.S.A.*, International Publishers, New York, 1980.

Mankiw, N. Gregory, David Romer, and David N. Weil, "A Contribution to the Empirics of Economic Growth," *Quarterly Journal of Economics*, Vol. 107, December 1992.

Mann, Arthur J., "Economic Development, Income Distribution and Real Income Levels: Puerto Rico, 1953–1977," *Economic Development and Cultural Change*, 1985.

Marqués Velasco, René, *Nuevo Modelo Económico para Puerto Rico*, Editorial Cultural, Río Piedras, Puerto Rico, 1993.

Martínez, Francisco E., "Los centros bancarios internacionales y las posibilidades de las zonas de incentivos económicos," in Carmen Gautiér Mayoral and Néstor Nazario Trabal, eds., *Puerto Rico en los 1990*, Centro de Investigaciones Sociales, Universidad de Puerto Rico, Río Piedras, 1988, 80–105.

Mass, Bonnie, "Puerto Rico: A Case Study of Population Control," *Latin American Perspectives*, Winter 1977, 66–81.

McLanahan, Sara, and Lynne Casper, "Changes in Marriage, Parenthood, and Living Arrangements: 1980–1990," In Reynolds Farley, ed., *The State of the Union*, Russell Sage Foundation, New York, 1995, 1–46.

McManus, Walter, W. Gould, and F. Welch, "Earnings of Hispanic Men: The Role of English Language Proficiency," *Journal of Labor Economics*, Vol. 2, February 1983.

Meléndez, Edwin, "Crisis económica y estrategia de desarrollo en Puerto Rico," in Carmen Gautiér Mayoral and Néstor Nazario Trabal, eds., *Puerto Rico en los 1990*, Centro de Investigaciones Sociales, Universidad de Puerto Rico, Río Piedras, 1988, 160–222.

———, "Los que se van, los que regresan: Puerto Rican Migration to and from the United States, 1982–1988," mimeo., September 1991.

Mintz, Sidney, "Puerto Rican Emigration: A Three-Fold Comparison," *Social and Economic Forces*, Vol. 1, December 1955.

Montaner, Carlos Alberto, *Impacto de la emigración cubana en el Puerto Rico actual*, Editorial San Juan, Río Piedras, Puerto Rico, 1971.

Montano, Agnes, and Antonio Gomez, "Caos en datos de Junta de Planificación," *El Mundo*, October 4, 1990.

Mulero, Leonor, "Desigual para la mujer la lucha profesional," *El Nuevo Día*, November 28, 1990.

Muñoz Vázquez, Mayra, "La experiencia del divorcio desde la perspectiva de un grupo de mujeres Puertorriqueñas," in Yamila Azize Vargas, ed., *La Mujer en Puerto Rico: Ensayos de Investigación*, Ediciones Huracán, Río Piedras, Puerto Rico, 1987, 155–70.

Muñoz Vázquez, Mayra, and Edwin Fernández Banzó, *El Divorcio en la Sociedad Puertorriqueña*, Ediciones Huracán, Río Piedras, Puerto Rico, 1988.

Murphy, Kevin, and Finis Welch, "Industrial Change and the Rising Importance of Skill," in S. Danziger and P. Gottschalk, eds., *Uneven Tides: Rising Inequality in America*, Russell Sage Foundation, New York, 1993, 101–32.

Murray, Charles, *Losing Ground: American Social Policy, 1950–1980*, Basic Books, New York, 1985.

Navarro, Mireya, "After Carjacking Surge, Puerto Rico Is Wary behind the Wheel," *New York Times*, July 31, 1994.

Nieves Falcón, Luis, *Diagnóstico de Puerto Rico*, Editorial Edil, Río Piedras, Puerto Rico, 1975.

———, *El Emigrante Puertorriqueño*, Editorial Edil, Río Piedras, Puerto Rico, 1975.

Nuñez, Lisette, "Se redefine el rol de la mujer," *El Nuevo Día*, October 9, 1990.

Ortiz, Vilma, "Changes in the Characteristics of Puerto Rican Migrants from 1955 to 1980," *International Migration Review*, Vol. 20, 1987, 612–28.

———, "Circular Migration and Employment Among Puerto Rican Women," mimeo., April 1992.

Pantojas-García, Emilio, *Development Strategies as Ideology: Puerto Rico's Export-Led Industrialization Experience*, Lynne Rienner, London, 1990a.

———, "Crisis del modelo desarrollista y re-estructuración capitalista: hacia una redefinición del rol de Puerto Rico en la economía hemisférica," in C. Gautier-Mayoral, A. Rivera-Ortiz and I. Alegría-Ortega, eds., *Puerto Rico en la Economía Política del Caribe*, Ediciones Huracán, Río Piedras, Puerto Rico, 1990b.

Pérez, Sonia, *Moving from the Margins: Puerto Rican Young Men and Family Poverty*, National Council of La Raza, Washington, D.C., 1993.

Perloff, Harvey S., *Puerto Rico's Economic Future: A Study in Planned Development*, University of Chicago Press, 1950.

Picó, Isabel, "Estudio sobre el empleo de la mujer en Puerto Rico," in R. Duncan, ed., *La Investigación Social en Puerto Rico*, Interamerican University Press, San Juan, Puerto Rico, 1980, 209–32.

Presser, Harriet B., *Sterilization and Fertility Decline in Puerto Rico*, Institute of International Studies, University of California at Berkeley, 1973.

Pyatt, Graham, and Erik Thorbecke, *Planning Techniques for a Better Future*, International Labour Organization, Geneva, 1974.

Quintero Rivera, Angel, "Base clasista del proyecto desarrollista del 40," in E. Rivera Medina and R. Ramírez, eds., *Del Cañaveral a la Fábrica: Cambio Social en Puerto Rico*, Ediciones Huracán, Río Piedras, Puerto Rico, 1985, 139–46.

Ramírez, Rafael, "Los arrabales y caceríos de Cataño," in R. Duncan, ed., *La Investigación Social en Puerto Rico*, Interamerican University Press, San Juan, Puerto Rico, 1980, 119–52.

Ramos, Fernando, "Out-Migration and Return Migration of Puerto Ricans," in George J. Borjas and Richard Freeman, eds., *Immigration and the Work Force*, University of Chicago Press, 1992, 49–66.

Reyes, Belinda, "Moving Back or Moving On: Puerto Rican Migration and Poverty," mimeo., Institute of Public Policy Studies, University of Michigan, October 1994.

Reynolds, Lloyd G., and Peter Gregory, *Wages, Productivity, and Industrialization in Puerto Rico*, Yale University Press, New Haven, Conn., 1965.

Ríos, Palmira N., "Gender, Industrialization and Development in Puerto Rico," in Christine Bose and Edna Acosta-Belén, eds., *Women in the Latin American Development Process*, Temple University Press, Philadelphia, 1995, 125–47.

Rivera, Marcia, "El proceso educativo en Puerto Rico y la reproducción de la subordinación femenina," in Yamila Azize Vargas, ed., *La Mujer en Puerto Rico: Ensayos de Investigación*, Ediciones Huracán, Río Piedras, Puerto Rico, 1987, 113–38.

Rivera-Batiz, Francisco L., "Child Labor Patterns and Legislation in Relation to Fertility," in George J. Stolnitz, ed., *Quantitative Approaches to Analyzing Socioeconomic Determinants of Third World Fertility Trends*, The Futures Group, Washington, D.C., 1984.

———, "Can Border Industries Reduce Immigration to the United States?" *American Economic Review*, Vol. 76, May 1986.

———, "Is There a Brain Drain of Puerto Ricans to the United States?" *Puerto Rico Business Review*, July 1987.

———, "The Characteristics of Recent Puerto Rican Migrants: Some Further Evidence," *Migration World*, October 1989.

———, "The Effects of Literacy on the Earnings of Hispanics in the United States," in Edwin Meléndez, Clara Rodríguez, and Janis Barry-Figueroa, eds., *Hispanics in the Labor Force: Issues and Politics*, Plenum Publishers, New York, 1991, 53–76.

———, "Trends and Patterns of Educational Attainment in Puerto Rico," mimeo., Consejo General de Educación, Hato Rey, Puerto Rico, October 1992a.

———, "Quantitative Literacy and the Likelihood of Employment Among Young Adults," *Journal of Human Resources*, Vol. 27, Spring 1992b.

———, "The Multicultural Population of New York City: A Profile of the Mosaic," in F. Rivera-Batiz, ed., *Reinventing Urban Education: Multiculturalism and the Social Context of Schooling*, IUME Press, Teachers College, Columbia University, New York, 1994a, 23–68.

———, "Education and the Economic Status of Women in Puerto Rico," paper presented at the Consejo General de Educación, Hato Rey, Puerto Rico, April 22, 1994b.

———, "A Profile of the Immigrant Population of Puerto Rico," Background Paper, U.S. Commission of Immigration Reform, Washington, D.C., January 1995.

———, "La formación de maestros y la reforma educativa," in *La Preparación de Maestros y la Reforma Educativa en Puerto Rico*, Consejo General de Educación, Hato Rey, Puerto Rico, Forthcoming, 1996a.

———, "The Economics of Technological Progress and Endogenous Growth in Open Economies," in G. Koopman and H. E. Scharrer, eds., *The Economics of High-Technology Competition and Cooperation*, Nomos Verlagsgesellschaft, Hamburg, 1996b, 31–63.

Rivera-Batiz, Francisco L., and Carlos Santiago, *Puerto Ricans in the United States: A Changing Reality*, The National Puerto Rican Coalition, Washington, D.C., 1994.

Rivera-Batiz, Francisco L., and Selig Sechzer, "Substitution and Complementarity Between Immigrant and Native Labor in the United States," in Francisco Rivera-Batiz, Selig Sechzer, and Ira Gang, eds., *U.S. Immigration Policy Reform in the 1980s: A Preliminary Assessment*, Praeger Publishers, New York, 1991, 89–116.

Rivera-Quintero, Marcia, "Incorporación de las mujeres al mercado de trabajo en el desarrollo del capitalismo," in Edna Acosta-Belén, ed., *La Mujer en la Sociedad Puertorriqueña*, Ediciones Huracán, Río Piedras, Puerto Rico, 1980, 41–66.

Roberts, Sam, *Who We Are: A Portrait of America Based on the Latest U.S. Census*, Times Books, New York, 1993.

Robinson, J. Gregory, and Jeffrey S. Passel, "Evaluation of Coverage of the 1980 Census of Puerto Rico Based on Demographic Analysis," paper presented at the annual meetings of the Population Association of America, Chicago, Illinois, April 30–May 2, 1987.

Rodríguez, Clara E., "Circulating Migration," *Journal of Hispanic Policy*, Vol. 3, January 1988, 5–9.

———, *Puerto Ricans: Born in the U.S.A.*, Unwin Hyman, Boston, 1989.

Rodríguez, Meriemil, "Cuestionables las estadísticas del empleo," *El Nuevo Día*, December 21, 1995.

Rodrik, Dani, "Getting Interventions Right: How South Korea and Taiwan Grew Rich," *Economic Policy*, Vol. 9, October 1994, 55–107.

Rohter, Larry, "Puerto Rico's Coastline: New York's Back Door," *New York Times*, December 13, 1992, 30.

———, "As Crime Rises, Puerto Ricans Retreat," *New York Times*, January 13, 1993a.

———, "National Guard Joins Puerto Rico Police on Beat as Crime Rises," *New York Times*, July 28, 1993b.

———, "A Puerto Rican Boom for Florida," *New York Times*, January 31, 1994.

Román, Elizabeth, "Brain Drain to the Mainland," *Caribbean Business*, September 13, 1990, 1–2.

Rosario Natal, Carmelo, *Exodo Puertorriqueño: Las Emigraciones al Caribe y Hawaii, 1900–1915*, Ramallo Brothers Printing, San Juan, Puerto Rico, 1983.

Ruíz, Angel L., "Desarrollo económico de Puerto Rico: Evaluación de una estrategia de desarrollo basado en importación de capitales y tecnología," Serie de Ensayos y Monografías 25, March 1982.

Sachs, Jeffrey, Aaron Tornell, and Andrés Velasco, "The Collapse of the Mexican Peso: What Have We Learned?" National Bureau of Economic Research working paper 5142, June 1995.

Safa, Helen Icken, *Familias del Arrabal: Un Estudio Sobre Desarrollo y Desigual-*

dad, Editorial Universitaria, Universidad de Puerto Rico, Río Piedras, 1980.

————, "Female Employment in the Puerto Rican Working Class," in June Nash and Helen Safa, eds., *Women and Change in Latin America,* Bergin and Garvey Publishers, South Hadley, Mass., 1986, 84–106.

Sánchez, Luis Rafael, "La guagua aérea," in Asela Rodríguez de Laguna, ed., *Imágenes e Identidades: El Puertorriqueño en la Literatura,* Ediciones Huracán, Río Piedras, Puerto Rico, 1985, 23–30.

Sánchez Korrol, Virginia E., *From Colonia to Community: The History of Puerto Ricans in New York City,* University of California Press, Berkeley, 1983.

Santiago, Carlos E., "How Significant Is the Discouraged-Worker Effect in Puerto Rico?" *Puerto Rico Business Review,* Vol. 6, Nos. 7–8, July/August 1981a, 3–8.

————, "Male-Female Labor Force Participation and Rapid Industrialization," *Journal of Economic Development,* Vol. 6, No. 2, December 1981b, 7–40.

————, "Closing the Gap: The Employment and Unemployment Effects of Minimum Wage Policy in Puerto Rico," *Journal of Development Economics,* Vol. 23, No. 2, 1986, 293–311.

————, "The Impact of Foreign Investment on Export Structure and Employment Generation," *World Development,* Vol. 3, No. 2, 1987a, 317–28.

————, "Policy Intervention and Forecasting: An Application to Minimum Wages," *International Journal of Forecasting,* Vol. 3, No. 2, 1987b, 289–98.

————, "The Dynamics of Minimum Wage Policy in Economic Development: A Multiple Time Series Approach," *Economic Development and Cultural Change,* Vol. 37, October 1989, 1–30.

————, "Wage Policies, Employment and Puerto Rican Migration," in Edwin Meléndez, Clara Rodríguez, and Janis Barry-Figueroa, eds., *Hispanics in the Labor Force: Issues and Policies,* Plenum Publishers, New York, 1991, 225–46.

————, *Labor in the Puerto Rican Economy: Postwar Development and Stagnation,* Praeger Publishers, New York, 1992a.

————, "The Changing Role of Migration in Puerto Rican Economic Development: Perspective from the Past and a Look to the Future," in C. A. Torre, H. Rodríguez, and W. Burgos, eds., *The Commuter Nation: Perspectives on Puerto Rican Migration,* University of Puerto Rico Press, Río Piedras, 1992b.

————, "The Migratory Impact of Minimum Wage Legislation: Puerto Rico, 1970–1987," *International Migration Review,* Vol. 27, No. 4 (Winter 1993), 772–95.

Santiago, Carlos E., and Kisalaya Basu, "Theory and Evidence of Circular Migration: The Puerto Rican Case," mimeo., Department of Economics, State University at Albany, New York, 1993.

Santiago, Carlos E., and Rosemary Rossiter, "A Multiple Time Series Analysis of Labor Supply and Earnings in Economic Development," *Journal of Development Economics,* Vol. 17, No. 3, April 1985, 259–75.

Santiago, Carlos E., and Erik Thorbecke, "Regional and Technological Dualism: A Dual-Dual Development Framework Applied to Puerto Rico," *Journal of Development Studies,* Vol. 20, No. 4, July 1984, 271–89.

————, "A Multisectoral Framework for the Analysis of Labor Mobility and Development in LDCs: An Application to Postwar Puerto Rico," *Economic Development and Cultural Change*, Vol. 37, No. 1, October 1988, 127–48.

Santiago, Esmeralda, *When I Was Puerto Rican*, Vintage Books, New York, 1993.

Schultz, Theodore Paul, "Education Investments and Return," in H. Chenery and T. N. Srinivasan, eds., *Handbook of Development Economics*, North Holland, Amsterdam, 1989, 412–76.

Schultz, Theodore W., ed., *Economics of the Family*, University of Chicago Press, 1973.

Seda Bonilla, Eduardo, *Interacción Social y Personalidad Social en Una Comunidad de Puerto Rico*, Editorial Juan Ponce de León, San Juan, Puerto Rico, 1964.

————, "Que hay sobre la llamada transformación social de Puerto Rico," in E. Rivera Medina and Rafael Ramírez, *Del Cañaveral a la Fábrica: Cambio Social en Puerto Rico*, Ediciones Huracán, Río Piedras, Puerto Rico, 1985, 109–14.

Silvestrini de Pacheco, Blanca, "La violencia criminal en Puerto Rico: de 1940 a 1973," in R. J. Duncan, ed., *Investigación Social en Puerto Rico*, Interamerican University Press, San Juan, Puerto Rico, 1980.

Soto, Pedro Juan, *Ardiente Suelo, Fría Estación*, Editorial Cultural, San Juan, Puerto Rico, 1983 (first edition, 1961).

Sotomayor, Orlando, *Poverty and Income Inequality in Puerto Rico 1970–1990: A Decomposition Analysis*, Unpublished Ph.D. Dissertation, Department of Economics, Cornell University, August 1994.

————, "Poverty and Income Inequality in Puerto Rico, 1969–1989: Trends and Sources," *Review of Income and Wealth*, Vol. 42, March 1996, 1–13.

Steward, Julian H., *The People of Puerto Rico*, University of Illinois Press, Urbana, 1956.

Stycos, J. M., *Family and Fertility in Puerto Rico: A Study of the Lower Income Group*, Columbia University Press, New York, 1955.

Tienda, Marta, "Puerto Ricans and the Underclass Debate," *Annals of the American Academy of Political and Social Science*, Vol. 501, January 1989, 105–19.

Tienda, Marta, and William Díaz, "Puerto Rican Circular Migration," *New York Times*, August 28, 1987.

Tobin, James, et al., *Report to the Governor of the Committee to Study Puerto Rico's Financial Issues*, Editorial Universitaria, Universidad de Puerto Rico, Río Piedras, 1976.

Torre, Carlos Antonio, Hugo Rodríguez Vecchini, and William Burgos, eds., *The Commuter Nation: Perspectives on Puerto Rican Migration*, Editorial de la Universidad de Puerto Rico, Río Piedras, 1994.

Torres, Andrés, and Frank Bonilla, "Restructuring and the New Inequality," in Rebecca Morales and Frank Bonilla, eds., *Latinos in a Changing U.S. Economy*, Sage Publications, Thousand Oaks, Calif., 1993, 85–108.

Torruellas, Luz M., and José L. Vázquez, *Puerto Rican Return Migrants during 1965–70 and Their Impact in the Labor Market*, Centro de Investigaciones Sociales, Universidad de Puerto Rico, Río Piedras, 1976.

Tumin, Melvin M., and Arnold Feldman, *Social Class and Social Change in Puerto Rico*, Princeton University Press, Princeton, N.J., 1961.

United Nations, *The World's Women: Trends and Statistics, 1970–1990*, United Nations, New York, 1991.

Valdivia, Yadira, "Limitadas las oportunidades de empleo para las mujeres," *El Nuevo Día*, April 30, 1992.

Vázquez Calzada, José L., "Tendencias y patrones de la fecundidad en Puerto Rico," *Revista de Ciencias Sociales*, Vol. 10, September 1966, 257–76.

———, "La dinámica poblacional y el futuro de Puerto Rico," in R. Duncan, ed., *La Investigación Social en Puerto Rico*, Interamerican University Press, San Juan, Puerto Rico, 1980.

———, *La Población de Puerto Rico y su Trayectoria Histórica*, Raga Printing, Río Piedras, Puerto Rico, 1988.

Vázquez Calzada, José L., and Zoraida Morales del Valle, "Características de la población extranjera residente en Puerto Rico," *Revista de Ciencias Sociales*, Vol. 21, September 1979, 245–88.

———, "Female Sterilization in Puerto Rico and Its Demographic Effectiveness," *Puerto Rico Health Sciences Journal*, Vol. 1, April 1982.

Vega, Bernardo, *Memoirs of Bernardo Vega*, Monthly Review Press, New York, 1984 (edited by César Andreu Iglesias).

Viglucci, Andrew, "Migration a Fact of Life That Could Be Facilitated," *San Juan Star*, February 6, 1994.

Villamil, José Joaquín, "Puerto Rico 1948–1979: The Limits of Dependent Growth," in J. Heine, ed., *Time for Decision: The United States and Puerto Rico*, North-South Publishing, Lanham, Md., 1983, 95–116.

Weisskoff, Richard, "Income Distribution and Economic Growth in Puerto Rico, Argentina and Mexico," *Review of Income and Wealth*, December 1970, 303–32.

———, *Factories and Food Stamps: The Puerto Rican Model of Development*, Johns Hopkins University Press, Baltimore, 1985.

Wilson, William Julius, and Kathryn M. Neckerman, "Poverty and Family Structure: The Widening Gap between Evidence and Public Policy Issues," in S. Danziger and D. Weinberg, eds., *Fighting Poverty: What Works and What Doesn't*, Harvard University Press, Cambridge, 1986.

World Bank, *Population and Development: Implications for the World Bank*, World Bank, Washington, D.C., 1994.

———, *World Development Report 1995: Workers in an Integrating World*, Oxford University Press, New York, 1995.

Zell, Stephen, *A Comparative Study of the Labor Market Characteristics of Puerto Rican Migrants*, Puerto Rico Planning Board, San Juan, Puerto Rico, 1976.

Index

Boldface numbers refer to figures and tables. Numbers followed by *n* refer to notes.

Puerto Rico (*cont.*)
  showcase, 3–8; unemployment crisis, 85–109; and U.S., 17–19, 163.
  See also specific municipios
Puerto Rico Fertility and Family Planning Assessment (PRFFPA), 61
PUMS. *See* public-use microdata samples

Quebradillas: population, **172**

race: and socioeconomic status, 68–71
racial discrimination, 70, 83
racial groups: household income in
  New York City, 148–50, **149**;
  household income in U.S., 128–29,
  129
racial identity, 70
Reading, Pennsylvania: Puerto Rican
  economic influence, 140, **141**;
  Puerto Rican household income,
  135–38, **139**; Puerto Rican movers
  and non-movers, 144–45, **145**;
  Puerto Rican population, 133–35,
  136; Puerto Rican presence, 133–
  35, **137**
Reagan administration, 16
real estate: labor force, 86, **86**
recession, 12
regional dualism, 105
regions: unemployment rates and,
  106, **106**, 109. *See also municipios*
return migrants, 158; characteristics
  of, 55–58; definition of, 58; demographic characteristics of, **56**, 56–
  57; educational distribution of, 57,
  57; occupational distribution of,
  57–58, **58**
return migration, 55, **55**, 61
Rincon: population, **172**
Rio Grande: population, **172**
Rochester, New York: Puerto Rican
  economic influence, 140, **141**;
  Puerto Rican household income,
  135–38, **139**; Puerto Rican movers
  and non-movers, 144–45, **145**;
  Puerto Rican population, 135, **136**;
  Puerto Rican presence, 133–35, **137**
Rossello, Pedro J., 8
rural areas: economy, 109; fertility
  rates, 34; population, 3; real annual
  earnings, 106–7, **107**; unemploy-

ment rates, 106, **106**, 109; urban migration, 83

Sabana Grande: population, **172**
salaries. *See* earnings; income; wages
Salinas: population, **172**
San German: population, **172**
San Juan, 2, 71; per capita income, 13,
  71, **75**; population, 71, **74**, **172**; unemployment rate, 13, 71, **75**
San Lorenzo: population, **172**
San Sebastian: population, **172**
Santa Isabel: population, **172**
Santiago, Esmeralda, 153
scientific instruments, 12
secondary school enrollment, 79, **79**,
  84
section 936 funds, 11, 16–17
service sector: labor force, 86, **86**, 87,
  108
single parenthood, 29–31, 41–42;
  among women, 31, **32**
single women: definition of, 31*n*
slavery, 70
socioeconomic transformation, 63–84,
  128–31; fertility and, 33–34; race
  and, 68–71; summary, 82–84;
  trends, 154–60
South Americans: household income
  in New York City, 148–50, **149**;
  household income in U.S., 128–29,
  129; population in Puerto Rico,
  113, **113**
Spain: cultural contact with, 2
Springfield, Massachusetts: Puerto
  Rican economic influence, 140, **141**;
  Puerto Rican household income,
  135–38, **139**, 151; Puerto Rican
  movers and non-movers, 144–45,
  145; Puerto Rican population, 135,
  136, 150, 159; Puerto Rican presence, 133–35, **137**; unemployment
  rate, 151
standard of living, 17
states (U.S.): Puerto Rican population
  dispersion in, 132–33. *See also specific states*
stereotypes about immigrants, 116
sterilization, 33
student enrollment, 79, **79**

Tampa, Florida: Puerto Rican economic influence, 140–41, **141**;